ONE-DAY CRICKET

WITH FULL COVERAGE
OF THE FOUR WORLD CUPS

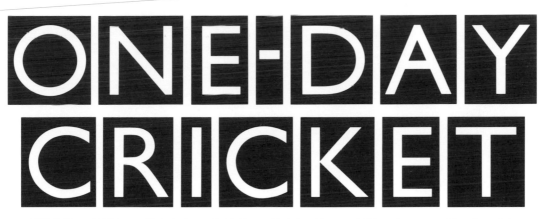

ONE-DAY CRICKET

WITH FULL COVERAGE OF THE FOUR WORLD CUPS

DAVID LEMMON

FOREWORD BY
CHRISTOPHER COWDREY

St Michael

This edition published for
Marks and Spencer plc in 1988
by Century Benham Ltd, Brookmount House,
62–65 Chandos Place, London WC2N 4NW

Copyright © David Lemmon 1988

ISBN 0 7126 2478 3

Designed by Tom Deas

Typeset in 'Monophoto' Garamond
by Vision Typesetting, Manchester

Printed and bound in Great Britain by
Butler and Tanner, Frome and London

Cover photographs

Front: left, a jubilant Alan Border, World Cup Final 1987; centre, David Gower; right, Ian Botham during the Benson and Hedges World Series, 1987.

Back: above, Mike Gatting; below, Viv Richards during a 48-ball century, Somerset v Glamorgan, June 1985.

CONTENTS

FOREWORD

CHRISTOPHER COWDREY
Kent & England

By the time I began my career as a professional cricketer in 1977, one-day cricket in England was fully established. Indeed, my own county, Kent, had already won all three of the major one-day competitions. I took to the limited-over game from the outset. I see professional sport as an entertainment, and the one-day game has proved itself as an entertainment, attracting huge crowds and providing a sense of occasion which makes it an exhilarating game to play.

It has a special appeal for me, too, in that I have always loved fielding, and that long-neglected aspect of cricket has been brought to the forefront in limited-over matches. It is possible to win a one-day game through the quality of your fielding, and that is how it should be. One-day cricket has turned average fielders into good fielders, and poor fielders into adequate fielders. In Kent, we had one of the greatest bowlers that the game has known, Derek Underwood, but in his early days, Derek was only a moderate fielder. The amount of one-day cricket he played, and the demands it made, allied to his own hard work, turned him into a very good fielder indeed. The value of the good fielder in one-day cricket is recognized by the crowd who are appreciative of every run saved. In a three-day or four-day match, the failure to back up bowler or wicket-keeper when a throw comes in from the field becomes forgotten in the general course of events. In one-day cricket, such a slip or piece of negligence can cost the match, and the spectators know it.

There are those who criticize limited-over cricket for they believe that it has a detrimental effect on a batsman's technique. This is a grave mistake. Batting in one-day cricket is not a matter of blocking or slogging; it is an art which demands high technical application, much work and a great deal of serious thought. Every shot that a batsman like Alan Knott has played has been calculated. He was quick to realize that each bowler poses different problems, and he fashioned his game accordingly. It is not simply a question of slogging aimlessly. It is better to hit some bowlers over mid-wicket. Others should be driven straight, and some must be hit over cover. It is not a matter of chance. It is batting that demands technical assessment and application.

Batting in one-day cricket has a fascination of its own. If you bat in the first four, there is pressure on you from the score-book. You must build an innings, but you must not allow too many overs to evaporate before you get the score moving. If you bat number five or six, you are faced with the question of when to accelerate, knowing that to lose your wicket can slow the rate of scoring because those that follow may not be so adept as yourself. Bowlers plan to attack and to contain, and the batsman must cope with their schemes. He must improvise and even be prepared to take risks, and it is this element of risk which excites and entertains the crowd.

In three- or four-day cricket, the bowler concentrates on a line and a length which may vary little over the whole course of the match; in the one-day game he must be prepared for instant variation, adjusting a length or a direction to every ball that he bowls. What few people appreciate though is that the mental aspect of one-day cricket is probably more demanding than that required by the longer game but the excitement of the contest is stimulating and the response of a capacity crowd is most rewarding.

My interest and joy in the one-day game is manifold, and I am delighted that my friend David Lemmon has turned his attention to this form of cricket with zest and understanding. His career as a writer on the game has occupied almost the same length of time as mine as a professional cricketer. He never fails to see the fun and the passion, he always focuses on the people which is ultimately what cricket is all about.

1 THE RISE OF ONE-DAY CRICKET

Wherever and whenever it originated, by the eighteenth century cricket had become a popular pastime. It was patronized and played by the gentry, and large sums of money were wagered on the outcome of matches. Technique, equipment and pitches were primitive; protection was non-existent. Injuries were suffered and tempers were lost. When defeat loomed it was not unusual for one or two of the players on the losing side to disappear from the ground in order to escape from paying their debts. There are records of matches ending in disagreement, fights and duels. Scores were low, and the aim was to complete a match in a single day. So, on 6 September 1737, at Moulsey Hurst in Surrey, London scored 81 and 31 for 5 to beat Chertsey, 45 and 66, by five wickets. The games lasted between four and six hours and were invariably followed by a hearty supper and then some hearty drinking.

By the beginning of the nineteenth century, techniques had developed; the surfaces on which games were played, although inadequate by today's standards, had improved; the heyday of the first great cricket side, Hambledon in Hampshire, was over, and scores were becoming higher. On 11 July 1837, at Saffron Walden in north Essex, the home side hit 474, and this was one of the earliest incidents of a team scoring as many as 400. The opponents were Bishop's Stortford, and the hero of the game was the Saffron Walden opening batsman, a local butcher named Alfred Adams, who scored 279. At the time, this was the highest score ever recorded.

Adams was never to be recognized as one of the great players of his day, but his achievement, at a time when to be credited with six a batsman had to hit the ball out of the ground, was a fine one. He hit one five and twenty-five fours, and the innings lasted from ten in the morning until seven at night. Bishop's Stortford did not bat. Faced by such a large score, they did what was customary in the circumstances and conceded the match.

Within the next thirty years, the game changed dramatically. The development of the railways and the movement of large sections of the population from the country to the towns brought about great social changes, and cricket was not unaffected by this revolution. In 1846, William Clarke formed his All-England XI. Gathering together the finest players of the age, he took them to towns and villages all over the country, and they would often compete against fifteen to twenty local cricketers. A business argument caused a split in the side after 1851, and another touring side, the United All-England XI, came into existence. In September 1859 a team of English cricketers set sail for North America, and this was the first English side to undertake an overseas tour. Cricket was growing fast.

William Clarke, like those who played with him, such as Wisden and Parr, was a professional and earned a great deal of money from the game, but in the second half of the nineteenth century the amateurs began to dominate. This dominance was really due to one man, W.G. Grace, the greatest all-rounder of his day and arguably the greatest player in the history of the game.

Grace first appeared in major cricketing events in 1864 and was active in the game until the early part of the twentieth century. His arrival on the scene coincided with the formation of several of the leading county clubs. Lancashire, Middlesex, Yorkshire and Warwickshire are among the county cricket clubs which came into existence between 1863 and 1865, and it is from 1864 that we date what is known as first-class cricket.

A single day proved insufficient for a game between two first-class counties. Cricket had become an altogether more leisurely affair, and it took three days to decide a match. Even then, many games were left drawn. At the top level, one-day cricket disappeared. Australia met England in Melbourne in 1877 for the first Test match. Three years later, The Oval saw the first Test match to be played on English soil. South Africa's entry into Test cricket came in 1889, and the following year the County Cricket Championship was organized by the MCC and was established as the premier domestic competition.

W.G. Grace. Arguably the greatest cricketer of all time and one who would have been as dominant in one-day cricket as he was wherever he played for nearly half a century.

Learie Constantine, the West Indian all-rounder, who played in the Lancashire League in the 1930s and excited people all over England in one-day matches during the Second World War.

Joe Hulme, Middlesex cricketer, Arsenal and England footballer, captained the London Counties team during the Second World War and helped raise thousands of pounds for charity.

status. The first BBC radio broadcast commentary on a cricket match was transmitted in 1927.

For the mass of the population, the choice of leisure interests was simple – soccer in the winter, cricket in the summer. People would queue all night to see a Test match or cling precariously to a telegraph pole to watch Kent play Surrey at Blackheath, yet by the late thirties three-day cricket no longer had the hold on people that it had enjoyed a decade earlier. The fact was that fewer people could spare the time. The leisured class had diminished in size, and the average working man worked far longer hours than he does today and would enjoy only two weeks holiday a year at most. The Second World War was to bring a great many changes.

In the Great War cricket had come almost to a complete stop, although league cricket in the North had continued to offer rich entertainment. The Lancashire League had been founded in 1890 and thrived in the 1930s when, on a Saturday afternoon, clubs like Nelson and Todmorden, all from within a radius of twenty square miles around Blackburn and Burnley, would play before packed houses. Each club was allowed to engage a professional, and great players such as the West Indians Constantine, Martindale and Headley, the Australian fast bowler McDonald and the Indian all-rounder Amar Singh graced the League. Continuing this tradition, equally great players, culminating in Viv Richards with Rishton in 1987, have played in the northern leagues since the Second World War.

During the First World War there had been a few charity matches in the South, but little else. In the Second World War, however, not only did the leagues in the North continue to thrive, but a full programme of Saturday matches was arranged at Lord's.

Two sides – the London Counties XI and the British Empire XI – came into existence and toured the country playing week-end matches against local club sides and raising money for war funds. They met at Lord's in an annual fixture, but the majority of wartime games at Lord's were organized by Sir Pelham Warner, one of the grand old men of cricket.

Warner had fought in the First World War, considering that it would have been wrong to have continued to play cricket, but he, and many others, believed that to continue cricket at Lord's during the Second World War was essential both for morale and for the war effort. He wrote later, 'If Goebbels had been able to broadcast that the war had stopped cricket at Lord's, it would have been valuable propaganda for the Germans.'

The majority of the matches arranged at Lord's were highly successful. They involved

The Edwardian period was the golden age of cricket, and even the butchery of the First World War did nothing to alter the pattern of the game. By the 1930s, the pre-war heroes such as Fry, Jackson and Trumper had been replaced by Chapman, Hobbs, Larwood, Hammond and Bradman. It now took four days, or longer, to play a Test match between England and Australia, and India, West Indies and New Zealand were also soon to be elevated to Test

many of the finest players of the day, attracted large crowds and provided exciting cricket and memorable moments. On 6 September 1941, for example, 10,000 people watched The Army play a Lord's XI. Denis Compton scored 114 for The Army, whose side included Test cricketers Leyland, Nichols, Peter Smith and Gover. The Lord's XI had Wyatt, G.O. Allen, Jim Sims and Bill Edrich among their number, and shortly before he came out to bat it was learned that Bill Edrich had been awarded the DFC for his part in a low-flying bomber raid. He was cheered all the way to the wicket.

On 29 July 1944, The Army met the RAF at Lord's, and during the course of the match a flying bomb was heard approaching the ground. The fielding side and the two batsmen threw themselves to the ground, but the bomb exploded harmlessly in Regent's Park. The game continued, and Middlesex batsman Jack Robertson celebrated the resumption by hitting the next ball for six.

Much of the cricket at this time was breathtakingly exciting. Whitsun weekend 1943 provided two magnificent games of cricket. On the Saturday, The Army (with Maurice Leyland of Yorkshire and England hitting 93) scored 252 for 8 declared and left the Civil Defence two and three-quarter hours in which to reach the target. Two wickets, those of John Langridge and Laurie Fishlock, went for 39 runs, but two former England players, Jim Parks senior and Harold Gimblett, added 200 runs in 100 minutes. Gimblett reached his century in 86 minutes and finished with 124, which included three sixes and fifteen fours. One of his sixes, off Nichols, the Essex and England all-rounder, ended high in the Mound Stand and split the fingers of an elderly man who tried to catch the ball. Civil Defence won by six wickets, with five minutes to spare.

Two days later, on Whit Monday, The Army were again in action, this time against the RAF. There was a crowd of 22,000, who

Ray Smith (Essex) hits out in a county game against Sussex. Smith captained the British Empire XI in the Second World War and played in one-day matches throughout the country which helped to raise money for the war effort.

The Leicestershire opening batsman Les Berry who played a memorable innings to help the Royal Air Force to victory over The Army, Lord's 1943.

suffered four interruptions for rain in the early part of the day. At one time the ground was left covered with a layer of white hailstones. The Army batted first and lost their first five wickets to Austin Matthews, the Glamorgan and England pace bowler. The first four to fall were all caught behind by the New Zealand and Northamptonshire wicket-keeper Ken James. At 5.15, with the score on 168 for 8, Tom Pearce, The Army's captain, declared so leaving the RAF 95 minutes in which to score 169 runs.

The RAF opening pair were Cyril Washbrook of Lancashire and Les Berry of Leicestersh.re. Washbrook was never quite able to get on top of the bowling, but they put on 55 in 40 minutes before Washbrook fell to Reg Perks of Worcestershire. Berry was now joined by Bill Edrich of Middlesex. They scored the 114 runs needed for victory in 44 minutes of exhilarating stroke-play. The crowd roared approval throughout the innings.

So successful were matches like these when players of the calibre of Edrich, Compton, Ames, Constantine, Hutton, Leyland, Gimblett, Wright and Barnett were gathered together that Sir Pelham Warner was asked whether it might be a good idea to continue such matches after the war, for centres other than Lord's had staged exciting one-day games. Warner said that he could see no point in continuing them, for when the world was back to normality the public would not support a one-day game between Middlesex and Surrey or Lancashire and Yorkshire. They would want only what they had always wanted – three-day county matches and Test cricket.

Initially, it seemed that Warner was right. In 1946, cricket continued to follow the same pattern it had had in the summer of 1939, and for a time the game thrived, with large crowds flocking to matches. It was a time of austerity. Goods were in short supply. Sweets and some foods were still rationed. People turned to sport, with the enthusiasm of a population that had

SOME CRICKETING STATISTICS, 1939–45

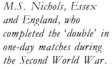

M.S. Nichols, Essex and England, who completed the 'double' in one-day matches during the Second World War.

BRITISH EMPIRE XI

The British Empire XI, generally led by Ray Smith, the Essex all-rounder, played 243 matches between 1940 and 1945, winning 150 and losing 36.

H.P. Crabtree hit 4328 runs during these five years, average 36.30. Crabtree was an Essex opening batsman who did much to establish cricket coaching on a firm basis in the years after the war.

Ray Smith hit 2157 runs, average 21.78, and took 308 wickets, average 13.98.

The outstanding success, however, was C.B. Clarke, the West Indian leg-break bowler who had played Test cricket in 1939. In six seasons with the British Empire XI he took 665 wickets at 9.82 runs each.

LONDON COUNTIES

Under the captaincy of Joe Hulme, the Middlesex cricketer and former Arsenal, Huddersfield and England footballer, London Counties won 115 of their 196 games and were beaten only 19 times.

The two leading batsmen in the side were Hulme himself who hit 4340 runs, average 39.00, and F.S. Lee, the Somerset opener, who hit 4360 runs, average 32.00.

Jack Young, the Middlesex slow left-arm bowler who had not established himself in county cricket before the war even though he had been at Lord's for six years, took 295 wickets in five seasons at 9.02 runs each.

LEADING CRICKETERS IN WARTIME CRICKET

In all matches played during the war years, some of them two-day fixtures, the leading players were as follows.

Batsmen

	runs
F.S. Lee (Somerset)	5324
J. Hulme (Middlesex)	4578
H.P. Crabtree (Essex)	4512
A. Fagg (Kent)	3511
R.E.S. Wyatt (Warwickshire)	3259
L.J. Todd (Kent)	3257

Bowlers

	wickets
C.B. Clarke (West Indies)	746
R. Smith (Essex)	335
J.A. Young (Middlesex)	303
P.F. Judge (Glamorgan)	262
A.R. Gover (Surrey)	208
F. Appleyard (Yorkshire)	165

All-round cricket

As well as scoring 3257 runs, L.J. Todd took 146 wickets.

M.S. Nichols (Essex and England) also completed a 'double' with 113 wickets and 1141 runs.

been starved of entertainment and excitement for six years. It was not unusual for 30,000 people to watch a Third Division football match, and cricket, too, enjoyed a bonanza.

The second season of cricket after the war brought the great deeds of Denis Compton and Bill Edrich. Both batsmen passed 3000 runs. Compton hit a record 3816, with 18 centuries, another record. The two men took Middlesex to win the County Championship in 1947. At Leicester, 663 runs were scored on the second day, and 1405 runs in all, when Middlesex went there. When they went to Cheltenham to play Gloucestershire, their nearest rivals, in August, the gates were closed nearly two hours before the start of play, so many people wanted to see the match. A week earlier, 54,000 people had seen Middlesex beat Surrey at The Oval. The first day, Saturday, had seen the gates closed with 30,000 people in the ground.

These were heady days, and there was no decline in enthusiasm when Bradman brought his all-conquering Australians to England in 1948. In 1950 the West Indians, with two unknown spinners, Ramadhin and Valentine, made history by beating England in England for the first time. Peter May emerged as the first great English batsman of the post-war period (Compton, Edrich and Hutton had all been Test players before 1939), and nearly two million people regularly watched county cricket. Fifteen years later, the number was to drop to 500,000.

The reasons for the decline in attendances at matches are numerous. The euphoria that had pervaded society at the end of the war and at the exciting establishment of the new Welfare State gave way to a sense of boredom and self-interest. There were no longer shortages, and England became a consumer society. Sports such as tennis, golf, badminton and squash gradually came within the reach of more people. Television became commonplace, and other interests suffered in consequence. Where once a young man had had only the prospect of football in the winter, cricket in the summer, and cinema or dancing in the evenings, he was now spoilt for choice. To worsen matters, cricket moved into a dull period. Bad play dominated, and while there still were great players and achievements, there was also much dross.

The amateur cricketer who had been the backbone of the game in the golden age of the Edwardians had been becoming rare before 1939; by the 1960s he was almost obsolete. The season of 1962 marked the end of the demarcation between amateurs and professionals, Gentlemen and Players. Thereafter there were only cricketers, and the game became professional in both substance and attitude.

The abolition of the distinction between amateurs and professionals had been brought about as one result of investigations into the state of cricket and its finances in the late fifties. The MCC set up a committee under the chairmanship of Harry Altham to look into the decline in gate receipts and into the general state of the game. One of the committee's recommendations was that a new national knock-out tournament should be introduced, and that it should be a one-day limited-over competition.

The idea of a knock-out competition – cricket's answer to the FA Cup – had long been mooted, but previous suggestions had always seen the competition as being integrated into the pattern of first-class cricket and the three-day game. The idea of a limited-over tournament was a revolutionary one, for even the one-day matches so successful at Lord's and elsewhere during the Second World War had relied upon generous declarations to provide a result. Limitations on the length of an innings or on the number of overs that a bowler was allowed to bowl were seen by many as a betrayal of the basic principles of the game, but with the overall financial position of cricket deteriorating rapidly, radical remedies were needed, and 1963 saw the first knock-out competition in English cricket. Importantly for the future of the game, Gillette agreed to act as sponsors of the tournament, and a new era in English cricket began.

The first Gillette Cup competition was restricted to the seventeen first-class counties. The first match to be played in the new tournament was the preliminary round game at Old Trafford, where Lancashire entertained Leicestershire. The rules of the competition allowed for sixty-five overs per innings with no bowler to bowl more than fifteen overs. Play was supposed to last from 11.00 a.m. until 7.30 p.m., but the uncertain weather of 1 May in Manchester took the opening match into a second day. By the second season, the number of overs for each innings had been reduced to sixty, with bowlers restricted to a maximum of thirteen overs. In 1966, the bowler's quota was reduced to twelve overs, and the competition has remained in that format ever since.

In spite of the sixty-five-over allowance, the inaugural match at Old Trafford was the only one to go into a second day in 1963. Maurice Hallam, the Leicestershire captain, won the toss and asked Lancashire to bat first. Without ever suggesting foolhardiness, Lancashire scored at a rate of 4.67 an over to reach 304 for 9. The backbone of the innings was a fourth-wicket stand of 136 by skipper Ken Grieves and Peter Marner, who hit 121, the first century in the competition, and was named Man of the Match. Ironically, Marner was to move to Leicestershire two years later. When Leicestershire batted, the England fast bowler Brian Statham dismissed Bird (later to win renown as an umpire), Wharton and Jayasinghe with only 23 scored. Maurice Hallam played a courageous captain's innings of 106, but Leicestershire were all out for 203 in 51.3 overs. Statham finished with 5 for 28 from twelve overs, and Marner added three wickets to his century to clinch the individual award.

Marner's 121 was to remain the highest Gillette Cup score of that opening season, but, surprisingly, Statham's 5 for 28 was to be bettered twice. Lancashire's Dyson took 5 wickets against Essex in the next round, while at Worcester the home side's Jim Standen took 5 Surrey wickets for 14 runs. (Dyson and Standen were both also professional footballers.) In the quarter-final, another Worcestershire pace bowler, Jack Flavell, took 5 for 43 against

Brian Statham took 5 for 28 for Lancashire in the first game ever played in the Gillette Cup, England's first one-day tournament.

Glamorgan, and in the semi-final at Worcester, he captured 6 Lancashire wickets for 14 runs in thirteen overs. The Red Rose side were bowled out for 59, and Worcestershire scored the necessary runs in 10.1 overs for the loss of Kenyon.

In the final, Sussex beat Worcestershire by 14 runs in a low-scoring game which ended in drizzle and bad light. Nevertheless, the crowd of 25,000 stayed to the end, and there were scenes of great jubilation. The first year of the new tournament had had its teething problems, but it had captured the public imagination and it brought fresh hope to cricket in England.

If initial approaches to the knock-out competition were in some cases naive, most of those connected with the game realized the advantages in terms of finance and publicity that it could bring. For the second season of the Gillette Cup, as well as the change in the number of overs, five of the leading Minor Counties – Cambridgeshire, Cheshire, Durham, Hertfordshire and Wiltshire – were invited to play in the competition, and today, with Scotland, Ireland and thirteen Minor Counties included, the first round consists of thirty-two sides. The National Westminster Bank succeeded Gillette as sponsors in the 1981 season.

The success of the Gillette Cup made many business houses aware of the value to be derived from sponsoring cricket, particularly if matches were played at a time when they could draw large crowds and enjoy substantial coverage on radio and television.

In the early 1960s, great players from the past from all over the world got together on Sunday afternoons and, using the name 'Cavaliers', played matches against professional county sides or sides composed of top county players for the aid of charity or for a particular beneficiary. The matches were sponsored by the cigarette company Rothmans. They proved to be highly entertaining, and although they were played in a light-hearted manner with nothing at stake, they attracted good crowds and were televised, to the delight of a large audience watching at home. The Advisory County Committee realized the potential of Sunday afternoon cricket and its large television audience. With the sponsorship of another large cigarette company, John Player, the Sunday League came into being in 1969. Its arrival meant the death of the Cavaliers who, denied both quality opposition and television coverage, disbanded in 1970.

Due to the Sunday Observance Laws in Great Britain, the John Player Sunday League matches could not begin until 2.00 p.m., although this was amended to 1.30 in 1985 mainly for the convenience of television

Following in the wake of the disbanded Cavaliers, the Lord's Taverners play Sunday matches to raise money for charity. Their side consists of former professional cricketers and show-business personalities. Barry Norman is a regular supporter.

Greg Chappell, later to be captain of Australia, hit the first Sunday League century, June 1969.

coverage. Each innings was limited to forty overs which had to be bowled by 3.50 p.m. If only thirty-eight or thirty-nine overs had been bowled by that time, the side batting second would also have its innings restricted to thirty-eight or thirty-nine overs. No bowler was allowed to bowl more than eight overs, and the run-up was limited to 15 yards. In the event of bad weather, plans were set down regarding reduction in the number of overs etc. which tried to ensure that a result would always be possible within the span of the afternoon's play.

The Sunday League, sponsorship of which was taken over by the Refuge Assurance Company in 1987, differs from the other limited-over one-day competitions in that it is on a league basis as opposed to being a knock-out tournament and that it is played exclusively on a Sunday. In fact, both of these distinctive features underwent minor alterations for the 1988 season when it was decided that the top four sides in the League should play off for the title, and that the semi-finals of the competition would be on the Wednesday prior to the final Sunday of the season.

In recent years the BBC has tended to restrict its television coverage of Sunday League matches, but initially the whole of a match was televised and the game, as well as the sponsor, would enjoy an armchair audience of between three and five million every Sunday.

The first matches in the Sunday League were played on 27 April 1969, when Essex beat Nottinghamshire by 37 runs at Chelmsford; Warwickshire beat Gloucestershire at Bristol by 59 runs; Kent beat Hampshire at Canterbury by 70 runs; Middlesex beat Yorkshire at Lord's by 43 runs; Glamorgan beat Northamptonshire at Northampton by 7 runs; Leicestershire beat Somerset at Weston-super-Mare by 5 wickets; Surrey beat Worcestershire at The Oval by 5 runs; and Lancashire, the eventual champions, beat Sussex at Hove by 5 wickets.

In that first round of matches, Don Shepherd of Glamorgan and Charles Spencer of Leicestershire both took 5 wickets. In a year in which the bowlers held the upper hand, the first century in the new League was not hit until 15 June when Greg Chappell, later to become captain of Australia, hit 128 not out for Somerset against Surrey on the Brislington ground at Bristol. Chappell's innings came out of a stand of 170 in an hour and three quarters with Roy Virgin, who finished with 42 not out. Chappell hit nineteen fours and gave Somerset their first win in the competition.

One of the excitements of the Sunday League is that it offers so many incentives. There is prize money for bowlers who take 4 wickets in a match, for batsmen who hit sixes, and for the fastest televised half-century. In the 1969 season Keith Boyce of Essex, the West Indian all-rounder, hit the most sixes with sixteen, while Derek Underwood (Kent) and Tom Cartwright (Warwickshire) each took 4 wickets in an innings on three occasions.

There were other spectacular performances, however. At Leicester on 20 July, Peter Marner hit 99 in 53 minutes, and his innings included eight sixes. At Johnson Park, Yeovil, Brian Langford of Somerset bowled eight consecutive maidens against Essex so that his quota read 8–8–0–0. It is a record that has never been beaten in the nineteen seasons since. On 29 June, Richard Hutton took 7 Worcestershire wickets for 15 runs in 7.4 overs at Headingley, a bowling analysis which has been bettered only once in the League, as will be seen.

Lancashire were to retain the John Player League trophy in 1970, the year in which they also beat Sussex in the Gillette Cup Final at Lord's. That final was watched by a capacity crowd of 25,000, while a week earlier at Old Trafford, 33,000 people had seen Lancashire beat Yorkshire to win the Sunday League title. The gates had been closed at Old Trafford for the first time since 1948. One-day cricket had provided a great fillip to dwindling county receipts, and it had unquestionably caught the imagination of the public. In 1972 a third limited-over competition was added to the

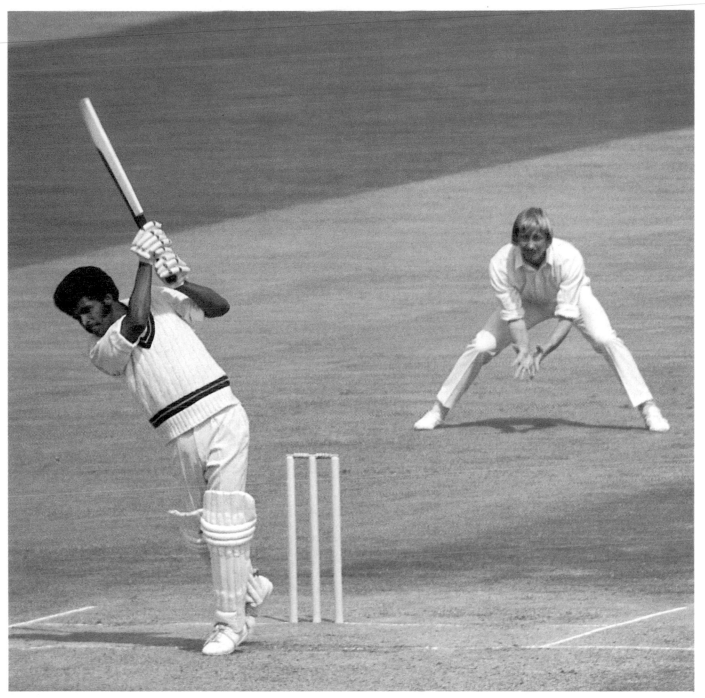

Keith Boyce, Essex and West Indies, hit the most sixes in the inaugural season of the John Player League.

Colin Cowdrey hit 107 not out for Kent against Middlesex in the first Benson and Hedges Cup match played at Lord's.

The adjudicator's decision as to who should win the Gold Award has not always met with approval. Don Wilson's five wickets against Lancashire, 1972, went unhonoured much to the annoyance of the Yorkshire captain. Wilson is now head coach at Lord's.

cricket calendar – the Benson and Hedges Cup.

The Test and County Cricket Board welcomed another generous offer of sponsorship, but the problem that confronted them was to devise a one-day competition which differed from the two existing competitions and would assert a personality of its own. What was agreed was a fifty-five over competition which would begin on a league basis to allow eight teams to qualify for a later knock-out stage of the competition. Initially the seventeen First-Class Counties, two sides representative of the Minor Counties and, in alternate seasons, the universities of Oxford and Cambridge were split into four zones. In 1975 Oxford and Cambridge joined to make a Combined Universities side which, since 1987, more sensibly and more representatively, has included players from Durham, Exeter and other universities affiliated to the UAU. Since 1980 the Minor Counties have entered one fully representative side, so allowing Scotland to compete as the twentieth team in the competition.

Colin Cowdrey hit 107 not out for Kent against Middlesex at Lord's in the opening match in the Southern Section, but his side lost, and at Swansea, Sadiq Mohammad hit 108 as Gloucestershire beat Glamorgan. Mike Procter took 5 wickets in the same match.

Don Wilson was another bowler to take 5 wickets in an opening match. His slow left-arm spin brought him figures of 5 for 26 for Yorkshire against Lancashire at Bradford. Lancashire were bowled out for 82, and Yorkshire won by 9 wickets. The match adjudicator, Bill Voce, the former Nottinghamshire and England fast bowler, gave the Gold Award for the outstanding individual performance of the match to Barry Wood, the Lancashire all-rounder, who scored 31 and took the only Yorkshire wicket to fall at a personal cost of 13 runs. This judgement caused a storm, for Wilson had taken the wickets of Wood, Pilling, Clive Lloyd, Sullivan and Engineer, numbers two to six in the Lancashire batting order, and the Yorkshire captain, Geoff Boycott, roundly condemned Voce's adjudication.

Yorkshire went on to reach the final, where they were beaten by Leicestershire who were led by former Yorkshire player Ray Illingworth. Another ex-Yorkshire player, Chris Balderstone, took the Gold Award on that occasion.

The final, played on the third Saturday in June, was watched by 18,000 people, an indication that the Benson and Hedges Cup was taking longer to establish itself than the other one-day competitions. The problems had been the timing of the zonal rounds, and the weather. The competition had begun on 29 April and was due to finish on 3 June. With three days set

One-day cricket has always been the norm for club sides like Windsor.

aside for each game to compensate for disruptions by the weather, this virtually excluded first-class cricket from the month of May. Of the forty matches played in the zonal rounds in 1972, only sixteen were completed in one day, and as many as eight required the three bad-weather days allocated in order to be completed. For the public, limited-over cricket meant one-day cricket, the guarantee of seeing a result in a single day's play. People were not enamoured by the idea of watching the closing overs of a game held over to a third day and then played in gloomy weather.

In 1980, however, the timing of the zonal rounds was changed. Only two days were allocated to each game, and the whole of the qualifying part of the competition was condensed into what was little more than a fortnight. This seemed to give added excitement and interest, and full television coverage and capacity crowds have since attended the knock-out stages of the competition, with the July final at Lord's providing a mid-season highlight.

While the FA Cup in soccer often provides giant-killing shocks, the NatWest Trophy and the Benson and Hedges Cup have seen comparatively few. In soccer, Third Division sides have reached the semi-final of the FA Cup and have even won the Football League's Littlewoods Cup, but in cricket none of the

Advertising and excitement. Sussex v Essex, Benson and Hedges Cup match at Hove, 1986. Brian Hardie of Essex is the batsman.

minor sides has ever reached the later stages of either of the game's cup competitions.

It was 1973, the eleventh season of the Gillette Cup, before a Minor County triumphed over a First-Class County. The surprise was all the greater in that the victims were Yorkshire, who were beaten at home (Harrogate) by Durham. The initial inspiration for the Minor County came from John Wilkinson, a thirty-one-year-old seam bowler, who bowled Geoff Boycott for 14. At the time, Boycott was not only captain of Yorkshire but he was indisputably the finest batsman in England. Wilkinson's example was followed by Brian Lander, a medium-pace bowler from Bishop Auckland, who was captain of the Durham side. In 11.4 relentlessly accurate overs Lander took 5 for 15, and Yorkshire were bowled out for 135. Durham won by 5 wickets with 8.3 overs to spare.

In 1974 Lincolnshire beat Glamorgan, and two years later Hertfordshire beat Essex at Hitchin. In 1984 Shropshire beat Yorkshire at Telford, so that the White Rose county had the unenviable record of becoming the first First-Class County to lose to a Minor County in both the Gillette and NatWest competitions.

The Minor Counties have been far less successful in the Benson and Hedges Cup, in which they failed to win a match between 1972 and 1979. Their initial success came in 1980 when they beat Gloucestershire at Chippenham by 3 runs. It should be pointed out, however, that their side included several players with first-class experience, one of whom was New Zealand

Test player Lance Cairns who hit 54, took 2 for 35 and won the Gold Award.

Oxford University, with a side that included Imran Khan and Tim Lamb, beat Northamptonshire by 2 wickets at Northampton in 1973, the first year in which they participated in the tournament; and in 1976 Yorkshire were once more the victims of a less fancied side when they were comprehensively beaten by 7 wickets by the Combined Universities side. Peter Roebuck, Chris Tavare, Vic Marks, Paul Parker and Steve Coverdale were all members of the Universities side, but the Gold Award went to the Cambridge opening batsman Pathmanathan, a Sri Lankan, who launched a violent assault on England opening bowler Chris Old.

Scotland, who first played in the Benson and Hedges Cup in 1980, did not record a victory until their twenty-sixth match. This was at Perth on 10 and 11 May 1986, when their opponents were Lancashire. Put in to bat, Scotland reached 156 on a difficult wicket, with several batsmen making useful contributions. Lancashire lost Graeme Fowler in the third over, but they appeared to be well on course for victory when Gehan Mendis and John Abrahams put on 60 for the second wicket. Then came collapse, and in spite of a late flurry from Allott and Simmons, Scotland snatched an historic victory by 3 runs. The Gold Award went to the Scottish captain Richard Swan, who had not only handled his side admirably, but had made an invaluable 31.

By 1987, prize money for the NatWest Trophy had been increased to £53,500, while of

the £436,770 sponsorship that Benson and Hedges put into their competition, £84,900 was in the form of prize money. The National Westminster Bank sponsored their competition, and the counties participating, to the extent of almost another £400,000 over and above prize money. When they took over sponsorship of the Sunday League in 1987, Refuge Assurance plc committed themselves to an expenditure of two and a half million pounds over a period of five years.

There have been other benefits, but it was the enormous revenue brought in by one-day cricket that initially saved and ultimately revitalized and reshaped the game.

One-day cricket has its detractors, mainly purists who feel that it has sullied first-class cricket. Yet without it, one doubts whether three-day cricket would have survived. Some counties would certainly not have done, and it is interesting to note that when, in 1988, it was decided to introduce some four-day games into the County Championship programme, it was first thought that the only way to do this would be to abolish the quarter-final stage of the Benson and Hedges Cup. The counties had second thoughts. When they weighed the income to be derived from a Benson and Hedges quarter-final match with its capacity crowd against the attendance likely on the fourth day of a County Championship match, they saw the necessity of keeping the Benson and Hedges Cup competition intact. What began as an experiment has become the lifeline of the game. The one-day game had insured the survival of cricket.

GILLETTE CUP/NATWEST BANK TROPHY RECORDS

WINNERS

Gillette Cup

1963	Sussex	1972	Lancashire		
1964	Sussex	1973	Gloucestershire	*NatWest Bank Trophy*	
1965	Yorkshire	1974	Kent	1981	Derbyshire
1966	Warwickshire	1975	Lancashire	1982	Surrey
1967	Kent	1976	Northamptonshire	1983	Somerset
1968	Warwickshire	1977	Middlesex	1984	Middlesex
1969	Yorkshire	1978	Sussex	1985	Essex
1970	Lancashire	1979	Somerset	1986	Sussex
1971	Lancashire	1980	Middlesex	1987	Nottinghamshire

Moment of jubilation. Clive Rice holds the NatWest Bank Trophy after Nottinghamshire had beaten Northamptonshire at Lord's in 1987.

HIGHEST TEAM SCORE

404 for 3, Worcestershire *v* Devon, Worcester, 1987.

LOWEST TEAM SCORE

39, Ireland *v* Sussex, Hove, 1985.

HIGHEST SCORE IN FINAL

317 for 4, Yorkshire *v* Surrey, Lord's, 1965.

LOWEST SCORE IN FINAL

118, Lancashire *v* Kent, Lord's, 1974.

BIGGEST VICTORY

By 299 runs, Worcestershire beat Devon, Worcester, 1987. Six counties have gained victories by ten wickets.

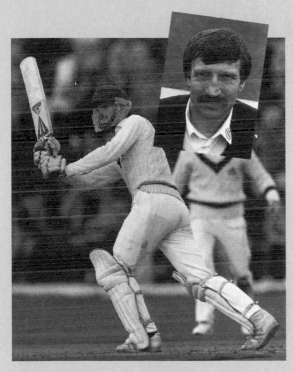

HIGHEST INDIVIDUAL SCORE

206, A.I. Kallicharran, Warwickshire *v* Oxfordshire, Edgbaston, 1984.

HIGHEST INDIVIDUAL SCORE IN FINAL

146, G. Boycott, Yorkshire *v* Surrey, Lord's, 1965.

MOST CENTURIES

5, G.M. Turner (Worcestershire)

FASTEST CENTURY

77 minutes, R.E. Marshall, Hampshire *v* Bedfordshire, Bedford, 1968.

Alvin Kallicharran hit the highest score ever made in the NatWest Bank Trophy, 206 for Warwickshire against Oxfordshire at Edgbaston, 1984

Ian Anderson . . .

. . . and, inset, Alan Hill, who shared a record stand in the NatWest Bank Trophy, 286 for Derbyshire against Cornwall, 1986.

RECORD PARTNERSHIPS FOR EACH WICKET

1st	227	R.E. Marshall & B.L. Reed, Hampshire *v* Bedfordshire, Bedford, 1968.
2nd	286	I.S. Anderson & A. Hill, Derbyshire *v* Cornwall, Derby, 1986.
3rd	209	P. Willey & D.I. Gower, Leicestershire *v* Ireland, Leicester, 1986.
4th	234*	D. Lloyd & C.H. Lloyd, Lancashire *v* Gloucestershire, Old Trafford, 1978.
5th	166	M.A. Lynch & G.R.J. Roope, Surrey *v* Durham, The Oval, 1982.
6th	105	G.StA. Sobers & R.A. White, Nottinghamshire *v* Worcestershire, Worcester, 1974.
7th	160*	C.J. Richards & I.R. Payne, Surrey *v* Lincolnshire, Sleaford, 1983.
8th	71*	R.C. Ontong & T. Davies, Glamorgan *v* Staffordshire, Stone, 1986.
9th	87	M.A. Nash & A.E. Cordle, Glamorgan *v* Lincolnshire, Swansea, 1974.
10th	81	S. Turner & R.E. East, Essex *v* Yorkshire, Headingley, 1982.

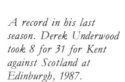

Dennis Amiss. More runs in the sixty-over competition than any other batsman.

A record in his last season. Derek Underwood took 8 for 31 for Kent against Scotland at Edinburgh, 1987.

MOST RUNS IN A CAREER

1950 (average 39.00), D.L. Amiss, Warwickshire, 1963–87.

MOST WICKETS IN A MATCH

8, D.L. Underwood, Kent *v* Scotland, Edinburgh, 1987; full analysis 11.1–2–31–8.

MOST ECONOMICAL BOWLING

J. Simmons, Lancashire *v* Suffolk, Bury St Edmunds, 1985, 12–9–3–1.

MOST EXPENSIVE ANALYSIS

D.A. Gallop, Oxfordshire *v* Warwickshire, Edgbaston, 1984, 12–0–106–2.

MOST WICKETS IN A CAREER

81 (average 14.85), G.G. Arnold, Surrey and Sussex, 1963–80.

HAT-TRICKS

J.D.F. Larter, Northamptonshire *v* Sussex, Northampton, 1963.
D.A. Sydenham, Surrey *v* Cheshire, Hoylake, 1964.
R.N.S. Hobbs, Essex *v* Middlesex, Lord's, 1968.
N.M. McVicker, Warwickshire *v* Lincolnshire, Edgbaston, 1971.
G.S. le Roux, Sussex *v* Ireland, Hove, 1985.
M. Jean-Jacques, Derbyshire *v* Nottinghamshire, 1987.

'Flat' Jack Simmons whose 1 for 3 in 12 overs is the most economical bowling return in the history of the sixty-over competition, for Lancashire against Suffolk, Bury St Edmunds, 1985.

Bob Taylor in action at Arundel. His 66 dismissals between 1963 and 1984 constitute a record for the sixty-over competition.

WICKET-KEEPING

MOST DISMISSALS IN A CAREER

66, R.W. Taylor, Derbyshire, 1963–84

MOST DISMISSALS IN A MATCH

6, R.W. Taylor (c 5/st 1), Derbyshire *v* Essex, Derby, 1981.
6, T. Davies (c 4/st 2), Glamorgan *v* Staffordshire, Stone, 1986.

2 THE IMPACT OF ONE-DAY CRICKET

The financial rewards that the advent of one-day cricket brought to the game are undeniable. Not only did cricket benefit from the direct involvement of companies such as Gillette, Benson and Hedges, John Player, the National Westminster Bank and Refuge Assurance, but counties drew revenue from smaller firms who recognized the one-day game as an ideal occasion on which to entertain guests. Hospitality boxes and tents became oversubscribed.

Where once it had been difficult to find anyone willing to advertise at cricket matches, it was now possible to sell space on boundary boards, for the advertisers knew that, at a Sunday League match or in the later stages of the Benson and Hedges or NatWest tournaments, their names would be seen in four million homes as games received extensive television coverage. One-day cricket was born of financial necessity, and that it provided the cure for the malaise that was gripping the game is indisputable. Financially, cricket is in the healthiest position it has enjoyed for well over half a century.

The arrival of the one-day game was received by purists with trepidation. They saw it as a violation of a tradition that had its roots in all that was best in Britain. Certainly it brought about a more fundamental change in the game than anything since the legalizing of overarm bowling in 1864, yet the limited-over game settled down easily alongside the three-, and now four-day game. Moreover, it excited a new, young following for cricket.

The NatWest Trophy Final and the Benson and Hedges Cup Final are sold out before the season begins, as are, in the main, the first three days of Test matches and the one-day internationals. The extensive television coverage and publicity given to one-day games has attracted some to the game who were previously uninterested in cricket. Many of those unwilling or unable to take time to see a three-day match have found it possible to take leave on a Wednesday or Tuesday to see a Benson and Hedges Cup game or a Nat West Trophy tie.

Weather permitting, the limited-over game allows for a result to be reached in one day. Invariably, the finishes to the matches are thrilling and dramatic, yet to suggest that the followers of the one-day game are impressed only by what is sensational is to belittle their interest. Many have acquired a sensitivity to the finer points of the game which makes them appreciative of good fielding and intelligent bowling.

A new breed of spectator may have been attracted, but he has not restricted his interest to one-day cricket. Encouraged by what he has seen, he has frequently returned to watch a Championship match the following Saturday and, in many cases, has taken out club membership. Counties like Essex and Somerset, both of which fervently embraced the one-day game from the outset, now boast record memberships, while others, such as Kent, Surrey, Warwickshire and Leicestershire, have developed executive suites and luxurious areas where companies may entertain.

Yet for many, the doubts persist. The purists blame one-day cricket for any decline in standards at international level and for weaknesses in technique. There is concern and some complaint among players that they are asked to play too much cricket, that they are now working a seven-day week. On close examination it seems unlikely that this is the case. By comparison, in the 1930s with a full programme of Championship matches and other fixtures, a cricketer was in action for six days every week without the breaks now afforded by rest days after NatWest Trophy and Benson and Hedges Cup matches.

In 1933, 'Tich' Freeman, the Kent leg-break and googly bowler, sent down 1829.4 overs, and in 1962, the last season before the arrival of one-day cricket, twenty bowlers delivered more than a thousand overs, with Hampshire's Derek Shackleton bowling 1717.1 at medium pace. In the same year, twenty batsmen played 60 innings or more. Jack Bond, Lancashire, and Richard Langridge, Sussex, each went to the wicket 67 times.

In 1987, with three one-day competitions, a

'Tich' Freeman bowled 1829.4 overs in 1933, but it is doubtful whether the great Kent leg-spinner would find a regular place in a one-day side today.

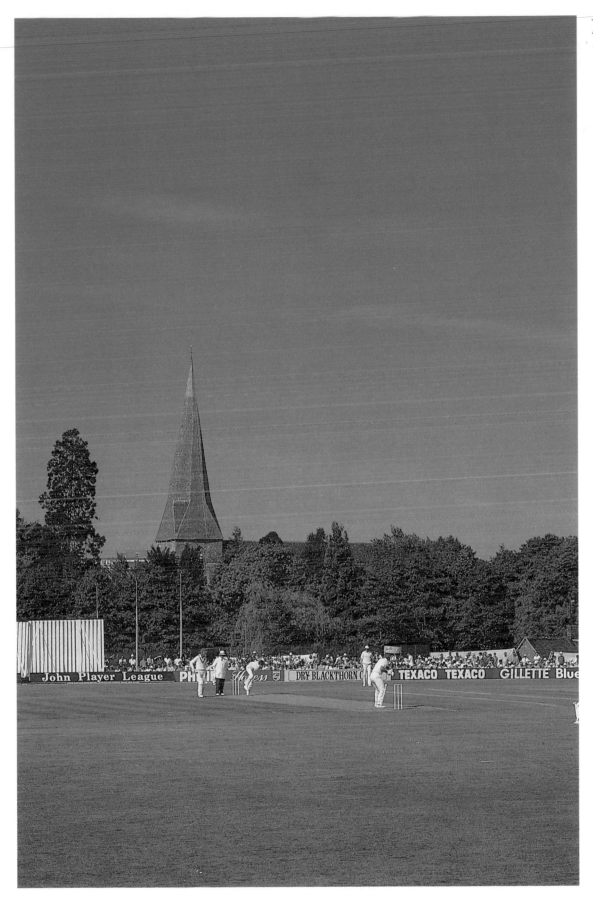

Sunday full house at Horsham, Sussex v Nottinghamshire, 1985.

Warwickshire floundered in the County Championship, but Bob Willis led them to the John Player League title in 1980.

contemporary professional cricketers are overworked when compared with their predecessors.

Another argument is that before 1963 a cricketer had to play only the three-day game, whereas today he has to adapt from Championship matches to the sixty-over game, to the fifty-five-over game to the forty-over slog, sometimes within the space of a few days. This is true, but such adaptability should be within the scope of a man who is earning his living from the game. The prizes are far higher than they used to be, and the chances of winning them are far greater.

Before 1963 there was only one domestic competition, the County Championship. Now there are four, and hope of success can be maintained for longer into the summer. From May 1935 to May 1939, Northamptonshire did not win a match. They finished bottom of the Championship table five years in succession, lifting themselves one place to sixteenth in 1939. Their support and morale dwindled, but it is unlikely that such a thing would happen today when the Sunday games offer perpetual hope.

In 1980 Warwickshire finished fourteenth in the County Championship, but won the John Player League under Bob Willis' leadership, while in 1983 the mighty Yorkshire, embarrassed at finishing last in the Championship, had the compensation of winning the Sunday title. From 1931 until 1962 the County Championship was dominated by the two counties of Yorkshire, who won the title eleven times and shared it once, and Surrey, who won it seven times in succession from 1952 to 1958 and shared it once in 1950. Since the Championship was officially constituted in 1890, four of the seventeen counties, Gloucestershire, Northamptonshire, Somerset and Sussex, have never won the title, but since the advent of the one-day game, only Glamorgan have failed to carry off any of the trophies, and only Hampshire, three times John Player League winners, have failed to reach a Lord's final.

Captains, assessing the strengths and weaknesses of their sides, concentrate their efforts in the area where they think they will bring most success. When he became captain of Kent in 1972 Mike Denness believed that his side was better equipped for the one-day competitions than for the County Championship. The bowling was strong in medium-pacers – John Shepherd and Bernard Julien, the West Indians, Bob Woolmer, Norman Graham and the incomparable Derek Underwood whose left-arm spin was bowled at a pace quicker than others of the type. The strength of the batting was the ability of Shepherd, Julien, Asif Iqbal, Johnson and Denness himself to score runs quickly, while

five-Test series against Pakistan, three one-day internationals, the MCC's Bicentenary Match and various other fixtures as well as the Britannic Assurance County Championship, only five batsmen played as many as 60 innings, and only Matthew Maynard of Glamorgan as many as 65. Of the bowlers, in all matches, only Eddie Hemmings, with 1025.4, bowled as many as a thousand overs. Worcestershire's Neal Radford sent down 918.1 overs. This hardly suggests that

the fielding was of the highest quality, with Ealham and wicket-keeper Alan Knott particularly outstanding.

Denness' assessment of his side was correct. Playing to their strengths, Kent won the John Player League three times, the Benson and Hedges Cup twice and the Gillette Cup once during Denness' five years as captain. The prize money for winning these competitions was large – Kent took £2000 and a trip to the West Indies for winning the John Player League in 1972 – but the other benefits were equally significant. When Worcestershire came to Canterbury on 10 September for the game that was to decide the championship of the Sunday League, 12,000 people were packed into the ground. Capacity

crowds always attended their home matches in the later stages of the Benson and Hedges Cup and Gillette Cup tournaments. Nor did the financial rewards for either club or players end with the excellent gate receipts and winning bonuses.

Sponsors and businesses were eager to be associated with the county, and when in 1977, close to the end of Kent's dazzlingly successful run, Norman Graham took his benefit he was rewarded with a staggering £80,000, a record for the time. Graham was an honest, fast medium-pace bowler. He was the type of player who serves a county well but who is never in contention for an England place. In 186 first-class matches for Kent he took 600 wickets at

Mike Denness believed that his Kent side was best equipped to succeed in one-day competitions in the 1970s, and was proved right.

A crowd of 12,000 packed into Canterbury to see Kent play Worcestershire in the John Player League in September 1972.

22.44 each, and he was always popular, although so were Underwood, Knott and Denness, all Test players, who received little more than a quarter of what Graham received.

Two years after Graham's benefit, Stuart Turner, the Essex all-rounder, took a benefit which exceeded Graham's and established a record for the eastern county. Turner was aided by the fact that during his benefit year, 1979, Essex won the Benson and Hedges Cup and went on to take the Championship. The Cup Final victory at Lord's in July aroused tremendous enthusiasm (it was the first time in their 103-year history that Essex had ever won a trophy), and Turner's benefit prospered as a result.

Both Graham and Turner worked exceedingly hard and deserved the large sums that they received, as did Jack Simmons of Lancashire who, in 1980, topped the hundred-thousand mark. While all three men gained a just reward for long and honourable service, their benefits had been given a tremendous boost by the advent of the one-day game and the publicity it afforded them and cricket in general. The record amounts they received have now become something of a norm. Cricket has learned to profit from its business connections, just as it has had to learn to be more professional and more businesslike in itself. The one-day game has wrenched many counties into the twentieth century and made them aware of economics and the need for financial stability.

If the monetary rewards have become greater, so also has the responsibility thrust upon administrators and players. Spectators have demanded more comfort and better facilities. Those companies and individuals who entertain guests wish to do so with grace and style. Adequate catering and bar management have become essential. Non-Test grounds such as Canterbury, Taunton, Leicester and Chelmsford

Prosperity and development. A full house is normal for an Essex one-day match. An attentive crowd watches the game against Warwickshire at Chelmsford at the beginning of the 1986 season.

Fitness is all. Phil
Edmonds receives
treatment before a one-
day international in
Sharjah.

*Fitness is all. Phil
Edmonds receives
treatment before a one-
day international in
Sharjah.*

have undergone exciting redevelopment so that
they can cope with capacity crowds and cater for
their needs. In the ten years since they first won
the Benson and Hedges Cup, Essex have
transformed the County Ground at Chelmsford.
New stands, a new scoreboard development, a
riverside restaurant, an executive suite and brick-
built arbours for entertaining have all appeared,
yet in the 1960s Essex had been faced with the
possibility of extinction because of financial
problems.

Where the county administrators have had
to become more adept at meeting the needs and
demands of the public, so, too, have the players.
Cricket is no longer such a leisurely game,
carried on with a sense of remoteness from the
onlookers. In the limited-over game, the period
between lunch and tea cannot be played in a
gentle state of lethargy which encourages the
audience to doze in the sunshine. Every over is
of importance; there is a constant feeling of
urgency.

It is this sense of urgency which demands a
standard of fitness of today's players which was
unknown to many cricketers of the past. It is a
fitness of mind and body, for in the one-day
game there can be no respite in concentration.

The concession of a leg-bye can prove to be an
error which costs the match. To bowl a wide or
a no-ball has become a heinous crime. Not only
does it concede a vital run, but it also gives an
opposing bowler an extra delivery, a bonus on
top of his quota of overs.

Concentration has always been an essential
part of cricket, and the great batsmen of the
1930s, such as Hammond, Bradman and
Ponsford, were noted for their ability to bat for
long periods. Yet arguably one-day cricket has
brought about a need for a more intense form of
concentration over shorter periods, particularly
in the field. When a capacity crowd and a large
television audience has its attention riveted on
every ball and is counting the value of every run,
a miss in the field becomes the greatest
embarrassment and an outstanding catch or
excellent stop can make a player a hero.

In the NatWest Bank Trophy semi-final
match at The Oval in August 1986, Surrey made
a splendid start, dismissing the Lancashire
openers, Fowler and Mendis, for 0 and 1.
Lancashire were eventually bowled out in the
fifty-ninth over for 229. This was a total which
Surrey should have found well within their
grasp, but a series of injudicious strokes marred

32

Graeme Fowler. His single contribution to Lancashire's win over Surrey in the NatWest Bank Trophy semi-final at The Oval in 1986 was a brilliant running catch which ended the match.

Triumph for Lancashire in the Benson and Hedges Cup Final of 1984.

their challenge. One man, Trevor Jesty, stood firm. He displayed a most glorious array of shots to reach 112, even though he was hampered by a leg injury and batted with a runner from the time he had scored 79. When the ninth wicket fell, however, Surrey were still 24 short of victory, but Jesty's brilliance took them to within five runs of victory.

Hayhurst bowled the fifty-ninth over, and with eight balls of the match remaining Jesty hit the ball high towards the long-on boundary. It seemed that the shot would level the scores, but Fowler sprinted round the boundary to take a memorable catch. As Fowler himself said afterwards, 'I had done nothing in the game. I'd been out for a duck and had hardly touched the ball in the field. Then, just as we looked like being beaten, I managed to hold on to a catch and we're at Lord's.'

To have been out of the game for much of its duration, but to be called upon to make the most significant and dramatic contribution at the last demands a total fitness of mind and body. It is also symbolic of an attitude that has been brought about by the one-day game, an attitude which has had a great impact on the game as a whole.

Worcestershire take the Refuge Assurance Sunday League, 1987.

Impact. A charity one-day game at Harrogate between India and Pakistan in July 1985 attracts a capacity crowd.

Sunday at Hastings.

3 TACTICS AND SKILLS

The semi-final of the Gillette Cup between Lancashire and Warwickshire at Old Trafford on 29 July 1964 was not a happy affair. A fine innings of 76 by the former Lancashire left-hander Bob Barber helped Warwickshire to a formidable total of 294 for 7 in their sixty overs. In reply, the home side began well, with Green and Worsley hitting 67 off the first twelve overs, but thereafter things went wrong. Mike Smith, the Warwickshire captain, took two good catches on the leg side to account for Entwistle and Grieves, and he then set his field deep, surrounding the boundary as bowlers maintained accuracy of length and line. The Lancashire batsmen, Marner and Clayton in particular, showed their frustration and displeasure at the tactics adopted by Warwickshire by making little attempt to score runs and simply blocking the ball. Lancashire crawled to 209 for 7. Warwickshire won by 85 runs, and the game ended with the large crowd barracking angrily.

Nor did the matter end there. The Lancashire committee asked for a survey from team manager Cyril Washbrook which was to make special reference to the behaviour of several players following complaints by other counties and following the way in which Lancashire had batted in the Gillette Cup semi-final. Having read Washbrook's report, the committee decided to dispense with the services of their captain, Ken Grieves, and to dismiss both Marner and Clayton 'on the grounds that their retention was not in the best interests of the playing staff or the club'. Marner, the first Gillette Cup hero, joined Leicestershire, and Clayton moved to Somerset.

The rumpus caused by Lancashire's reaction to Warwickshire's field-settings was nothing new. There had been grave concern the previous year, the first of the competition, when, most notably in the final at Lord's, Tex Dexter had placed every available fielder on the boundary in the closing overs of the match in an attempt to prevent Worcestershire from scoring rapidly. Like those of Mike Smith, Dexter's tactics seemed justified in that his side, Sussex, won the game. It was to be nearly twenty years, and then only in support of the example set by the Australians, before the legislation was brought in which stipulated that in all the one-day competitions a minimum of four fieldsmen (plus

Ted Dexter. A great attacking cricketer who adopted defensive and negative field-placings when he led Sussex to victory in the first Gillette Cup Final, 1963.

the bowler and the wicket-keeper) must be within a radius of thirty yards from the wicket at all times. This rule has meant that captains have had to consider more thoughtful and subtle field-placings than in the early days of the Gillette Cup, when reasoning was often naive.

Two other rules have been introduced in recent years as a result of incidents which have occurred in matches – one in England and one in Australia.

On 24 May 1979, Somerset met Worcestershire at Worcester in the final zonal match in Group A of the Benson and Hedges Cup. Gloucestershire had already completed their programme and were out of the reckoning. Somerset had won their three matches, and Worcestershire and Glamorgan had won two games each. Glamorgan's last fixture was against Minor Counties (South), a game they were expected to win with ease, so that if Worcestershire beat Somerset there was a possibility that three counties would finish on nine points and the two qualifying places for the quarter-finals would be decided on the bowlers' striking rates. In this area, Somerset entered their last match ahead of their rivals.

Batting first at Worcester, Somerset opened with Brian Rose, their captain, and Peter Denning. The Worcestershire bowling was opened by the West Indian pace-man Vanburn Holder. After one over in which the only run scored was a no-ball, Rose declared the Somerset innings closed. Following the customary interval, Worcestershire began their innings. It lasted for ten balls, and Glenn Turner scored two singles which gave his side victory by ten wickets.

The whole match had lasted for under twenty minutes, and Somerset had deliberately forfeited the game, but in doing so they had preserved their superior striking rate and finished top of their group.

Not unnaturally, Worcestershire were incensed, and the hundred or so paying spectators who had braved miserable conditions to see the match had their money returned. It was not only Worcestershire who were angered, for Rose's action was condemned by most people connected with cricket. In his defence it should be stated that his sole concern was that his county should win a trophy, something which by May 1979 they had never done, and if, in the minds of many, he had violated the spirit of the game, he had broken no rules.

Brian Rose, who declared
the Somerset innings
closed after one over in
the Benson and Hedges
Cup match at Worcester,
May 1979. Rose's action
caused a storm of
protest. Somerset were
disqualified from the
competition, and the rules
were amended.

Trevor Chappell looks at his bat, but it was as a bowler that he caused a rumpus by bowling the last ball of the match underarm to prevent New Zealander McKechnie from hitting a six.

This last fact was the only point offered in defence of Somerset when the matter was debated at a special meeting of the Test and County Cricket Board at Lord's on 1 June. Derbyshire alone stood by Somerset, supporting them in that their action contravened no rule, but by seventeen votes to one Somerset were disqualified from the competition for bringing the game into disrepute.

Ironically, Rose need never have made his declaration, for Glamorgan's game at Watford was abandoned after only four balls and the Welsh county took only one point, so leaving Somerset clear at the top of the table. Rose's action did, however, lead to a hasty amendment of the rules governing one-day competitions, and thereafter declarations were forbidden.

The second incident which brought about a change in the rules took place in Melbourne nearly two years later. A crowd of 53,000 had gathered at the Melbourne Cricket Ground to see the third and deciding final of the Benson and Hedges World Series between Australia and New Zealand. In their fifty overs Australia made 235 for 4, but not without controversy.

The argument surrounded the Australian captain, Greg Chappell, who hit 90. When he had scored 58 he skied a ball from Cairns to mid-wicket, where Martin Snedden ran some thirty yards and dived to hold a seemingly brilliant catch. The fielder held up the ball in triumph, but Chappell stood his ground and it was left to the umpires to arbitrate. After discussion they gave Chappell not out, arguing that neither of them had seen the catch as both had been watching the popping creases. If New Zealand were upset by this decision, they were even more disturbed by events at the end of the game.

Wright and Edgar gave New Zealand a splendid start with 85 in twenty-four overs, but the middle order failed to give the innings the boost that it needed. With three overs remaining, New Zealand still wanted 32 runs to win. Eleven runs were taken from an over by Trevor Chappell and six from an over by Dennis Lillee, so that when Trevor Chappell began the last over New Zealand needed 15 to win.

Richard Hadlee drove the first ball for four and was lbw to the second. Smith hit the next two deliveries for twos, but he was bowled by the fifth ball of the over. This meant that McKechnie, a renowned hitter, came in to face the last ball of the match which he had to hit for six in order to tie the game. Greg Chappell went into consultation with his brother, and Trevor Chappell bowled the last delivery underarm along the ground. McKechnie threw down his bat in disgust, and the New Zealand outrage did not end there. There were exchanges at prime-ministerial level and between the respective boards of control. No Man-of-the-Match award was made, so bitter were the feelings. Rules were redrawn. Underarm bowling in a one-day match was made illegal.

The three incidents which we have mentioned and which have led to a change in the rules governing one-day competitions point, directly or indirectly, to what many see as the essential tactical weakness pertaining to the limited-over game. From the earliest days of cricket, the object of the fielding side has been to bowl out the opposition. In the one-day game, this is no longer necessary. The key word has become containment, so that a bowler is seen as being of more value to his side if he restricts run-scoring than if he takes wickets but concedes runs at a rate of four or more an over.

In the Benson and Hedges Cup Final of 1980, for example, Keith Pont, the Essex all-rounder, took the wickets of the first three Northamptonshire batsmen, Cook, Larkins and Williams, and later had Sharp caught, but these four wickets, all of them valuable, cost him 60 runs from his eleven overs. When Essex batted, Tim Lamb captured the one important wicket of Graham Gooch, and conceded only 42 runs in his eleven overs. Northamptonshire won the game by six runs, and in the context of a match in which Northamptonshire were all out and Essex lost only 8 wickets, Tim Lamb's 1 for 42 had more significance than Keith Pont's 4 for 60.

The emphasis on containment rather than on wicket-taking has tended to influence sides in their choice of players. There was a lament after the first Gillette Cup competition in 1963 that the majority of counties were reluctant to include even one slow bowler in their sides, and that this fact, coupled with the deep-set fields, would create tedium. Yet this criticism was only partly justified. In the match between Gloucestershire and Middlesex at Bristol, two England off-spinners, David Allen and Fred Titmus, had outstanding matches. Allen took 4 for 28 while Titmus' 2 for 32 in fifteen overs was instrumental in bringing victory to Middlesex. At Old Trafford, where Lancashire beat Essex, the hero was another off-spinner, Dyson, who took 5 for 47. In the final at Lord's, the Man-of-the-Match award went to Worcestershire's Norman Gifford, who took 4 for 33 in fifteen overs and still finished on the losing side.

Among the record-holders in one-day competitions are spinners Underwood, Simmons and Langford, while Ray East, the Essex slow left-arm spinner, was the leading wicket-taker in the first John Player League season.

Spin bowling is, however, an art that is mastered only with much practice. The development of a spinner is a long process which demands application on the part of the bowler and sensitivity and intelligence on the part of his captain. By its very nature, spin bowling asks for thought and courage, and that courage must often be used in experimentation, which is at odds with a style of cricket that asks for containment rather than wickets.

One can point to a spin combination like Emburey and Edmonds of Middlesex and England, who have been highly successful in

Off-spinner John Emburey takes advice from England manager Mickey Stewart. A highly effective defensive bowler in the one-day game, Emburey's recent failure to take wickets in first-class cricket is ascribed by some critics to the negative style he has developed in limited-over cricket.

both the Benson and Hedges Cup and the NatWest Bank Trophy matches, yet there are those who would argue that Emburey's ability to restrict run-scoring in one-day cricket has affected him at Test and county level, where he has found it harder and harder to take wickets. It seems almost as if he has so tailored his bowling to deny batsmen that he is no longer able to show the variety and adventure necessary to lure them to destruction.

For all the success of the slow bowlers mentioned, and it is probably safer to refer to them as slow bowlers rather than spinners, for most are content to bowl flat at leg stump in the one-day game rather than to try to spin the ball, most sides opt to go into a limited-over match with five seam bowlers. It is this fact which arouses so much adverse criticism. Five bowlers bowling at medium pace just short of a length implies a lack of variety and imagination. It seems a recipe for dullness, particularly when such emotive terms as 'trundler' and 'military medium' are used to describe the members of the attack in a one-day side. The obsession for pace or medium-pace bowling, however, is not restricted to the limited-over game. At Test level, the West Indies under Clive Lloyd consistently operated with an attack consisting of four pace bowlers, and Lloyd showed little subtlety in manipulating such an attack, simply replacing one fast man with another when tiredness seemed imminent. The way in which a five-man attack is deployed in a limited-over game demands more thought and skill than that.

In the first place there is a restriction on the number of overs that a bowler can bowl which, considering that nobody makes a batsman retire when he has faced a certain number of deliveries, is in many ways unfair, but a captain none the less has this limitation to consider in all his tactical decisions. Very few attacks consist of five bowlers of equal quality, and some sides carry six players who are able to bowl with the intention either that one is held in reserve in case a front-line bowler is off form, or that the 'fifth' bowler's quota is shared between two people. Whatever the composition of an attack, the captain has two main decisions to make – how best to use his strengths and how best to hide his weaknesses.

Several captains have fallen into an unwavering system of opening with their two main bowlers who, having bowled half or two-thirds of their quota, return for the closing overs of the innings. Yet even this simple, and obvious, tactic can be challenged. If one of the main strike bowlers takes quick wickets, the captain has to decide whether to rest him, so that he has overs left for the final spurt; or to continue to attack in the hope of breaking the

Geoff Boycott's style of batting was considered by some to be alien to the one-day game, but his gentle medium-pace bowling was used to tactical effect on several occasions.

back of the batting side.

Such a problem was posed to England's captain Mike Brearley in the Prudential World Cup match against Pakistan at Headingley in 1979. Put in to bat, England were 4 for 2, but they recovered to reach 165 for 9 in their sixty overs, a total which hardly looked likely to trouble the Pakistanis, who were strong in batting. Willis and Hendrick opened the England bowling, and in a memorable spell Mike Hendrick took 4 wickets in eight balls for 3 runs. With Botham accounting for Zaheer Abbas and Javed Miandad, Pakistan disintegrated to 34 for 6 and looked hopelessly beaten. Brearley had, however, persevered with Hendrick, allowing him to bowl out his ration of twelve overs and finish with 4 for 15.

The problem was that as Asif Iqbal, Wasim Raja, Imran Khan and Wasim Bari began to revive Pakistan's hopes, Brearley was unable to use his most economical bowler, Hendrick, because he had completed his quota. The difficulty was compounded by the fact that the England side was not strong at bowling in depth. Edmonds, the fifth bowler, found his left-arm spin unsuited to the occasion and the wicket, and Gooch, a relatively inexperienced player at the time, and Boycott were pressed into action. In the event, Boycott took the last two wickets with his slow medium pace, and England won by 14 runs. Welcome as Hendrick's success had been, it had presented Brearley with a dilemma, which he resolved happily as it turned out, but had Bob Taylor and Hendrick not taken fine catches it might well have gone the other way. Boycott's 2 for 14 was to represent his best bowling figures in limited-over internationals, in which his career total was 5 wickets.

Some captains, Mark Nicholas of Hampshire being amongst them, have arrived at the view that whoever bowls the closing overs of an innings it is likely to be expensive in the final wild slog for runs. Believing this, Nicholas has frequently used his most economical and lethal bowlers Malcolm Marshall and Tim Tremlett in mid-innings, hoping to frustrate the batsmen and induce some rash strokes as they seek to break the shackles.

Such a policy may mean utilizing one of the less effective bowlers over the last stages of the innings, but the question as to when to use the weak link is always a difficult one. In a Sunday League match, all bowlers are reduced to something of a mundanity by the limitation placed upon their run-ups, so that the timing of the use of the 'fifth' bowler becomes even more complex. Each competition, and each occasion, demands a reassessment of tactics.

In his early days with Essex, Neil Foster, although an England bowler, found himself left

Neil Foster struggled to adapt to the needs of one-day cricket in his early days with Essex.

out of the county's Sunday League side, for he was unable to come to terms with the special needs of the forty-over game. While his colleague, the experienced John Lever, could tax batsmen in the closing overs by consistently moving the ball in to them on a very full length so that they were constantly tucked up around their pads, Foster would maintain a line on and outside the off stump, admirable in a three-day match when bowling with the new ball to three slips and a gully, but offering the batsman room and scope to hit hard on the off on a Sunday afternoon.

In the longer competitions, the NatWest Bank Trophy and the Benson and Hedges Cup, tactical thinking in terms of deployment of the field and the use of bowlers can be closer to that of the first-class game, but always with the additional problem of the limitation on the number of overs that a bowler is allowed to bowl. To have to entrust eleven or twelve overs to an inexperienced bowler at a time when the main strike bowlers have given you the initiative can mean the surrender of that initiative, so the moment when such a bowler is used is vital in the tactical pattern of the game. There is always the desire to hold some overs in reserve from the quota of the main strike bowlers against a turn of fortune or against the inevitable plunder for runs that comes in the closing overs.

Northamptonshire entered the 1987 NatWest Bank Trophy Final against Nottinghamshire with a formidable attack – West Indian pace-man Winston Davis, medium-pacers Capel and Walker, slow left-arm spinner Nick Cook and off-break bowler Richard Williams. Also in the side and capable of bowling were Duncan Wild, a most useful medium-pacer, Robert Bailey and Wayne Larkins, so that Northamptonshire had the comfort of depth in reserve, a luxury given to few sides. In contrast, their opponents had to survive on five bowlers, with no room for manoeuvre.

Put in to bat, Northamptonshire made 228 in their sixty overs. Winston Davis produced a furious opening spell during which he accounted for the England opening pair Broad and Robinson. Walker had Johnson lbw, and Nick Cook bowled Randall with a ball which he tossed into the evening sun and which descended into the shadows. The game had been disrupted by rain and had to be continued on the Monday afternoon, but Nottinghamshire had seemingly lost the match on the Saturday evening when Davis' blast and excellent support bowling had reduced them to 38 for 4.

The problem that faced Geoff Cook, the Northamptonshire captain, when play resumed on the Monday, was how to use what remained of Davis' allocation. Rice and Birch were the not-out batsmen, and the quick dismissal of one of them would virtually assure Northamptonshire of victory. Cook opted to try for this and use Davis for two overs, but he failed to produce the fire of the Saturday evening and the batsmen survived. What was worse from the Northamptonshire point of view was the inability of David Capel, an England all-rounder, to find any sort of form with his medium-pace bowling. Wild was used too late, at a time when the batsmen were confident, established and going for runs, and Capel was brought back to share the closing overs with Davis.

Nottinghamshire had begun play on the Monday needing 172 from twenty-nine overs to win a match which rain had reduced to fifty overs an innings. Rice and Birch negotiated the difficult opening overs, and Hadlee and French launched the final assault. Richard Williams had taken 1 for 33 in nine overs, but 15 runs were scored off his last over and two catches were missed. Nottinghamshire needed 51 off the last five overs, and French and Hadlee reduced this to 16 off the last two.

The penultimate over was bowled by Winston Davis who produced two splendid deliveries, but four runs were scored from the next three balls and the last ball of the over Hadlee slashed to the Mound Stand for four.

The unhappy Capel bowled the last over. French was run out in bizarre fashion off the first ball. The batsmen went for a comfortable single, but the ball hit Hadlee on the inside of the foot and rebounded into Capel's hands to leave French well out of his ground. It mattered little. The next ball Hadlee pulled furiously to the Tavern boundary, and the following ball was hit gloriously over long-off for six to give Nottinghamshire a glorious victory.

It had seemed that Northamptonshire had had the match in their grasp, but Nottinghamshire had wrenched it tactically from them. Clive Rice, leading by example, assured his team before play began on the Monday that victory was still possible, that all that was necessary was to combat Davis with care and common sense and to wait patiently for the bad over that was sure to come. Cook could have anticipated this tactic, but he failed to respond quickly enough to Capel's lack of form and fitness, trusting in the England all-rounder when the signs suggested otherwise. Cook's failure to use Wild adequately and at the right time was a tactical flaw, although when the correct time would have been remains debatable, so keen was the Northamptonshire captain to maintain the pressure on the Nottinghamshire batsmen. It is also hard to remain true to a formula when confronted by batsmen of the calibre of Rice and Hadlee.

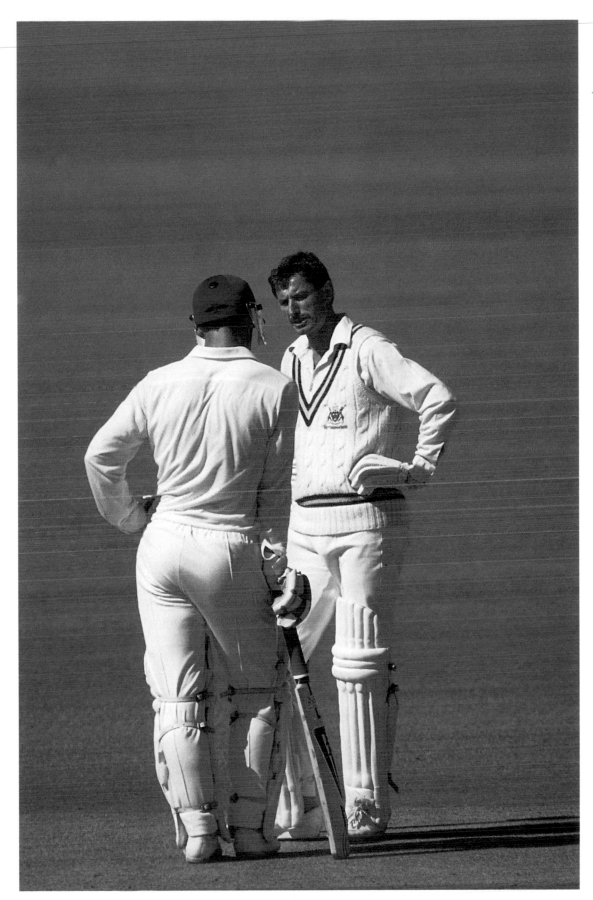

Richard Hadlee, Man of
the Match in the 1987
NatWest Bank Trophy
Final, wrecked
Northamptonshire's
plans and took
Nottinghamshire to
victory.

'Larry' Gomes who was
often the vital fifth
bowler for the
triumphant West Indian
side, but was more at
home as a batsman.

The tactical opportunity that the sixty-over and fifty-five-over games present that the Sunday League does not is that an innings is spread either side of a lunch or tea interval. Clive Lloyd, successful as captain of both West Indies and Lancashire, was one tactician who grasped the advantages that the break had for the fielding captain.

In Test cricket Lloyd was able to permutate his four fast bowlers, but the limited-over game imposed upon him the need to use a fifth bowler who was frequently of a standard well below that of the pace-men of whom the West Indies always seem to have an abundance. At various times Lloyd himself, Kallicharran, Gomes and Richards have filled the fifth bowling spot, for the composition of the West Indian side before the advent of Roger Harper was invariably six batsmen, a wicket-keeper and four fast bowlers, leaving one of the batsmen (or a combination of two or three) to bowl a quota of overs in the one-day game.

It needed no great intelligence to recognize that, spared momentarily from the bombardment of pace, batsmen would attempt to score freely off the makeshift West Indian bowler, and Lloyd's tactic was to use his weaker member of the attack either side of an interval. By doing this he created a sense of uncertainty in the mind of the batsman, who was eager to score runs while he could but who also realized the importance of not losing a wicket as an interval approached. Kapil Dev adopted the same policy with his Indian bowlers, and it is a tactic which many see as making great sense, although some have even opened the bowling with the weakest member in an attempt to get overs out of the way before batsmen settle.

We have tended to concentrate so far on the bowling aspect of one-day cricket, when most people would argue that the attraction of such cricket is the entertaining batting it provides. Again it is necessary to draw a distinction between the forty-over Sunday League and the other competitions, both domestic and international. Professional cricketers will argue that the forty-over game allows only the opportunity to slog, that there is neither time nor incentive to build an innings. The whole game is a form of instant cricket, a lottery which breeds a violation of technical and aesthetic standards.

The longer competitions, on the other hand, allow a batsman time to build an innings and do not demand that he attempts to score runs off every ball from the outset. Against this view can be set the opinion that this is only the case for the earlier batsmen and that the late middle order, often young players learning their craft, still has to indulge in batting eccentricities and

blasphemies in the charge which accompanies any attempt to accelerate the run rate. The critics point to the one-day game as the reason for what they see as a decline in the quality of batting, and several examples are given of shots which epitomize this drop in standards.

Certainly, a shot which has crept into the game at all levels is the angled bat to divert the ball through the slip area. In most one-day competitions slips are removed after one or two overs, and running the ball down to third man with an angled bat has become highly productive of singles. Those captains who are brave enough to persevere with slip fielders are often rewarded with wickets like Emburey's thrilling catch to dismiss Chris Cowdrey in the 1986 Benson and Hedges Cup Final. Cowdrey was the victim of a brilliant one-handed catch and of the angled-bat shot. Other captains argue that if they keep a slip fielder, the batsmen will score by slashing the ball over the top of the fielder.

The problem with the angled-bat shot is that not only is it ugly and dangerous, but it has almost killed the art of cutting, and the cut was one of the most beautiful shots in cricket.

For some, it has been replaced by the reverse sweep, seen by many as one of the great abominations directly attributable to the one-day game. In simple terms, the reverse sweep is really an attempt by a right-handed batsman momentarily to play left-handedly, crossing his hands and sweeping a ball pitched on or outside leg stump round to the off. The object is to frustrate the bowler and to score runs because it is virtually impossible to set a field in anticipation of such a shot; but it violates all the precepts of batsmanship, and while many players will argue that they have prospered by using it, they have also looked very silly when it has been responsible for their dismissal. Two of its greatest exponents, Ian Botham and Mike Gatting, have also succumbed because of it at

The offending shot produced by one-day cricket. Botham plays the reverse sweep.

Botham in more orthodox mood as Worcestershire beat Northamptonshire and take the Refuge Assurance Sunday League, 1987.

most crucial moments in important matches.

At Old Trafford in May 1985, England met Australia in the first of three Texaco Trophy matches. England were 27 for 3 when Botham came in to play with customary majesty. He hit five massive sixes and his 72 came off 82 balls at a time when his side had been in a wretched position. Having added 116 in twenty-eight overs with Gooch, who was caught on the square-leg boundary, Botham was just threatening to establish another big stand with Gatting when he was out. Greg Matthews tossed his off-breaks at the off stump, and Botham was bowled by a ball which hardly turned when he attempted to play the reverse sweep. England added only another 59 runs and were all out for 219, with one over unused. Botham was named Man of the Match, but Australia won by three wickets.

Peter May, the Chairman of the England selectors, banned the reverse sweep by his players after this match, but the ban does not seem to have stayed in operation for very long, for the shot was to claim another victim just over two years later.

Mike Gatting has always maintained that the reverse sweep brings him many runs, but his injudicious use of the shot in the World Cup Final in India in 1987 will long remain in the memory. Australia had made 253 in their fifty overs, and after thirty-one overs England were 135 for 2. Gatting and Athey were at the wicket, and there were signs that Australia were losing confidence and were in some disarray. The Australian captain, Allan Border, decided to introduce himself into the attack although his slow left-arm bowling was not seen consistently as part of the Australian attack. Border's object in bowling himself, it seemed, was to calm his young side. To his first delivery, pitched on leg stump, Gatting attempted a reverse sweep. It was hard to see the reasoning for the shot. The area where he would have hoped to send the ball was tenanted, and as this was Border's first delivery in the match it must have been difficult for the batsman to make an accurate assessment of flight, line and whether or not the bowler was able to turn the ball. The ball was pitched on leg stump and Gatting swept it on to his shoulder from where it looped into the hands of Greg Dyer, the Australian wicket-keeper. From that moment, Australia regained the initiative and they won the match.

If one has dwelt on the grotesqueness of the reverse sweep and the way in which the use of it by two great players in important matches has cost their side victory, this is because it is the most flagrant example of a shot which profanes the text-book and which is attributable to the one-day game. Equally, one must condemn the

No need for profanities. David Gower hits out.

tendency of many players to step outside the leg stump in an attempt to force through the off-side balls which may well be pitched outside leg stump. To see players of top quality bowled while attempting such shots is an undignified sight. The problem is that many seem to see the bizarre and grotesque as the only way to bat in limited-over cricket, tending to scorn the orthodox. They do so at their peril.

When Essex went to Leicester on 10 August 1975 for a John Player League match, they soon had the home side in trouble at 81 for 5. Leicestershire were rescued by a stand of 81 by Jack Birkenshaw and David Gower, an eighteen-year-old left-hander new to the side. Recognizing Gower's inexperience and technical orthodoxy, Essex were content, in their own words, 'to keep him in', but Gower has never had need to violate the orthodox or the aesthetic in order to score runs. He finished with 57 not out, and Essex were well beaten. Within three years Gower was an England player.

The truth is that while the one-day game is blamed by some for a drop in batting standards, it also gives the sensible county player the opportunity to increase the range of his stroke-play. Bill Athey is an example of a batsman who has reached Test level through application and sound technique and who is now in need of a greater sense of freedom, improvisation and variety if he is to score runs consistently against international bowling. Certainly none of the overseas batting stars such as Richards, Rice, McEwan, Hick, Martin Crowe or Javed Miandad seems to have had his batting technique impaired by the amount of one-day cricket that he has played in England. Gordon Greenidge held the batting record in all three one-day competitions in England at one time, but he was still scoring prolifically, quickly and stylishly in the County Championship and in Test cricket.

Viv Richards has given several examples as to how genius can reshape any game without offending the connoisseur greatly. In the World Cup Final of 1979 he recovered from an uncertain start to hit 138 not out. The last over of the West Indian innings was bowled by Mike Hendrick, the most economical of the England bowlers. Hendrick's last ball was an intelligent delivery, aimed at preventing runs being scored. It was an attempted yorker on off stump. The unhappy result from the English point of view was that Richards' agile cricket brain anticipated Hendrick's attempted yorker as the logical delivery. As the ball left the bowler's hand he had adjusted his position on to the line of the off stump and, taking the ball on the full toss, he hoisted it into the Mound Stand for six. It was a stroke of daring and intelligence from a batsman supremely confident of his own ability, and it was a shot of skill and invention that owed much to the one-day game.

Graham Gooch has prospered in all forms of cricket while rarely deviating from his constant desire to attack the bowling. His team-mate Ken McEwan, who retired from English cricket in 1985, delighted wherever he went with his classical stroke-play which remained as consistent in the one-day game as it did in the three-day variety.

In the Benson and Hedges Cup Final at Lord's in 1979, Gooch and McEwan shared a stand of 124 which delighted all who saw it and which offered no offence to the purists. It was batting of a richness that needed no recourse to the vulgar. McEwan's 72 came off 99 balls and included ten fours. A reverse sweep would have been to him a denial of his art. As he helped to seize the initiative from the bowlers he twice drove thunderously to the cover boundary, and when the bowler dropped short he hooked and pulled the ball ferociously for four.

Gooch, who had opened the innings, was out in the fifty-third over for 120. Ever belligerent, he had hit three sixes and eleven fours and always sought to dominate the bowling with an exciting range of shots that exuded power. When Roger Knight, the Surrey captain and medium-pace bowler, threatened to curb the rate of scoring, Gooch moved down the wicket and hit the ball high back over the bowler's head to the Nursery End sight-screen for six. As Hugh Wilson raced in on his long run which started almost at the pavilion steps, Gooch ambled forward and picked up the ball on the full pitch, flicking it off his toes into the Mound Stand. Disdainfully he repeated the shot, this time landing the ball on the roof of the Mound Stand.

It was perhaps appropriate that the first time that Gooch profaned the craft of batsmanship he was punished. He swung across the line at Wilson and was bowled. It was an inelegant end to an innings of majesty.

Batsmen like Gooch, Viv Richards and David Gower have sufficient confidence in their armoury of strokes and in the surety of their timing to find it generally unnecessary to resort to reverse sweeps and dabs down to third man. Why push for a single when you are capable of driving for four? The one-day game has tended only to extend their repertoire, and they have never found that the need to accelerate the tempo of an innings has to be made at the expense of the more subtle skills of the game.

If Ian Botham has been singled out for some criticism because of his injudicious use of the reverse sweep in a one-day international match, it is because of the feeling that a man who is more capable of tearing apart a Test-match attack than any other batsman in the world has no need to play such shots. Botham's record in nearly a hundred one-day internationals is somewhat disappointing. His figure of fourteen Test-match hundreds is matched by a highest score of 72 in one-day internationals, where one would have thought that his talents would have flourished. That they have not done so is, of course, because he has often batted so low down the order and has had no opportunity to play a substantial innings. Recognizing that the capabilities of one of the world's great attacking batsmen were being wasted, England promoted Botham to opener in the Benson and Hedges World Series in Australia in 1987, while a few months later his new county, Worcestershire, also cast Botham in this role for their one-day matches. The move met with enormous success. Botham and Tim Curtis ended the season with four successive century partnerships in the Refuge Assurance Sunday League, and Worcestershire carried off the title.

Graham Gooch ready for action. The raised bat was a technique evolved to combat quick bowling. It was not a product of the one-day game — Gooch maintains style and approach in all forms of cricket.

Botham's prowess at the one-day game has never been in doubt, for there is no greater hitter of the ball anywhere in the world; arguably, there never has been. Returning from suspension in August 1986, he played an amazing innings at Wellingborough where Somerset's opponents were Northamptonshire.

In this John Player League game, he hit 175 not out off only 122 balls and established a record for the competition by hitting thirteen sixes. He also hit twelve fours and would surely have reached the highest individual score ever made in the competition but for the fact that the innings was restricted to thirty-nine overs rather than the

Graeme Hick (Worcestershire). The most exciting batting prospect in the world.

prescribed forty because so much time had been lost in retrieving the ball after Botham's massive hits.

A year later, now with Worcestershire, Botham reached a hundred off 92 balls in a first-round NatWest Bank Trophy match against Devon. He hit three sixes and ten fours, but he was overshadowed by Graeme Hick. The young batsman from Zimbabwe reached his hundred off 81 balls and, astonishingly, made 172 not out off 111 deliveries. Four of Hick's eight sixes came off successive balls, and he also hit thirteen fours. Capable of the most powerful driving and pulling and of piercing the field by the way in which they place their shots, batsmen like Hick, Botham and Gooch approach the one-day game as they would any other, and, allowing for Botham's occasional aberrations which stem from his supreme self-confidence and his lust for adventure rather than from anything else, they have shown emphatically that a limitation in overs has in no way placed limitations on their technique, nor caused them to pervert it.

If some have argued that one-day cricket has had an adverse effect on batting, no one has denied that it has helped to raise the quality of fielding to a level never seen before. We have already touched on this in the examination of the impact that limited-over cricket has made on the game as a whole, but it is worth reiterating. Preventing runs from being scored is a requisite of one-day cricket, and it demands a high standard of athleticism and consistent throwing power. It is no longer possible to hide a less-than-nimble member of the side in the slips or fine-leg. Slips invariably disappear after a few overs, if posted at all, and fine-leg, like all other positions, may be constantly tested. A throw from the boundary fence can turn a match so that a weak arm can no longer find a place in a side, and fielding has now become as important a part of the game as batting and bowling.

Inspired by Jack Bond, Lancashire owed much of their one-day success in the early years of the domestic competitions to their excellence in the field, and players such as Alan Ealham of Kent and Alan Lilley have been chosen for their qualities as fielders above all else.

Ealham was dynamic in the field, bringing off spectacular running catches and diving stops as well as running out batsmen with lightning flat throws from the boundary. To see him field in the highly successful Kent side of the 1970s was one of the greatest joys of the game. He was one player who introduced a new dimension to cricket and brought the realization that every ball bowled was important.

Ealham became captain of Kent and has now retired, but Alan Lilley is still a regular member of the Essex side, although he took a

Alan Ealham, whose brilliant fielding helped to lift Kent cricket to new heights and to success.

long time to establish himself. His career began sensationally with a century on the occasion of his county debut in a Championship match at Trent Bridge at the end of the 1978 season. The following year he opened the innings for Essex in one-day matches, and he and Gooch shared what was then a record partnership of 223 in a Benson and Hedges Cup match against Combined Universities. But his technical vulnerability outside the off stump was exploited in later matches, and he lost his place in the Essex side before the final at Lord's. He remained a fringe cricketer, but the brilliance of his fielding was always apparent. He seems capable of catching anything, moves very fast and throws with the speed and accuracy of a bullet. He won a place back in the Essex side, as a number seven batsman able to provide some ferocious hitting towards the end of an innings, and as a fielder who could turn the course of a game.

In a Benson and Hedges Cup match at Chelmsford in 1985, Essex were defending a total of 202 for 8 which, with Gatting going strongly, looked inadequate. At 63 for 1, Middlesex were cruising to victory and Gatting had begun to find the boundary with regularity. He slashed fiercely at a short ball from Turner, and it seemed that the ball would race to the fence, but Lilley, square at cover, held the ball in his left hand as he was knocked back by the force of the shot. It was a breathtaking catch

The importance of fielding in the one-day game. Jack Heron (Zimbabwe) is run out by Madan Lal, and Kapil Dev leaps clear. India v Zimbabwe, Tunbridge Wells, 1983.

symptomatic of Essex fielding, which snatched victory after a less than satisfactory batting display.

The increasingly exciting fielding that is so much an aspect of the one-day game, is, of course, not restricted to that type of cricket. In the past decade, the fielding of the England side has reached levels never before attained. Derek Randall became renowned for his swoops on the ball, his pick-up and throw, and for the joy he exuded in the sheer pleasure of fielding. Where once bowlers were prone to rest in the field when not actually bowling, now players of the calibre of Foster, De Freitas, Emburey and Ellison contribute significantly with their catching and throwing.

To the one-day game cricket owes thanks for the advance and development in the skill of fielding and in more thoughtful field-placing. Those who follow the game are now more appreciative than ever before of this most important aspect of the game, and even the role of the wicket-keeper, so long undervalued, is now studied with greater understanding.

There have been occasions when the significance of a top-rate wicket-keeper has been underestimated, and sides have elected to take the field with a lesser keeper who had the potential to score more runs than the first choice. This proved to be a false economy. The run contribution turned out to be minimal, and the loss in expertise costly. Some would argue that with most wicket-keepers spending their time standing back to medium-pace bowlers the job of the keeper has been reduced to that of a catcher with gloves on, but that is far from the case. With slips withdrawn, the keeper often has to cover an area far in excess of what was once expected. The full-length dive to take a catch somewhere in the position of third slip or wide down the leg side has now become the norm rather than the sensational, and the keeper remains the hub of the side.

While many keepers do spend most of their time standing back, there are those like Downton, Rhodes and, before his retirement, Taylor who inhibit batsmen by standing up and attacking from the rear. In some ways the wicket-keeper's job has become less varied, but it has also become, of necessity, more athletic.

Neither has this increased athleticism been restricted to the art of fielding. The whole art of running between the wickets has been revitalized. Where every run is vital, no chance of a run must be lost. In this area, the big hitters of the ball like Gooch are more reluctant quick runners, perhaps, but the eager sprinting for singles of Fowler, the Cowdrey brothers, Radley, Randall and the rest have given the game a new excitement.

*Fitness fanatic. Gooch
trains with West Ham
United Football Club in
the winter months.*

None exemplifies the modern attitude to running between the wickets better than Javed Miandad of Pakistan, and formerly of Sussex and Glamorgan. From the moment he comes to the crease, Javed, one of the most prolific scorers in one-day international cricket, is on the look-out for runs. His instinctive philosophy is that if a ball is hit, the shot should be worth nought, two or four. The purely defensive shot is obviously worth no runs, and the boundary shot is equally obvious, but Javed maintains that with one-day field-placings, once the inner ring is pierced a shot should be worth two, and his attitude to running is geared accordingly. He adheres to the maxim of running the first run quickly, very quickly, and he is always looking for another. His eagerness at the wicket is one of the most attractive features of his batting.

The tactics and skill born of the one-day game have enhanced cricket as a whole, and it would seem that the benefits of limited-over cricket outweigh the liabilities if the amount of such cricket played is kept in proportion, which sadly does not seem to be the case in Australia. There can be good one-day cricket with thrilling finishes and high-quality batting, bowling and fielding; and there can be boring one-day matches in which the side that bats first scores either too many runs or too few to give an even

contest, and the rest is tedium – but such is the danger in any sport, not only in cricket.

There are those, too, who argue that as the one-day game must always offer a result, the removal of the possibility of batsmen forcing a draw deprives the game of interest and excitement, but this is why the one-day and first-class games co-exist and replenish each other.

One-day cricket inherited the technique and philosophy of the traditional game. At its best it does not violate traditions, but it has shaped its own personality, tactics and skill to its own needs. It offers a batsman a chance to widen his range of strokes, and helps the wise to become inventive without being foolhardy. To the bowler it offers the opportunity to develop accuracy and control and to exploit a batsman's weaknesses. To the fielder it has given a new, exalted status and helped him to reach standards of achievement previously undreamed of. It has breathed energy into every aspect of the game.

It does present pitfalls and dangers to the unwary and unthinking, but the master craftsmen – Richards, Greenidge, Lloyd, Kapil Dev, Rice, Hadlee, Gooch, Gower, Gatting, Imran, Qadir, Crowe, Border – have taken sustenance from it which has sharpened their response to the game as a whole and has in no way diminished their great powers.

BENSON AND HEDGES CUP RECORDS

WINNERS

1972	Leicestershire	1980	Northamptonshire
1973	Kent	1981	Somerset
1974	Surrey	1982	Somerset
1975	Leicestershire	1983	Middlesex
1976	Kent	1984	Lancashire
1977	Gloucestershire	1985	Leicestershire
1978	Kent	1986	Middlesex
1979	Essex	1987	Yorkshire

HIGHEST TEAM SCORE

350 for 3, Essex *v* Combined Universities, Chelmsford, 1979.

LOWEST TEAM SCORE

56, Leicestershire *v* Minor Counties, Wellington, 1982.

HIGHEST SCORE IN FINAL

290 for 6, Essex *v* Surrey, Lord's, 1979.

LOWEST SCORE IN FINAL

130, Nottinghamshire *v* Somerset, 1982.

BIGGEST VICTORY

By 214 runs, Essex beat Combined Universities, Chelmsford, 1979. Ten victories have been obtained by ten wickets.

HIGHEST INDIVIDUAL SCORE

198 not out, G.A. Gooch, Essex *v* Sussex, Hove, 1982.

HIGHEST INDIVIDUAL SCORE IN FINAL

132 not out, I.V.A. Richards, Somerset *v* Surrey, Lord's, 1981.

MOST CENTURIES

5, G.A. Gooch (Essex) and C.G. Greenidge (Hampshire).

FASTEST CENTURY

62 minutes, M.A. Nash, Glamorgan *v* Hampshire, Swansea, 1976.

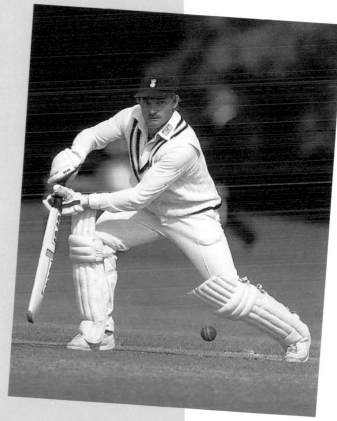

David Turner of Hampshire. One of the most consistently successful batsmen in one-day cricket, and an outstanding fielder. He and Gordon Greenidge hold the record for the highest partnership in the Benson and Hedges Cup.

RECORD PARTNERSHIPS FOR EACH WICKET

1st	241	S.M. Gavaskar & B.C. Rose, Somerset *v* Kent, Canterbury, 1980.
2nd	285*	C.G. Greenidge & D.R. Turner, Hampshire *v* Minor Counties (South), Amersham, 1973.
3rd	269*	P.M. Roebuck & M.D. Crowe, Somerset *v* Hampshire, Southampton, 1987.
4th	184*	D. Lloyd & B.W. Reidy, Lancashire *v* Derbyshire, Chesterfield, 1980.
5th	160	A.J. Lamb & D.J. Capel, Northamptonshire *v* Leicestershire, Northampton, 1986.
6th	114	Majid J. Khan & G.P. Ellis, Glamorgan *v* Gloucestershire, Bristol, 1975.
7th	149*	J.D. Love & C.M. Old, Yorkshire *v* Scotland, Bradford, 1981.
8th	109	R.E. East & N. Smith, Essex *v* Northamptonshire, Chelmsford, 1977.
9th	85	P.G. Newman & M.A. Holding, Derbyshire *v* Nottinghamshire, Trent Bridge, 1985.
10th	80*	D.L. Bairstow & M. Johnson, Yorkshire *v* Derbyshire, Derby, 1981.

MOST RUNS IN THE COMPETITION

3007, G.A. Gooch (Essex).

MOST WICKETS IN A MATCH

7, W.W. Daniel, J.R. Thomson and R.G.D. Willis. W.W. Daniel 7 for 12, Middlesex *v* Minor Counties (East), Ipswich, 1978. J.R. Thomson 7 for 22, Middlesex *v* Hampshire, Lord's, 1981. R.G.D. Willis 7 for 32, Warwickshire *v* Yorkshire, Edgbaston, 1981.

MOST WICKETS IN A CAREER

137, J.K. Lever (Essex).

MOST WICKETS IN A SEASON

19, C.E.H. Croft (Lancashire), 1982, and J.K. Lever (Essex), 1979.

MOST RUNS IN A SEASON

591, G.A. Gooch (Essex), 1979.

HAT-TRICKS

G.D. McKenzie, Leicestershire *v* Worcestershire, Worcester, 1972.
K. Higgs, Leicestershire *v* Surrey, Lord's (final), 1974.
A.A. Jones, Middlesex *v* Essex, Lord's, 1977.
M.J. Procter, Gloucestershire *v* Hampshire, Southampton, 1977.
W. Larkins, Northamptonshire *v* Combined Universities, Northampton, 1980.
E.A. Moseley, Glamorgan *v* Kent, Cardiff, 1981.
G.C. Small, Warwickshire *v* Leicestershire, Leicester, 1984.
W.K.M. Benjamin, Leicestershire *v* Nottinghamshire, Leicester, 1987.

FIELDING

MOST CATCHES IN A CAREER

46, G.A. Gooch (Essex).

MOST CATCHES IN AN INNINGS

5, V.J. Marks, Combined Universities *v* Kent, Oxford, 1976.

WICKET-KEEPING

MOST DISMISSALS IN A CAREER

114, D.L. Bairstow (Yorkshire) (c 109/st 5).

MOST DISMISSALS IN A MATCH

8, D.J.S. Taylor (Somerset) *v* Combined Universities, Taunton, 1982. All eight were caught. This is a world record for a one-day match.

David Bairstow, Yorkshire, the leading wicket-keeper in the Benson and Hedges Cup matches.

4 CROWD BEHAVIOUR

The money that has poured into cricket in recent years in the form of sponsorship, advertising, players' benefits and courtesy cars is in sharp contrast to the rewards that the game offered in the 1930s. In comparing the status of the pre-war cricketer with the cricketer of today, Bill Andrews, Somerset all-rounder of the thirties and one of the game's most endearing characters, tells how he asked his friend E.W. Clark what he thought about the standard of living that a player of the 1980s could expect to enjoy.

'Nobby' Clark, who bowled left-arm medium pace for Northamptonshire and England, had advertised for Guinness in the 1930s, and Andrews asked him what he had been paid for the advertisement. 'They sent my wife a

box of chocolates at Christmas,' Clark replied. It is hardly likely that one of today's cricketers, or his agent, would be satisfied with such payment.

A successful cricketer's basic county wage is often the smallest proportion of his income. The endorsement of goods, the gifts for opening a new kitchen centre or fashion store, can provide a substantial boost to salary. The more successful he is, and the more his face is seen in front of a television camera, the more a cricketer can expect to earn from sources not directly related to his cricketing prowess.

Victory in one-day competitions brings with it considerable prize money. Awards to individuals for outstanding performances in matches have a monetary as well as a prestigious value, and while the Gold Award winner retains his medal, the cheque (£125 in Benson and Hedges Cup zonal matches, rising to £200 in the quarter-finals, £275 in the semi-finals, through to £550 in the final) is paid into the players' pool which is shared among the first-team squad at the end of the season.

County success, too, brings increased sponsorship from companies eager to be patrons associated with a side doing well. Essex, highly successful in the 1980s, could boast that even second-team players who had not appeared in first-class cricket were driving cars that carried the names of sponsors on the side, which indicated some form of subsidy to club and player. A less successful county just to the north

A crowd-pleaser at any time. Tim Robinson pulls a ball to the boundary during his match-winning innings of 139 for Nottinghamshire against Worcestershire at Worcester, NatWest Bank Trophy semi-final, 1985

The Essex contingent at Lord's for the NatWest Final, 1985.

of them could, at the same period, hope for only four sponsored cars between players and administration.

As we have examined earlier, the rewards of the game have become greatly increased by the advent of one-day cricket, and many would argue that this has had a detrimental effect on the attitude of players and spectators. So great are the rewards today, so much is at stake, that there is a desire to win at any cost. We have noted this in the actions of Brian Rose declaring Somerset's innings closed at 1 for 0 in a Benson and Hedges match, and in the Chappell brothers' decision to bowl underarm to deny New Zealand any chance of victory. Such attitudes have sharpened the animosity between players, at least on the field, for winning has become paramount in a game where once simply to play and enjoy were sufficient. For many spectators new to the game, victory at all costs is the dominant

philosophy. They see no point in watching anything else.

When county championship matches provided the only form of cricket, there were few people able to be present for all three days of the game. Spectators would watch the first or second day of a match, anxious to see Hammond, Hutton, Compton or one of the other noted players of the day perform, and would not care greatly about the final outcome of the game, learning its result only from the newspapers. In any case, with Yorkshire and Surrey dominating the Championship for long periods, there was little point in getting too excited over a single victory, and to beat one of the top counties once every three or four years was excitement enough. In the 103 years before they finally won a trophy, for example, Essex counted their victory over Yorkshire at Huddersfield in 1935 as their greatest

Decoration at Hove during a Benson and Hedges Cup game.

achievement. Fifty years later, their supporters would feel a sense of failure and frustration if the county were not challenging strongly in the John Player League and were not also in the final stages of the knock-out competitions.

Winning has now become more important in cricket than ever before, and the price that clubs, administrators and players pay for failure now more closely resembles that paid by the football manager. Following their years of success in the seventies, Kent, with the retirement and departure of several key players, faced a period of rebuilding, and it was indicative of the scale of the problem that members of the administrative staff could say at the beginning of a season, 'We are in a transitional period. We are not going to win anything this year, and that will cost us two thousand members.'

Failure to succeed at both Yorkshire and Warwickshire has caused committee-room upheavals, the departure of players and officials, and public recrimination. The joy, and relief, when Yorkshire took the Benson and Hedges Cup in 1987 was enormous. Defeat can be a bitter disappointment for players and spectators alike.

We have already touched upon Trevor Jesty's innings of 112 for Surrey against Lancashire in the NatWest Bank Trophy semi-final of 1986, an innings which was ended by Fowler's running catch. There was no finer innings played in any type of match in England that summer, and for Jesty, Surrey's defeat was particularly bitter. He was thirty-eight years old and had had a distinguished career with Hampshire before joining Surrey, but he had never played in a Lord's final, which has become the summit of many cricketers' hopes as well as those of their supporters.

New floodlights at Perth, Western Australia, to satisfy the appetite for one-day cricket through the day/night matches.

One-day cricket has brought with it a demand for instant success which is commensurate with the pace of life in the closing years of the twentieth century, with that emphasis on financial reward which is characteristic of the age. The audience at a one-day match is guaranteed a result, and very few members of that audience are in any doubt as to what they want that result to be. There is a partisanship in cricket today which was undreamed of in years gone by.

When Gloucestershire came to Lord's to meet Kent in the Benson and Hedges Cup Final of 1977 they were accompanied by an army of supporters, many of whom were dressed in ostentatiously rural garb and carried banners claiming 'Prayers at Canterbury Won't Stop Procter' and 'Canterbury, We've Got a Hell of a Team'. Gloucestershire were nearing victory when, in the closing stages of the match, play was held up several times as fans invaded the pitch in premature excitement. When the presentation took place in front of the pavilion, supporters had to be forced back by squads of police and scuffles ensued. Jack Bailey, the MCC secretary, put the blame squarely on the

Gloucestershire supporters, saying that their behaviour had been 'disgraceful' and that cricket faced a sad future if crowds were to be controlled only by means of fences, barriers and police dogs.

If the Gloucestershire fans were singled out for censure because of their raucous behaviour in a Lord's final, they had been by no means the only, nor even the worst offenders. The supporters of Lancashire, Somerset and, on occasion, Yorkshire had been described as the equivalent of football hooligans and had attracted displeasure over a considerable period. Sussex followers had let down the tyres of the Essex team van after their side had been beaten in the NatWest Bank Trophy quarter-final match at Hove in 1981. A few weeks later, when Essex themselves were beaten in the semi-final of the same competition at Derby, the loutish behaviour of some of their supporters drew adverse comment. The Essex chairman, Doug Insole, following further trouble after a Sunday League game at Colchester, issued a statement to the effect that his county would rather be without supporters who were aggressively partisan and unpleasant.

As the result of a growing belief that rowdiness and bad behaviour at John Player League matches was caused by those who used the games as an excuse for an afternoon's drinking, bars were closed for a considerable part of the duration of matches. The climax to incidents of unruliness came at the Texaco Trophy one-day international at Edgbaston in 1987 when, during the game between England and Pakistan, a Pakistani supporter was stabbed. Yet to blame this dreadful incident and any of the others solely on one-day cricket would be short-sighted and stupid. Whatever violence and unruliness has occurred at cricket matches is only a minor eruption of a malaise that has gripped our society with ever-increasing vigour for the past fifteen to twenty years and which has its roots in social, economic and educational problems.

To their credit, the Test and County Cricket Board, administrators of the game in England, have responded swiftly and firmly to any breach of discipline and manners on the part of crowds. Pitch invasions have almost disappeared, for those who invade are evicted from the ground. Crowds are well marshalled and dangerous banners are not allowed, nor the importation of large amounts of alcohol into the ground. The MCC, too, have responded strongly. They forbade the sale of a popular cricket magazine because they considered its headline in the wake of the Edgbaston incident to be too lurid, and they now erect a temporary stand at Lord's in front of the Tavern on the occasion of big matches as a precaution against a gathering of noisy supporters who are the worse for drink.

This precaution has had a dual effect. It has certainly dispersed or prevented the gathering of a caucus of hard drinkers, but it has on occasions, perhaps, taken some of the atmosphere and excitement out of a match. One thinks particularly of finals between Kent and Middlesex when two bands of the more sedate followers of the game have failed to produce anything of the crowd sparkle that one associates with finals, with no compensatory wit from the Tavern area. For the one-day game has brought to cricket a cup-tie atmosphere which should be cherished. There is excitement and joy in the air, and a passion of support that should not necessarily be harmful to anyone.

Mike Denness recalls that when he went out to open the innings for Essex against Surrey in the Benson and Hedges Cup Final at Lord's in 1979, he was thrilled by the reception that greeted him and his partner Gooch. Denness had captained England in various parts of the world as well as at home. He had been to Lord's as captain of Kent in one-day finals and held the cup aloft, but he had never before experienced a reception like the one he received at Lord's that July. As he and Gooch appeared in the doorway to the pavilion, there was a roar of approval and goodwill so moving in intensity and so passionate in strength as to be both inspiring and frightening.

Drawing power. Rishton CC, Lancashire, 1987.

Police face the crowds during the tragic events at the Texaco Trophy match at Edgbaston, 1987.

Growing popularity. Dilip Vengsarkar batting before a capacity crowd in Sharjah, the latest and wealthiest of centres for one-day cricket.

One recalls, too, the sheer excitement and pleasure of the Yorkshire and Nottinghamshire supporters after their teams' cup-final triumphs in 1987 and the celebrations later that were never anything but friendly and good-humoured. In the Benson and Hedges Cup semi-final at Canterbury the same year, a pulsating match between Kent and Northamptonshire saw amazing fluctuations of fortune. In a thrilling display of hitting, Chris Cowdrey had seemingly put the game out of Northamptonshire's reach, but a series of misfortunes, including an injury to their main strike bowler Baptiste, reduced Kent's effectiveness, and an inspired century by

Allan Lamb took Northamptonshire to a memorable victory. To have remained impassive and unmoved by the deeds of daring and the cruel blows of fate on that day would have been to admit to emotional illiteracy.

The problem caused by the arousing of passions is that those passions need to be controlled so that the supporter does not remain blind to the more subtle skills and quieter aspects of the game. By its very nature, one-day cricket is an acceleration of the tempo of the traditional game, and it is likely to breed spectators who are at once noisier, more demonstrative and less informed than those who were brought up exclusively in the passivity of the three-day game. The lack of understanding or sensitivity of this new type of spectator can be irritating. When his side needs 240 in sixty overs he may quickly become vexed if they do not hit a six or a four in the opening over, for he has not yet judged the gradations in pacing an innings at which the modern batsman has become so expert. The uninitiated spectator may be guilty, too, of clamouring for sides to bowl their overs more quickly or set their fields more hastily when there is no urgency, for a requisite number of overs has to be bowled. He has come to expect, unwisely, instant cricket at every second, just as he has tended to sacrifice the leisurely social meal for fast-food service.

To emphasize the negative response of those drawn to the game by limited-over cricket, however, is to do an injustice to the new generation of spectators and to the game itself. Many who were drawn by what they saw of one-day cricket on television have become county members, have found enjoyment in the three-day game, too, and have become more aware of the finer points of cricket. The increase in membership in several counties has helped to combat and even obliterate any hint of unruliness, while it has accelerated a greater appreciation of the game and an insistence on high standards of performance and of accommodation and facilities. The coffers of county clubs have benefited accordingly.

A stroke of beauty and power is readily applauded by all, and there is now a deeper understanding of inventiveness, yet it is in fielding and bowling that the one-day game has educated the spectator more than in any other aspect of the game.

When Northamptonshire beat Essex in the Benson and Hedges Cup Final of 1980 they were greatly indebted to their bowlers and fielders, who defended a moderate total. At one time, off-break bowler Peter Willey exerted a stranglehold on the Essex batting and particularly on the experienced Keith Fletcher. With the ball consistently fired at his leg stump, Fletcher was

Crowd-pleaser. The victim of a Botham six.

left with little alternative but to sweep, but Sarfraz Nawaz was some 15–20 yards 'round the corner' on the leg side. Every time that Fletcher swept, Sarfraz would drop on the ball, frustrating any attempt at a run. It was not the Northamptonshire supporters alone who were appreciative of the intelligence of the tactic and the accuracy needed to make it effective.

For years, a maiden over was received with a polite ripple of applause. Onlookers in the one-day game have greeted it with as much fervour as they do a boundary and with cries of 'Well bowled!' The understanding of the skill necessary to restrict a batsman who is eager to score runs has become acute, and the game is the better for it.

There are still impatience and ignorance, but these are not the monopoly of those who have come to cricket only in the past twenty years. There has been rowdiness and drunkenness, but these ills have long been with us and that on occasion they have spilled into cricket is not the fault of the one-day game, but of a society that has lost some of its moral direction and concern for fellow humans.

If the new class of spectator has taken time to accept and be accepted into the ethical fabric of the game, he has more than compensated for that by the qualities he has brought, not least of which is a sense of passion and commitment.

5 THE LIMITED-OVER CRICKETER

The first one-day competition, the Gillette Cup in 1963, revealed very little original thinking or acute perception of the needs of the limited-over game, as we have noted. Fields were set deep, and there was a reluctance to include slow bowlers because it was believed that slow bowling was easier to hit than medium-pace or quick bowling. Apart from these rather naive attitudes, no other concessions were made in the one-day game to suggest that it was in any way different from the three-day county match. The selection of sides remained standard as did the batting orders, yet, by the arrival of the John Player Sunday League in 1969, attitudes had begun to change. The pioneers of this change were the Lancashire County Cricket Club and their captain from 1968 until 1972, Jack Bond, the first cricketer to win fame and fortune on the strength of his performances in and attitude to one-day cricket. He was, in effect, the first great product of one-day cricket.

We have already traced the reasons for the crisis in Lancashire cricket which came to a head in 1964 following defeat in the semi-final of the Gillette Cup. For one reason or another, Wharton, Barber, Marner, Clayton and Dyson all left the club, and Grieves was replaced as captain by Brian Statham. Statham, one of the finest fast bowlers to have played for Lancashire and England, was not an ideal captain, but he was well liked by the players, and he played an important part in encouraging young men in the side so that the nucleus of a good, new team began to take shape. After three seasons as captain Brian Statham retired from the game, and Lancashire needed a new leader. They had already found one in the board room where Cedric Rhoades, a fierce critic of the former administration, had first won a place on the committee, then been elected vice-chairman and, soon afterwards, chairman.

Rhoades' passion in life was the well-being of Lancashire cricket. He played the major part in a redevelopment which helped to save the club financially, and he was adamant that Lancashire should again become a major cricketing force in the land. He drew up new terms of agreement for the players which gave added incentive and pride in playing for Lancashire. When the new regulations were introduced to enable counties to sign overseas players on immediate contract, he tried first for Gary Sobers, but, outbid by Nottinghamshire, he signed Farokh Engineer, the Indian wicket-keeper and opening batsman, on immediate registration; he also signed Clive Lloyd, who became qualified to play for the county in 1969 after the West Indian tour of England had finished. Both were surprise acquisitions; both were inspired signings.

But however dynamic Rhoades was in committee and in convincing members that change was needed, it was on the field of play that the great revolution was required, and when Statham retired Lancashire caused another stir by naming Jack Bond as his successor.

Bond had first played for Lancashire in 1955, but he had not held a regular place in the side. Nevertheless, he had proved to be a most impressive captain of the second eleven. He was a man capable of getting the best out of others, and such a quality is not often found. In many respects, the Rhoades–Bond partnership mirrored those that Brian Clough was to have with McGovern and Bowyer when he was manager of Derby County and Nottingham Forest, for Clough in soccer, like Rhoades in cricket, selected a man to lead his side in whom he saw qualities that others had failed to perceive.

Bond's approach was again like Clough's in that he was a realist. He admitted the weaknesses of his side and forced individuals to face their limitations, some of which had been fostered by their attitude to the game. He resolved to remedy shortcomings by reinvigorating attitudes and approach. Firstly he stressed the importance of fielding, and he made it quite clear that he was not prepared to consider anyone for a place in the side who was not totally committed to raising the standard of fielding to a level not previously attained. He insisted on physical fitness, and set his players an example which many must have found daunting at first. Secondly, and allied to his demands on fielding,

Jack Bond, captain of Lancashire. The first man to realize the full potential of the one-day game.

David Hughes. Hero of a memorable Lancashire win and recalled as captain in an attempt to revive the fortunes of the county 16 years later.

was his emphasis on accurate bowling, tight field-placing, and a more zestful approach to batting which would increase the scoring rate. The apathy which had seeped through Lancashire cricket from pavilion to wicket and which had caused an erosion of support was at an end.

In 1969, the year of its inception, the John Player League was won by Lancashire. The margin of their victory – one point ahead of

70

Hampshire – is deceptive, for they actually took the title when they beat Warwickshire at Nuneaton on 24 August with three Sundays of the season still remaining.

They retained the title the following season, the deciding match being that against Yorkshire at Old Trafford on 30 August. We have already alluded to this match, in which the gates at Old Trafford were closed on a capacity crowd of 33,000 for the first time since 1948. Yorkshire were bowled out in 37.5 overs for 165 in spite of Boycott's 81, and it is interesting to note that 15.5 of the 37.5 overs bowled in the Yorkshire innings were bowled by off-break bowler Jack Simmons and slow left-arm spinner David Hughes. They took 2 wickets each and confirmed Bond's philosophy that if bowling was accurate enough, it was good enough.

Lancashire lost Engineer early on, but Snellgrove and Pilling added 58 for the second wicket and Lancashire went on to win by 7 wickets with 4.1 overs to spare. Harry Pilling finished on 55 not out, and Sullivan hit a very brisk 56 not out after Clive Lloyd had gone for 20. Pilling's knock, which was the cornerstone of the Lancashire innings, took him past 1000 runs in the John Player League. He was the first batsman to reach this aggregate, and won a hundred pounds for the feat.

At the end of the match against Yorkshire Bond was presented with the trophy, and such was the excitement in Lancashire caused by the success in the one-day game that the crowd engulfed the ground for more than an hour after the game had ended, and there were scenes of tremendous jubilation.

Those scenes were repeated at Lord's the following week, when Lancashire beat Sussex to add the Gillette Cup to the John Player League Trophy. Sussex had won the trophy in the first two years of its existence, but a third triumph was denied them by some accurate bowling supported by dynamic fielding.

Sussex struggled from the start, losing Geoffrey Greenidge at 7 and Richard Langridge at 34, although shortly after lunch, at 113 for 3 in the thirty-seventh over with Jim Parks and Tony Greig looking well set, they appeared to have recovered; but the need to attack was their undoing. The aggressive nature of the Lancashire fielding meant that Sussex had to take risks if they were to score runs, and Parks, Greig and Graves succumbed in quick succession to the slow left arm of David Hughes, so that Sussex had to settle for 184 for 9 from their sixty overs.

In spite of Clive Lloyd lifting Spencer over mid-wicket for six and driving him straight for four, Lancashire were 113 for 4 in the fortieth over, which was two runs fewer than Sussex had been at the same stage; but Pilling and Engineer now took the game by the scruff of the neck. Pilling, who finished on 70 not out, was again the cornerstone while Engineer provided the panache. Victory came by 6 wickets with 4.5 overs to spare. Bond's masterly field-setting, and the quality of the Lancashire out-cricket as a whole, was the real difference between the two sides.

Wherever Lancashire went under Bond, huge crowds turned out to see them. They surrendered their John Player League title to Worcestershire in 1971, but they retained the Gillette Cup after some pulsating matches on the way to the final.

The quarter-final paired them with Essex at Chelmsford. Boyce sent back Wood and Pilling, and David Lloyd was run out to leave Lancashire at 16 for 3. It was this running out which caused the first controversy. David Lloyd's partner Clive Lloyd set off on a foolish run, and the Essex players were convinced that it was he who had been run out; but David Lloyd set off for the pavilion, and umpires Jakeman and Constant supported the view that it was indeed David who was out. Clive Lloyd went on to make 109 before being caught and bowled by Stuart Turner. He was supported late in the innings by Simmons and Hughes, who helped him in stands of 91 and 23.

Lancashire's total of 203 was by no means out of the reach of Essex, but as the home side fretted for quick runs they lost Ward, Francis, Taylor and Fletcher for 34 runs. The hard-hitting Boyce and the steady Saville renewed hope, and Turner and Hobbs added 74 in thirteen overs. There was further controversy as Barry Wood seemed to take every opportunity of impeding Hobbs as the batsmen tried to run between the wickets. Tempers ran high among players and among the crowd of 8000, an attendance of a size which Chelmsford had not witnessed until that time. Eventually, Lancashire won by 12 runs in the last over of the match. Again, Bond's control of the Lancashire out-cricket had proved decisive.

If the quarter-final match had been exciting, the semi-final against Gloucestershire at Old Trafford was to pass into cricket legend. Once more the gates were closed before the start of play with thousands locked outside. Rain was to cause an hour's delay at lunch-time, and the game, which was officially played before 23,520 and had receipts of £9728, was to make Gillette Cup history, extending as it did from 11.00 a.m. until 8.50 p.m.

Tony Brown decided to bat first when he won the toss, and Green, another Lancashire player whose services at Old Trafford had been no longer required, and Nicholls negotiated the opening thrust of Lever and Shuttleworth. They looked set for a big score when, at 57, Green pushed Simmons to mid-on and called for a run. Clive Lloyd, at short mid-wicket, pounced on the ball before it could reach Sullivan at mid-on and threw down the stumps at the bowler's end to run out Green.

Nicholls played quite splendidly until he was second out, bowled by Simmons for 53. Mike Procter then began to thrash the ball with immense power. He was particularly severe on Hughes, but having hit 65, which included a six and nine fours, he got a thick edge to a ball from Peter Lever and was astonishingly caught behind by Farokh Engineer, diving wide to his left. Gloucestershire were restricted to 229 for 6, and the hero of the Lancashire bowlers was Jack Simmons whose twelve overs of off-breaks cost only 25 runs and, concentrating almost entirely on a leg-stump attack, brought him the wickets of Nicholls and Shepherd.

David Lloyd and Barry Wood, like the Gloucestershire openers, concentrated on blunting the pace attack, Procter and Davey, and they put on a solid 61, the first 50 taking seventeen overs. Wood and Pilling increased the tempo and took the score to 105 before Pilling was bowled by Brown. Clive Lloyd then set about the bowling with a vengeance. He took 16 off five balls from Procter, but Wood was run out attempting a sharp bye from the last ball of the over.

Gloucestershire now found a hero in off-spinner Mortimore. Clive Lloyd failed to treat him with sufficient respect and was beaten in the flight when he advanced down the wicket in an attempt to hit Mortimore out of the ground. Engineer was caught in two minds and hit his wicket while Sullivan fell to Davey. At 163 for 6, Lancashire were 67 runs short of their target; fourteen overs remained and only four wickets.

The light was fading fast, and Bond was asked by the umpires if he wished to go off and finish the game the following morning. He reasoned that if the finish was delayed until the following morning, the Gloucestershire bowlers would be refreshed and his own batsmen unlikely to get the runs required. He elected to stay, and in deepening gloom Simmons clouted well to add 40 with his skipper, but when Simmons was out 27 were still needed from the last five overs.

David Hughes now joined Bond. He was essentially a young left-arm bowler with a first-class career batting average of just over 13. His highest score in limited-over cricket was 38, and his maiden century was still ten years away. In an attempt to acclimatize himself to the light outside, he had sat in a gloomy corner of the dressing room as Simmons and Bond made their stand. It is generally reported that when he went to the wicket his captain said to him, 'Don't go daft. Take things as they come.' To this he had replied, 'If I can see them, skipper, I think I can hit them.'

John Mortimore began the fifty-sixth over with figures of 3 for 57 from ten overs. Perhaps, with hindsight, he was unwise to toss the ball up invitingly and try to spin out Hughes. Emburey, Marks and the off-spinners who came later would have kept it flat, but in any case, Hughes was quick on his feet and moved down the wicket to hit the first ball of the over beyond extra cover for four. The next ball he hit high over long-on for six. The third ball was slashed into the off-side field and the batsmen ran two. The fourth ball was hit wide of mid-on for another two, and the fifth was driven through the covers in classical style for four. The last ball of the over Hughes swung high over mid-on for six, and the scores were level. Twenty-four runs had come from an over which is now part of Lancastrian folk-lore.

Bond was as calm and authoritative as ever. He played four balls from Procter without event and nudged the fifth past gully for the winning run as the crowd surged on to the pitch. David Hughes was named Man of the Match for his romantic final flourish. Others might have given the award to Simmons, and many would have given it to Bond, whose tactical flair and astute cricketing brain had made the victory possible.

The final against Kent was almost as dramatic. This time, Lancashire batted first. Barry Wood was out to the second ball of the match, but Clive Lloyd rallied the side with an innings of 66 which he began with a six. Simmons and Hughes plundered mercilessly at the close, and Lancashire made 224 for 7.

Kent lost half their wickets for 105, and Lancashire seemed to be heading for a comfortable win, but Asif Iqbal took command and turned the course of the game. He hit a glorious 89 with wonderful inventiveness and vigour, and Kent needed only 28 to win from the last six overs with four wickets in hand.

Jack Simmons was bowling to a strong on-side field, and Asif gave himself room to hit to the sparsely populated off side. He hit cleanly and with great force, seemingly well wide of extra cover where Bond was fielding. But the Lancashire captain suddenly took off and, plucking the ball out of the air, he rolled over and over as he crashed to the ground. Amazed and forlorn, Asif trudged back to the pavilion almost too stunned to note the standing ovation he received. The last three Kent wickets fell for three runs, to give Lancashire victory by 24 runs. Bond's example and tactics in the field had once again brought a sensational triumph.

In 1972 Lancashire, still under Bond, won

the Gillette Cup for the third time in succession, and at the end of that season he announced his retirement. He had led Lancashire to one of the greatest and most exciting periods in their distinguished history, and he had grasped at what was offered by the one-day game to bring about the renaissance in the fortunes of the Red Rose county. He loved the weekly audience of thousands of people in the ground as well as millions at home watching on television. It was said that he hated Mondays more than anything else in cricket because he loathed leading his side out to field in front of rows of empty seats after the bubble and excitement of the previous day.

By the time he became captain of Lancashire, Bond's best days as a cricketer were behind him. His highest score in limited-over cricket was to be 43, which he made against Derbyshire at Old Trafford in the first year of the John Player League, but to judge him on figures would be a grave error. He was the first man to recognize the extra dimensions provided by the one-day game and the positivity and thought that were needed to take advantage of them. Players would move to their positions seemingly without direction, but those positions had in fact been decided by a cool, clinical cricketing brain, and the runs saved and the batsmen frustrated to destruction by the precision of those positionings were apparent to all.

Interestingly, Bond proved that it was accuracy rather than pace in bowling that was the vital factor in limited-over cricket, and in the years of Lancashire's triumphs, off-spinner Jack Simmons and slow left-arm spinner David Hughes were always to the fore. Both were to take more than a hundred wickets in the John Player League alone.

Hughes was to follow the pattern set by Bond in that he was to be called from second-eleven obscurity to attempt to lead another Lancashire revival in 1987. By then his spin bowling had almost totally given way to his late middle-order batting, although Simmons' off-spin still remained an important factor in Lancashire's one-day cricket.

A fallacy has arisen regarding the efficacy of spinners in the one-day game. In the first season of the John Player League, the leading wicket-taker was the Essex left-arm spinner Ray East. The most remarkable bowling return was by Brian Langford of Somerset against Essex at Yeovil: he bowled his eight overs without conceding a run from his off-breaks.

Indeed, the most economical bowling performances in the Sunday League have almost invariably been produced by spinners, which will surprise most followers of the game. It is worth studying the list.

Brian Langford (Somerset) 8–8–0–0, v Essex, Yeovil, 1969.
D.R. Doshi (Nottinghamshire) 8–7–1–1, v Northamptonshire, Northampton, 1977.
Fred Titmus (Middlesex), 8–6–2–3, v Northamptonshire, Northampton, 1972.
Arthur Robinson (Yorkshire), 8–5–3–3, v Derbyshire, Scarborough, 1973.
John Dye (Kent), 8–5–4–3, v Middlesex, Canterbury, 1969.
Don Wilson (Yorkshire), 8–5–4–2, v Glamorgan, Swansea, 1972.
Phil Edmonds (Middlesex), 8–5–4–2, v Northamptonshire, Milton Keynes, 1979.
B.S. Bedi (Northamptonshire), 8–4–4–2, v Nottinghamshire, Brackley, 1975.
David Hughes (Lancashire), 8–6–4–1, v Leicestershire, Old Trafford, 1972.

The left-arm spinner Dilip Doshi, highly successful in one-day cricket.

Peter Willey, Northants and Leicestershire, one of the most successful of cricketers in the one-day game.

the three-day game in many ways. Marks relies on control of line and length more than on any vast amount of turn, and his nagging accuracy, frustrating batsmen when overs are running short, has been of telling effect in limited-over cricket.

On Sundays, for example, he has proved to be far more economical than medium-pace bowlers such as Botham, Dredge and Burgess while, in the Benson and Hedges Cup Finals of 1981 and 1982, he had figures of 2 for 24 on both occasions. Five maiden overs crippled Surrey in mid-innings in 1981, while the following year he frustrated Nottinghamshire to such an extent that he accounted for Randall and Rice, their two most aggressive batsmen, and took the Gold Award.

Yet in spite of the success of Marks, Emburey, Simmons, Doshi and the rest, the majority of county captains remain unconvinced that a slow bowler is either necessary or of value in a one-day side. In the Benson and Hedges Cup Final of 1980, Keith Fletcher, the Essex captain, relied on five seam bowlers, denying a single over to Ray East. He adopted a similar policy three years later, and on both occasions Essex lost to their opponents, Northamptonshire and Middlesex respectively, who employed slow bowlers to great advantage, Willey in 1980 and Emburey and Edmonds in 1983. Some years earlier Essex had played leg-spinner Robin Hobbs, an excellent fielder, in all sixteen John Player League matches without allowing him to bowl a ball. Certainly, the treatment that they have received by their captains in one-day cricket has caused many slow bowlers to become both disheartened and cynical.

The argument of those who believe that the medium-pace bowler is of greater value in the one-day game is that with the pressure of time on the batsman he is always more likely to score runs against the slow bowler than the quicker man. By the very nature of his art, the spinner needs time to probe at a batsman and to buy his wickets. The one-day game needs instant returns from both batsman and bowler. To this end, it has fashioned its own ideal player – a medium-pace bowler who fields well and can hit hard and often when he bats.

When Harry Pilling took a £100 award in 1970 for becoming the first batsman to score 1000 runs in the John Player League, there was another prize winner, Kent all-rounder Bob Woolmer, who became the first bowler to reach the 50-wicket mark in Sunday matches. He was, in fact, the leading wicket-taker in the League in that year with 32 wickets, although in Kent's side in Championship matches he was the sixth or seventh member of the attack.

Woolmer's medium pace, just short of

Of those nine bowlers, two – Robinson and Dye – were left-arm medium pace. The rest were spinners, five of them – Doshi, Wilson, Edmonds, Bedi and Hughes – left-arm. These are facts worth pondering when the use of the spinner in one-day cricket is so readily dismissed by many people.

Dilip Doshi, an Indian Test bowler, assisted Warwickshire as well as Nottinghamshire, and he also played for the Minor County Hertfordshire. His success was not restricted to the Sunday League, for at Hitchin, in July 1976, he played a most significant part in Hertfordshire's Gillette Cup victory over Essex which made them the first Minor County to reach the quarter-final of the sixty-over competition. Hertfordshire made 153 with Ray East taking 4 for 28 in eleven overs. At 71 for 1, with Ken McEwan in full flow, Essex seemed set for victory, but Doshi and 'Robin' Johns, an off-break bowler, took four wickets each, and Hertfordshire won by 33 runs.

Equally and consistently successful has been the Middlesex and England off-break bowler John Emburey, while another England off-spinner, Somerset's Vic Marks, has found his talents better suited to the one-day game than

length, troubled few batsmen in the three-day game, but in one-day cricket, with the emphasis on getting on with things, his bowling became a different proposition. Although he was to become an England opening batsman, he frequently batted down the order in the successful Kent side of the seventies, played primarily for his restrictive bowling.

His team-mate John Shepherd is another example of the all-rounder beloved in one-day cricket. For Kent, and later for Gloucestershire, he took more than 300 wickets and scored more than 3000 runs in the limited-over game, and his furious hitting could turn the course of a match. In a Benson and Hedges Cup match at Lord's in May 1975, Kent were in a desperate plight. Middlesex's Tim Lamb removed Johnson and Denness in his fourth over, and when Titmus had Luckhurst caught at slip, Kent were 9 for 3. Edmonds then produced a spell of 4 for 11 in as many overs, and Kent were 53 for 8.

John Shepherd had come in at the fall of the third wicket and had opened his account with a six. He had continued to attack while all about him fell, but when Underwood offered sensible support he played with more restraint until, feeling more assured, he launched another

Bob Woolmer, Kent and England.

West Indian all-rounder John Shepherd who was of immense value to Kent, and later to Gloucestershire, in limited-over cricket.

violent attack on the bowling and hit three more sixes before being caught off Featherstone for 96. He and Underwood had added 81 for the eighth wicket, a competition record at that time.

Shepherd's 96 came out of 125 scored while he was at the wicket, but Kent's final score of 137 for 8 hardly looked likely to trouble Middlesex. The home side began as badly as Kent had done, however, and were 8 for 3 before Barlow and Featherstone joined in a partnership of 89 which looked certain to give Middlesex the game. At this point, John Shepherd returned for a second spell with his medium pace and dismissed Barlow, Featherstone and Murray so that Kent eventually won an extraordinary game by 2 runs.

The value of such a player as Shepherd in one-day cricket cannot be over-emphasized. In a match in which quick runs, top-class fielding, quick wickets or containment may be the need at any one moment, the player who can contribute in all these departments is of great worth. Keith Boyce, like Shepherd a West Indian, was the idol of Essex for many seasons because of his dynamic approach to every aspect of the game. He was a violent hitter of the ball – his sixteen sixes in the inaugural season of the John Player League put him ahead of any other batsman – and his electric running between the wickets turned singles into twos and twos into threes. In the field he moved with a feline rapidity which was a constant threat to the batsmen. By the fourth year of the Sunday League, he had achieved the 'double' with 1000 runs and 100 wickets, and he was to remain the leading wicket-taker in the competition until overtaken by his team-mate John Lever in 1976, by which time he had begun to be troubled by injury.

In 1971 he took 8 for 26 against the mighty Lancashire at Old Trafford, and this remains a record for a Sunday League match. A year later, at Westcliff, he and Lever bowled out Middlesex for 41 in the Gillette Cup tie. Boyce took 5 for 22 and a catch off Lever's bowling. He also became the first Essex batsman to hit a century in the Benson and Hedges Cup when he made 123 against Minor Counties (South) at Bedford in 1975. He was a player who thrilled to the one-day game, who also thrilled others and who could turn the course of a game by a single act of batting, bowling, catching or throwing.

Certainly, another player who was able to turn a game in a moment was Mike Procter, the Gloucestershire all-rounder who so stamped his authority on cricket in the West Country that W.G. Grace's old county became jokingly known as 'Proctershire'.

Procter had played in seven Test matches, in which he had taken an incredible 41 wickets at 15.02 runs each and, batting low down, had averaged 25.11 without the help of a fifty, before South Africa's excommunication from Test cricket. Finding himself thwarted in his ambition to play in Tests when still only twenty-four years of age, Procter came to England and qualified for Gloucestershire for whom he played from 1968 until 1981, captaining them from 1977 until his departure.

He bowled at a furious pace, hit ferociously hard and fielded magnificently in any position. To his adopted county he was a source of constant inspiration. 'The only problem with Prockie,' said one of his former team-mates, 'is that he was always doing something – catching someone, bowling someone or clouting a few sixes – and he couldn't understand why you weren't doing the same. He thought you weren't trying.'

In 1973 Procter prompted Gloucestershire to their first major success for ninety-six years. He was not fully fit for much of the season and missed the first round Gillette Cup match at Cardiff where Gloucestershire beat Glamorgan by 34 runs. In the second round, they recovered from a disastrous start to reach 169 for 7 in their sixty overs. At 122 for 5 Surrey looked set for a comfortable win, but Procter returned to finish with 3 for 21, and Gloucestershire won by 19 runs.

In the quarter-final Essex were beaten easily at Chelmsford, and this brought a local derby semi-final tie at Worcester. Worcestershire had been beaten semi-finalists in the Gillette Cup the previous year, and the tie against Gloucestershire aroused tremendous excitement and interest. A capacity crowd of 8500 packed into New Road, the biggest attendance at Worcester since Bradman's Australians had been the visitors in 1948 – another testimony to the impact that the one-day game had made.

Gloucestershire started badly, losing Nicholls and Roger Knight for 32. Procter came in at number four and, in two-and-three-quarter hours, hit 101 with the lazy, powerful majesty that made him one of the most attractive batsmen to have graced the game since the war. Nevertheless, Gloucestershire's 243 for 8 was hardly a decisive match-winning score on a perfect Worcester wicket. This became apparent when Ron Headley and Glenn Turner put on 123 in forty overs for the first Worcestershire wicket. Procter had been economical rather than penetrative in his opening spell, but he returned when Worcestershire were 188 for 3 and had Turner, who had hit 109, caught behind in his first over. With six overs remaining and six wickets in hand, Worcestershire needed only 41 to win, but Procter took two more wickets and Gloucestershire won by 5 runs.

Gloucestershire's opponents in the final

Mike Procter, one of the most exciting cricketers that the world has seen.

Trevor Jesty. An incomparable record in limited-over cricket.

were Sussex. Tony Brown won the toss, but Gloucestershire slipped to 27 for 3 after ten overs. Procter and David Shepherd then added 47 in thirteen overs. Procter had begun by hitting two short balls from Michael Buss for six, and he maintained an aggressive approach throughout his two-and-a-half-hour innings before he was finally caught at square-leg for 94,

made out of 158 scored while he was at the wicket. Tony Brown kept up the onslaught, and Gloucestershire reached 248.

Sussex started well enough and were 155 for 2 in forty-four overs, but the return of Procter again turned the match as he first slowed the run rate and then proved too formidable for the tailenders.

When Gloucestershire next returned to Lord's for a final, Procter had become the county captain. This time the success was in the Benson and Hedges Cup in 1977. In the zonal matches, victories over Somerset, Leicestershire and Lancashire had allowed Gloucestershire to qualify for the quarter-finals, even though they had been heavily trounced by Hampshire. Middlesex were the quarter-final opponents at Bristol, and when they restricted the home side to 194 and took their own score to 163 for 5, they looked easy winners. Once more it was the return of Procter which tilted the game, and Gloucestershire won by 18 runs.

It was the semi-final, however, which provided one of the most notable events in the history of the one-day game. Gloucestershire were drawn to meet Hampshire at Southampton. The date was 22 June 1977, and another capacity crowd saw an extraordinary match. In spite of an opening stand of 106, Gloucestershire were restricted to 180 and were bowled out in the fifty-fifth and last over.

Hampshire were considered to be the most formidable limited-over side in the country at the time, although in fact they have never reached a Lord's final. They won the John Player League in 1975 and 1978, and in Barry Richards they had the man considered to be the finest batsman in the world. Another South African and a friend of Procter's, Richards was the most prolific scorer in the John Player League with 4770 runs when he left English cricket in 1978. His opening partner was the West Indian Gordon Greenidge, a glorious stroke-player and a rapid scorer, and they were ably supported by the elegant Trevor Jesty and the left-handed David Turner, both of whom excelled in limited-over cricket.

Hampshire had reached 13 when, with the fifth ball of his third over, Procter bowled Greenidge. Five runs were taken off the next over, bowled by Brain, and Barry Richards now faced Procter who had chosen to bowl round the wicket. The first ball of the over saw Richards lbw, the next had Jesty trapped in a similar manner and the third bowled Rice off his pads. Procter had taken four wickets in five balls, including the hat-trick, and had effectively broken the resistance of the most feared batting combination in the land. Cowley narrowly survived an appeal for lbw first ball and went on to add 109 with David Turner. Procter came back to take two more wickets, and Gloucestershire won by 7 runs. Procter's final figures were: 11 overs, 5 maidens, 13 runs, 6 wickets.

In the final, a superb team effort saw Kent beaten by 64 runs, and Gloucestershire took the 1977 Benson and Hedges Cup, their second major trophy in five years. Kent's leading scorers in the final were Woolmer (64) and Shepherd (55), both of whom had also bowled their full quota of eleven overs.

In singling out Procter, Woolmer, Shepherd and Boyce, we have, in a sense, been unfair. All were Test cricketers. All prospered in every form of cricket, although Woolmer was never as useful a bowler in the three-day game as in the limited-over version. All were nourished by playing one-day cricket, but none was a product of the one-day game.

Arguably, however, Stuart Turner was such a product, for he never played for England, and until the arrival of limited-over cricket his place in the Essex side was tenuous, yet he was to become recognized as one of the outstanding performers in the form of cricket that rejuvenated the game in England. In July 1986, the last year that the Sunday League was sponsored by John Player, Les Hatton, whose meticulous statistical record of the League (published in 1987) had given a clear insight into the qualities best suited to the forty-over game, travelled from his home in Wolverhampton to Southend to present to Turner a commemorative record of his 300 wickets in the John Player League on behalf of the Association of Cricket Statisticians. Turner was to retire at the end of the 1986 season, and Les Hatton, in his history of the League, named Turner as 'The Cricketer of the John Player League'.

The choice of the Essex cricketer, Stuart Turner, as the outstanding player in the 18 seasons of the John Player League is based on his all-round contribution to his county over many years, rather than his achievements in a few specific matches. Turner is the only player to achieve the Double of more than 3000 runs and over 300 wickets in his JPL career, his final totals being 3165 runs and 303

More than 3,000 Sunday runs and more than 300 Sunday wickets – Stuart Turner, 'The Cricketer of the John Player League'.

wickets – he played in 255 Sunday League matches for his county. In addition to his batting and bowling, he is an excellent fielder, and had held 82 catches – the Sunday League has been responsible to a large extent for the overall improvement in fielding standards since the 1960s. Turner, who is a fast scoring batsman, has been extremely versatile over the years, batting in every position from no. 1 (he opened Essex's batting on 35 occasions) to no. 10. His fast bowling has also been utilized to the full.

Hatton's description of Turner is a description of the ideal cricketer for the limited-over game, the man who can do a bit of everything and, ideally, bowls brisk medium pace. Typical of Turner's value to his side were two performances in the Benson and Hedges Cup. At Chelmsford in 1982, he bowled his eleven overs for only 12 runs as Hampshire were dismissed for 130, but, at 14 for 6, Essex looked to be facing not only defeat but their lowest score in the competition. Turner then hit 55 not out in dreadful light and pouring rain, and Essex won by 1 wicket with nine balls to spare.

A year later, in the semi-final of the same competition at Canterbury, he took 2 for 15 in his eleven overs, and Kent, 62 for 1 at one time, were bowled out for 128. Essex went on to win by 9 wickets, and Turner took the Gold Award.

Turner had a hard road to success in cricket. He made his debut for Essex in 1965, but he was not retained in 1966. He was re-engaged in 1968, but he was twenty-seven years old before he was awarded his county cap. By now, however, one-day cricket had begun to play a prominent part in the English summer, and Turner thrived on the one-day game. His relentless accuracy as a bowler, his aggression as a batsman and his exuberance in the field were qualities highly suited to instant cricket. Whereas his bowling had seemed to lack penetration in the three-day game, it now became a decisive weapon in a restricted-over match where batsmen fretted for runs. The success and discipline that the one-day game gave him served to enrich the quality of his cricket in the first-class variety, and in 1974 he was named as the outstanding all-rounder in England. He played an integral part in the Essex triumphs of the late 1970s and early 1980s, and if, as he passed forty, he was not always included in the three-day side, he remained an essential member of the one-day team. More than any other cricketer, Stuart Turner was fashioned and heightened by limited-over cricket.

It was his consistency over a long period that marked Turner out. Others, such as Tom Cartwright of Warwickshire and Glamorgan, a bowler ideally suited in style and temperament to one-day cricket, enjoyed only a brief span. For one season – 1973 – Dennis Marriott of Middlesex was the most effective bowler in the Sunday League, finishing with 28 wickets and taking five wickets in an innings on four occasions, a record. Marriott was a fast medium left-arm bowler from Jamaica who had also assisted Surrey, but his career in cricket was short. Certainly, the two all-rounders to challenge Stuart Turner for consistency over a long period are Clive Rice and Trevor Jesty, yet neither was essentially a product of the one-day game, having achieved much at all levels.

It is appropriate to dwell on the records of these two men for a moment, for both recorded impressive achievements in one-day cricket. We have already mentioned Jesty's century for Surrey against Lancashire in the semi-final of the NatWest Bank Trophy in 1986, but before joining Surrey, whom he left at the end of the 1987 season, he played for Hampshire from 1966 to 1984. Indeed, all his best performances in limited-over competitions were made during his days on the South Coast, as can be seen below.

118 v Derbyshire, Derby, Gillette Cup, 1980.
6 for 46 v Gloucestershire, Bristol, Gillette Cup, 1979.
105 v Glamorgan, Swansea, Benson and Hedges Cup, 1977.
4 for 22 v Minor Counties, Southampton, Benson and Hedges Cup, 1981.
166 not out v Surrey, Portsmouth, John Player League, 1983.
6 for 20 v Glamorgan, Cardiff, John Player League, 1976.

Jesty has won six Man-of-the-Match awards in the sixty-over competition and nine Gold Awards in the Benson and Hedges Cup. In all matches in the John Player League he has scored over 4000 runs and taken over 200 wickets, while in 1982 he hit 499 runs and took 24 Sunday League wickets in the season. He played in eleven one-day international matches for England.

Clive Rice hit more than 6000 Sunday runs in his years with Nottinghamshire and took almost 200 wickets. In 1977 he played nine innings of fifty or more and scored a record 814 runs, average 58.14. He led Nottinghamshire to the Benson and Hedges Cup Final in 1982 and to the NatWest Bank Trophy Finals in 1984 and 1987, playing a vital part in the Nottinghamshire victory on the second occasion, as we have seen. He won nine Gold Awards in the Benson and

Wayne Larkins (Northants), capable of destroying an attack from the first over of the match.

Hedges Cup and took two Man-of-the-Match awards in the sixty-over competition. As well as his successes in England, Rice led Transvaal to dominance in the one-day competitions in South Africa, and South Africa itself to victory over the Australian XI which toured the Republic in 1985/6 and 1986/7.

Rice has four times been the winner of the Silk Cut Challenge, a competition to determine the most outstanding all-rounder in world cricket, and has captained his country in international encounters with considerable success. A great cricketer whatever the competition, Rice fashions his game to suit the needs of each style of contest; his cricket has not been fashioned by them.

The same can be said of great batsmen such as Viv Richards, Barry Richards, Graham Gooch, Zaheer Abbas, Javed Miandad, Glenn

Turner and Gordon Greenidge. They are players who have prospered in all types of cricket, from Test match to Sunday afternoon slog. Like Rice, they possess a genius which moulds itself to suit the moment.

In September 1985, playing for Somerset against Sussex in a John Player League match at Taunton, Viv Richards hit 66 not out off 31 balls as Somerset won by 8 wickets. He hit three sixes and eight fours, took a record 26 runs off the one over bowled by the Sussex captain John Barclay, and finished the match by hitting Garth le Roux for four consecutive fours. As, earlier in the same season, Richards had hit 322 off 248 deliveries, with eight sixes and forty-two fours, in a County Championship match against Warwickshire in the same ground, and as, in April the following year, he made a hundred off 58 balls in a Test match for West Indies against

A delightful setting for a Sunday League match – Knypersley, where Derbyshire hit 18 sixes in 1985.

England in St John's, Antigua, it can hardly be said that his attitude to the game changed dramatically according to the occasion.

Ian Botham is another batsman who maintains an aggressive approach to the game in all circumstances. The year before his record thirteen sixes in the John Player League at Wellingborough, he played a remarkable innings in the County Championship at Edgbaston, hitting an unbeaten 138 off 65 deliveries. He hit twelve sixes, and his hundred took just 26 scoring strokes. Five years before this, he had savaged the Australian attack in a Test series which his batting and bowling transformed.

A player who has not done himself justice at international level, but who has always adopted a positive attitude when opening the innings for Northamptonshire, is Wayne Larkins. A gloriously free stroke-player who has scored

over 17,000 runs in first-class cricket, Larkins is eager to attack from the very beginning of an innings, and has enjoyed the added freedom that the one-day game has given him. He has hit two of the highest scores ever recorded in the John Player League – 172 not out against Warwickshire at Luton in 1983 and 158 against Worcestershire on the same ground the previous year. Both innings contained six sixes and twelve fours.

One of the most appealing features of the one-day game for those new to watching cricket is the number of boundaries that are hit. Another delight is the variety of venues which have staged Sunday League matches – club grounds which take on a festive air for a day. In 1985 Derbyshire combined both pleasures when they allotted their Sunday League game against Worcestershire to Knypersley.

Another pleasant setting for a Sunday match – Milton Keynes.

Derbyshire made 292 for 9 in their forty overs and won by 33 runs, but the main feature of the game was that the home side hit a record eighteen sixes on the sloping pitch. Holding, Roberts and Newman each hit five, and Miller, Maher and Warner one apiece. Phil Neale, the Worcestershire captain, responded with three sixes in an over from Mortensen and one off Newman.

Six-hitting is encouraged on Sundays by the award of prize money, but to believe that batting in limited-over cricket is merely a question of clouting as many sixes as possible in the shortest period of time is a gross error. One of the most successful batsmen in the history of one-day cricket is Clive Radley, who is not renowned as a great hitter of sixes. When he retired at the end of the 1987 season his aggregate in the Sunday League was second only to that of Dennis Amiss, and he had taken seven individual awards in the sixty- and fifty-over competitions, three of them in finals.

In 1969, the first year of the John Player League, he hit the highest score of the season –

133 not out for Middlesex against Glamorgan at Lord's – and in the next seventeen seasons he was to prove one of the League's most consistent batsmen. A small, chunky right-hander, Radley was always an accumulator of runs rather than a fierce striker of the ball. He was a highly intelligent batsman, aware of his limitations and improvising and inventing within them. He watched the ball intently and cut, nudged and dabbed to great effect. He was never unattractive as a batsman because he was always so alert at the crease. His footwork was admirable as he moved down the wicket to dictate the length at which the bowler should bowl, and his running between the wickets was dynamic. Nothing was missed, for he appeared to work on the philosophy that it was not necessary to hit sixes and fours when field-positionings in one-day cricket invariably allowed six or seven runs an over if you were prepared to run them, and Radley was.

During his first benefit year, 1977, he was in the Middlesex side which reached the Gillette Cup Final at Lord's. Indeed, he had suffered

84

Clive Radley – the Man of many matches. Dipak Patel in attendance.

Brian Close left Yorkshire because of his dislike of one-day cricket, yet he improved Somerset's performances in the one-day game.

bitter disappointment along with his team-mates two years earlier when Middlesex had reached the finals of both the Benson and Hedges Cup and the Gillette Cup only to lose to Leicestershire in the first and to Lancashire in the second. This time, the opponents were Glamorgan.

Mike Brearley won the toss and asked Glamorgan to bat first. They stuttered to 50 for 3, but were momentarily inspired by Mike Llewellyn who began his account with four, six and four off the bowling of Mike Gatting. Later he hit Emburey, who had been bowling tightly, straight into the pavilion for six, the ball landing in the guttering near the BBC commentary box at the top of the pavilion, a colossal drive. Llewellyn was eventually caught off Featherstone for 62, and Glamorgan were restricted to 177 for 9 in their sixty overs.

Middlesex began disastrously. Malcolm Nash's first ball swung late and took the edge of

Brearley's bat for Eifion Jones to take the catch behind the stumps. Radley was next in, and when the score had reached 4 he touched a ball from Nash similar to the one which had accounted for Brearley. The ball flew straight into the hands of Collis King at second slip, and out again. Radley was to offer no other chance as he batted through 55.3 overs to finish with 85 not out. Middlesex won by 5 wickets, and Radley was named Man of the Match. He was to reappear in Lord's finals three times in the next ten years, and on two more occasions would receive the individual award.

A year after his initial triumph at Lord's he played in four limited-over international matches for England, scoring 79 and 13 against Pakistan, and 41 and 117 not out against New Zealand. Although he played in eight Test matches, he was never to play in another one-day international, and his average of 83.33 from his four innings and 250 runs remains unapproached by any other England player.

Radley's batting was founded on a totally professional application. He was ever eager and resourceful, quiet, determined and effective. He rarely produced the fireworks of a Gooch or a Botham, the belligerence of a Gatting or the majesty of a Gower, but he was a hugely successful batsman in one-day cricket, and in first-class cricket he was a brilliant fielder and eminently reliable in all that he did.

The example of Radley should not be forgotten, particularly by those impatient spectators who expect sixes and fours from the opening over when a side is chasing 200 runs at four an over. Michael Norman of Leicestershire, John Barclay of Sussex, Tim Curtis of Worcestershire and Peter Sainsbury of Hampshire all reached 1000 runs in the John Player League without the aid of a single six.

Radley was a master at pacing an innings, as are all the top players, and in this respect we would do well to consider the innings that Gordon Greenidge played for Hampshire against Warwickshire at Edgbaston in July 1979. His

Gordon Greenidge.

Keith Fletcher who has led Essex to success in all three one-day competitions and played on the first and last days of the John Player League.

score of 163 not out in the John Player League match was to remain a record for the competition until 1983, and although it has since been passed twice by Gooch, and once each by Botham, Larkins and Jesty, these four batsmen had the advantage of the fielding circles which demanded that a captain place four men within thirty yards of the wicket, the ruling on which was introduced in 1982.

Greenidge began his innings at Edgbaston with a single off the second ball of the match, and added another single off the fourth ball of the second over. The first ten overs ended with Hampshire on 44 for 0. There was no hint of aggression until Greenidge hit Oliver for two huge sixes in the fifteenth over, but still, at the end of twenty overs, Hampshire were 82 for 0, with Greenidge on 40.

John Rice, Greenidge's opening partner, was out in the twenty-sixth over with the score on 122; Rice had made 43. Greenidge's last eleven scoring shots had produced 44 runs. He had been particularly severe on Phil Oliver, whose seven overs cost 60 runs, but when Whitehouse sought to find refuge in one over from Andy Lloyd, Greenidge hit him for two, six, two, six and one, with Cowley, who had come in at 173 for 3, taking a single off the last ball of the over.

Cowley (14) and Greenidge added 73 in 24 minutes. Cowley was out off the second ball of the last over, having hit a six off the first. Greenidge managed four more runs from the rest of the over; Terry was caught off the fourth ball, so that the last four overs of the innings produced 42 runs, almost as profitable to Hampshire as the first ten. In fact, while the first twenty overs realized 82 runs, 168 came from the second twenty. Greenidge's 163, with ten sixes and thirteen fours, came off 120 balls, exactly half the number bowled during the innings, yet 123 of his runs had come in the second half of the innings and he did not hit a six until the fifteenth over.

Such an analysis reveals that even in a game limited to forty overs, a batsman of the calibre of Gordon Greenidge builds an innings, increasing momentum once he has gauged the pace of the pitch and the quality of the opposition's bowling.

Gordon Greenidge is, of course, an explosive batsman who has destroyed an England attack on the fifth day of a Lord's Test to score a double century and bring an unlikely victory. However, there are others who have emerged as essentially one-day specialists. Their technique may have been founded in the three-day game, but their temperament and attitude suit them better for the one-day variety.

Alan Lilley, the Essex batsman whose

Alan Lilley. His outstanding fielding has kept him a place in the Essex side.

fielding we have noted, is a case in point, and Steve O'Shaughnessy, formerly of Lancashire and with Worcestershire from 1988, is another. O'Shaughnessy is a batsman whose eagerness to hit the ball has often been his undoing in first-class cricket (in which, incidentally, he shares the record for the fastest century in the history of the game with Percy Fender), but who, in the one-day game, with his ability to bowl medium pace and to field outstandingly, is an invaluable player whose brisk scoring can turn a game.

Ian Gould's approach to the one-day game won him international recognition.

Another to prosper in one-day cricket – Geoff Humpage of Warwickshire.

Wicket-keepers Ian Gould of Sussex and Geoff Humpage of Warwickshire are others whose aggressive tendencies with the bat have made them vital players in one-day cricket. Both earned international recognition in this area, although neither was recognized as a wicket-keeper of the top flight.

One of the international selections harder to understand was that of Chris Cowdrey for a Test match before he had played in a limited-over international, for here, surely, is a cricketer

Chris Cowdrey hits out during his thrilling innings for Kent against Northants in the Benson and Hedges Cup semi-final at Canterbury, 1987.

whose talents and temperament are seen to best advantage in the one-day game. He is an exuberant character, son of the former Kent and England captain, Colin, who was noted for his classical stroke-play and element of restraint. Chris Cowdrey, also a captain of Kent, is by contrast anxious to hit the ball from the start of his innings which, batting as he does at number four or five, is often necessary. Yet it is not simply Chris Cowdrey's anxiety to hit the ball hard and often, nor his dynamic running

between the wickets and in the field, that makes him so at ease in one-day cricket, but also, like the legendary Jack Bond, that he rises to the occasion of the capacity crowd and the continuous murmur of excitement that attends a NatWest Bank Trophy or Benson and Hedges Cup tie. It stirs him because the atmosphere injects something into his play, whereas in the relaxed air of three-day county cricket he feels it incumbent upon *him* to inject something into the game. He has had exciting successes in first-class

Kevin Sharp, the Yorkshire left-hander, who found confidence and success in limited-over cricket.

cricket, but one is ever conscious that his is a spirit more at home in the one-day game.

The same could almost be said of Kevin Sharp, the Yorkshire left-hander, a batsman of immense potential which has never been fully realized in County Championship matches, but who has played some exciting cricket in the limited-over tournaments and contributed much to Yorkshire's recent successes.

But even a magnificent innings of 114 by Sharp against Essex at Chelmsford in September 1985 could not prevent the Southerners from taking the John Player League title in the last match of the season. Yorkshire reached 231 for 7, Sharp's 114 coming off 106 balls, and Essex's title hopes receded when Gooch and Hardie were out with 53 on the board in the fifteenth over. Ken McEwan, in what was his last Sunday League game for Essex, hit 62 off 67 deliveries. As ever, it was an innings of the greatest charm from one of the most delightful batsmen and personalities to have graced the game. McEwan was caught on the long-on boundary, and was given a standing ovation as he left the wicket on the ground where he had given so much pleasure to so many people.

Derek Pringle, too, played splendidly, hitting 60 off 54 balls, but when he was caught off Steve Oldham, Essex at 194 for 7 looked unlikely to win. Paul Prichard, a stylish young batsman whose technique and range of shots look as good as those of any other young player in England, was at number eight in the Essex side, for it was believed that it would be unfair to subject him to the inevitable slog that occurred in Sunday League matches and that he should be nurtured carefully. With the veteran Turner as his partner, he faced the prospect of having to score 30 from the last four overs if Essex were to hold on to the title.

Prichard never strayed from the orthodox. He drove Oldham through the covers for a majestic boundary. Twice he drove eloquently into the off side for twos, and then he late cut classically to the boundary. Perhaps, nerves having seized him with victory in sight, he lost concentration for a moment as he lofted Oldham to mid-off in the last over, with only two runs needed. Foster won the match with a ball to spare.

Prichard's innings of 25 is unlikely to stand out from the scorecard in years to come. The bare figures suggest nothing memorable, but for those lucky enough to see it, it was proof that there is no need to violate purity of technique in the quest for quick runs. As Viv and Barry Richards, Procter, Gooch and the rest have demonstrated, if you are good enough you will prosper whatever the number of overs.

Most players enjoy at least a fleeting

Ken McEwan, the South African batsman whose batting for Essex brought delight to millions.

Adrian Jones, 7 for 41, Sussex v Notts, 1986.

moment of triumph. At Trent Bridge in 1986, in the John Player League game between Sussex and Nottinghamshire, Adrian Jones, the Sussex right-arm fast medium-pace bowler who has since moved to Somerset, was not brought into the attack until the twenty-eighth over of the Nottinghamshire innings, by which time they were 142 for 1, Broad and Robinson having put on 89 for the first wicket. Jones took 7 for 41 in seven overs, and Nottinghamshire finished on 198 for 8.

Batting at number eleven, Jones came in with the score at 181 for 9. He hit 17 to win the game. Twelve of these runs came off the last over, and five came off the last ball when, with the scores level, he pushed a single which was overthrown to the boundary.

But the heroics do not always end in triumph. The 1976 Benson and Hedges Cup Final matched two sides, Kent and Worcestershire, who were then at the peak of form. Woolmer, displaying the powerful driving and sense of adventure which he was always able to find in the one-day game (but rarely outside it), and Johnson put on 110 for Kent's first wicket. Worcestershire's hope of containment lay with Basil D'Oliveira, a most difficult bowler to score from in limited-over cricket. He had the immediate effect of slowing the run rate, but Woolmer threw caution to the wind and attacked him, hitting 15 in one over.

Following a wild throw from the outfield, D'Oliveira chased after the ball to prevent overthrows, and in doing so tore a hamstring. He was helped from the field, and only with assistance could he reach the dressing room. The leg was packed with ice, but doctors stated that the injury was too severe from him to be allowed to bat. Kent made 236 for 7 from their

fifty-five overs.

D'Oliveira insisted that if his side needed him, he would bat. His skipper, Norman Gifford, knew only too well that Worcestershire would need him, particularly after Turner and Neale had gone quickly. The whole of D'Oliveira's left leg was strapped in an attempt to cut off all feeling, even from the toes, and at 90 for 4 he hobbled down the pavilion steps with Glenn Turner as his runner. He could only stand firm-footed at the crease and had to rely on powerful short-arm jabs. He later explained the tactics he had adopted.

> I decided to get as far over to the off stump as I could and then give it a slog on the leg side. I wanted to hit Derek Underwood over extra cover's head if I could, so I just stood there and carved. My left leg was giving me agony and I could only play off my back foot; I dreaded getting a bouncer because I wouldn't have had a hope of avoiding it. I took the middle and off guard so that I didn't have to worry too much about foot-work; if I missed a straight one, I was out, simple as that. I kept my left foot slightly off the ground and hit through the line of the ball whenever it came near me. My power and the fact that I was a back-foot player obviously helped me.

The Worcestershire run rate actually increased as D'Oliveira and Boyns added 35 for the sixth wicket, D'Oliveira and Hemsley having added 36 for the fifth. D'Oliveira bludgeoned and carved a succession of fours, and once hit Hills over mid-off into the crowd for six. The target was reduced to 75 from the last ten overs, and had D'Oliveira been able to maintain this aggression Worcestershire might well have won, but he

Basil D'Oliveira, now coach at his old county, was Worcestershire's limping hero in the Benson and Hedges Cup Final of 1976.

Gold Award winner in the 1976 final – Kent's Graham Johnson.

lashed out once too often at Jarvis and was bowled in the forty-seventh over. He had made 50 out of 76 in fourteen overs. It was heroic, but it proved forlorn: Kent won by 43 runs. Johnson, who had added four catches to the 78 he had scored earlier, took the Gold Award, but many will remember it as D'Oliveira's match.

All competitions produce some rather bizarre events. The John Player League saw two instances of batsmen being given out obstructing the field, which is a rarity in cricket. The first instance was at Lord's on 2 July 1972, when Leicestershire beat Middlesex by 19 runs.

Leicestershire suffered an early crisis when they lost both openers for 14, and Brian Davison was out at 50. Skipper Ray Illingworth joined Roger Tolchard in a stand of 79, and Paul Haywood helped Tolchard to add 77. Tolchard batted quite splendidly, being particularly strong on the back foot, and hit 103, the highest score he was to make in the Sunday League.

The last ball of the Leicestershire innings was driven straight by Haywood towards the bowler Keith Jones, but Tolchard at the non-striker's end diverted the ball out of Jones' reach with his bat and was adjudged to have obstructed the field, in that Jones had had the possibility of running out Haywood.

Eight years later, at Edgbaston on 7 September 1980, a week after Warwickshire had won the John Player League title, another wicket-keeper, Somerset's Derek Taylor, was the culprit. He had gone in at number eight and once again in the last over had kicked the ball away when Bob Willis attempted to run him out. Like Tolchard, Taylor ended on the winning side, Somerset beating the newly crowned champions by 26 runs.

A third eccentric dismissal in the John Player League also came towards the end of the season in 1982. On Saturday 4 September, Surrey beat Warwickshire to win the NatWest Bank Trophy. The following day they entertained Hampshire in a John Player League match. David Smith, the Surrey left-hander, was given out when, as the ball looped off his bat towards his stumps, he instinctively put out a hand to stop it and was given out 'handled ball'.

Nor was that the end of the entertainment in that particular match. Surrey made 139 for 9, and Hampshire began the last over of their innings on 138 for 7. The scores were levelled when, on the third ball of the over, bowled by Monkhouse, Rice, who had batted throughout the innings, was caught for 64. Off the last delivery of the innings, Tremlett attempted to turn the ball to leg for the winning single but skied to mid-wicket where Lynch caught him, so that the match ended in a tie.

Monkhouse was fortunate in this instance in

that Lynch held the catch, but there was an occasion in a John Player League match between Essex and Worcestershire when Phil Neale, the Worcestershire captain, pulled a ball to the boundary where Graham Gooch, in attempting to take the catch, tipped the ball over the boundary and into the crowd for six. Keith Pont was the unlucky bowler.

On that occasion the players were able to find the incident amusing, but the one-day game can bring its heartbreaks. On the last Sunday in August 1977, Essex travelled to play Yorkshire at Scarborough knowing that if they won they would almost certainly take the John Player League title. The enforced retirement of Keith Boyce through injury in mid-season had not helped their cause, but they went to Scarborough unbeaten in their last eight League matches. They made 178 for 7, and looked to have the game well in hand when Yorkshire did not reach 100 until the twenty-eighth over and had 4

wickets down. All seemed to be going well until the thirty-ninth over, bowled by Stuart Turner who had been the most economical of the Essex bowlers, when David Bairstow launched a violent attack. He hit four boundaries and Yorkshire went on to win the game with three balls to spare. Essex lost the title by virtue of the fact that, although they had the same number of points as Leicestershire at 52, Leicestershire had won one game more. As Essex had at that time never won a title, there was considerable disappointment.

Two years later, however, they took the Benson and Hedges Cup and the County Championship and started upon the golden period in their history which was to see them win all four competitions within the space of six years; and it was in 1987 that Stuart Turner, the agonies of Scarborough long forgotten, was to be named as 'The Cricketer of the John Player League'.

Roger Tolchard out 'obstructing the field for 103'.

JOHN PLAYER SPECIAL LEAGUE RECORDS

The Sunday League was sponsored by John Player from its inception in
1969 until 1986. In 1987 it was sponsored by Refuge Assurance, and the
format of the League was changed in 1988 to end with the four top
sides playing a knock-out competition. The records below refer to the league
between 1969 and 1986 when it was sponsored by John Player.

*One-day delight. Bernard
Julien, Kent and West
Indies all-rounder, in
spectacular mood.*

CHAMPIONS

Year	Champion
1969	Lancashire
1970	Lancashire
1971	Worcestershire
1972	Kent
1973	Kent
1974	Leicestershire
1975	Hampshire
1976	Kent
1977	Leicestershire
1978	Hampshire
1979	Somerset
1980	Warwickshire
1981	Essex
1982	Sussex
1983	Yorkshire
1984	Essex
1985	Essex
1986	Hampshire

Refuge Assurance
| 1987 | Worcestershire |

*Essex, who have won all
three one-day
competitions. Back row
(l to r): P.J. Prichard,
J.P. Stephenson, T.D.
Topley, C. Gladwin,
I.L. Pont, H.A. Page,
N.A. Foster, A.W.
Lilley, G. Miller. Front
row (l to r): D.E.
East, B.R. Hardie,
K.W.R. Fletcher, G.A.
Gooch, J.K. Lever,
D.L. Acfield, D.R.
Pringle.*

HIGHEST TEAM TOTALS

310 for 5, Essex v Glamorgan, Southend, 1983.
307 for 4 (38 overs), Worcestershire v Derbyshire, Worcester, 1975.

The latter is the only score of 300 to be recorded before the introduction of fielding circles.

HIGHEST MATCH AGGREGATES

604 for 15 wickets
Surrey 304 for 6
Warwickshire 300 for 9, The Oval, 1985

600 for 10 wickets
Essex 299 for 4
Warwickshire 301 for 6, Colchester, 1982

The latter is the only occasion on which a side batting second has scored more than 300 to win a match.

LOWEST TEAM TOTALS

23 (19.4 overs), Middlesex v Yorkshire, Headingley, 1974.
36 (25.4 overs), Leicestershire v Sussex, Leicester, 1973.

LARGEST VICTORIES

There have been 18 instances of counties winning by 10 wickets.

Warwickshire 180 for 0 (J.A. Jameson 123, D.L. Amiss 54) v Nottinghamshire, Trent Bridge, 1973.
Worcestershire 175 for 0 (J.A. Ormrod 90, G.M. Turner 75) v Surrey, Worcester, 1976.

It is noticeable that the introduction of fielding circles in 1982 brought about an increase in run-scoring. In the wet summer of 1979, Somerset won the title without ever once reaching 200, whereas in 1984 Derbyshire, with six scores of over 200, finished last in the competition.

HIGHEST INDIVIDUAL INNINGS

176 (1 six and 28 fours), G.A. Gooch, Essex v Glamorgan,
Southend, 1983.
175 no (13 sixes and 12 fours), I.T. Botham, Somerset v
Northamptonshire, Wellingborough, 1986.
C.G. Greenidge (Hampshire), G.A. Gooch (Essex), W. Larkins
(Northamptonshire) and K.S. McEwan (Essex) are the only batsmen
to have played two innings of 150 or more.

Sunday at Basingstoke.

CENTURIES

10 C.G. Greenidge (Hampshire).
 9 K.S. McEwan (Essex), B.A. Richards (Hampshire).
 7 G.A. Gooch (Essex), I.V.A. Richards (Somerset),
    P. Willey (Northamptonshire and Leicestershire),
    Zaheer Abbas (Gloucestershire).

Younis Ahmed (4 centuries) is the only batsman to have hit centuries for three different counties – Surrey, Worcestershire and Glamorgan. There were 282 centuries scored altogether in the John Player League.

MOST CENTURIES IN A SEASON

3 B.A. Richards (Hampshire), 1970; P. Willey (Northamptonshire), 1976;
   Zaheer Abbas (Gloucestershire), 1980; D.I. Gower (Leicestershire), 1982.

MOST RUNS IN A SEASON

814 (av. 58.14), C.E.B. Rice (Nottinghamshire), 1977.
720 (av. 60.00), C.L. Smith (Hampshire), 1984.

MOST RUNS IN A CAREER

6861, D.L. Amiss (Warwickshire).
6536, C.T. Radley (Middlesex).

Both of these batsmen retired at the end of the 1987 season. Their aggregates for the one season of the Refuge Assurance League were:

    Amiss   179 runs
    Radley   114 runs

Sixes

MOST SIXES IN A SEASON

26 I.V.A. Richards (Somerset), 1977.
23 I.T. Botham (Somerset), 1986.
21 C.G. Greenidge (Hampshire), 1978.
19 D.B. Close (Somerset), 1974; J.A. Jameson (Warwickshire), 1975;
    M.W. Gatting (Middlesex), 1984.

MOST SIXES IN A CAREER

146 I.V.A. Richards (Somerset).
131 C.G. Greenidge (Hampshire).
123 I.T. Botham (Somerset).
121 C.H. Lloyd (Lancashire).

MOST RUNS OFF AN OVER

34 I.V.A. Richards, Somerset against Gloucestershire, Taunton, 1977.
    Five sixes (a record) and one four.

The most runs conceded by a bowler in the one over that he bowled in the innings is 26 by J.R.T. Barclay (Sussex), Taunton, 1985, where Richards was again the destroyer, and by K.W.R. Fletcher (Essex), Trent Bridge, 1983.

SIXES AT A DECISIVE MOMENT

There have been eight occasions on which a batsman has hit the last ball of the fortieth over for six to win the match:

P.E. Russell (Derbyshire), off R.J. Bailey (Northamptonshire), Northampton, 1974.
J.C. Balderstone (Leicestershire), off G.A. Cope (Yorkshire), Leicester, 1975.
N.M. McVicker (Leicestershire), off A.A. Jones (Somerset), Yeovil, 1976.
J. Simmons (Lancashire), off R.D. Jackman (Surrey), Old Trafford, 1976.
C.J. Tunnicliffe (Derbyshire), off G.R.J. Roope (Surrey), Chesterfield, 1978.
S. Turner (Essex), off B. Roberts (Derbyshire), Derby, 1984.
I.T. Botham (Somerset), off W.W. Daniel (Middlesex), Taunton, 1986.
A. Sidebottom (Yorkshire), off N.A. Foster (Essex), Headingley, 1986.

Botham accomplished the feat in a televised match, hitting two of the last three balls for sixes.

RECORD WICKET PARTNERSHIPS

1st	239	G.A. Gooch (171) & B.R. Hardie (60), Essex *v* Nottinghamshire, Trent Bridge, 1985.
2nd	273	G.A. Gooch (116) & K.S. McEwan (162*), Essex *v* Nottinghamshire, Trent Bridge, 1983.
3rd	215	W. Larkins (158) & R.G. Williams (79*), Northamptonshire *v* Worcestershire, Luton, 1982.
4th	178	J.J. Whitaker (132) & P. Willey (106), Leicestershire *v* Glamorgan, Swansea, 1984.
5th	185*	M. Asif Din (108*) & B.M. McMillan (78*), Warwickshire *v* Essex, Chelmsford, 1986.
6th	121	C.P. Wilkins (94) & A.J. Borrington (56), Derbyshire *v* Warwickshire, Chesterfield, 1972.
7th	101	S.J. Windaybank (56*) & D.A. Graveney (49), Gloucestershire *v* Nottinghamshire, Trent Bridge, 1981.
8th	95*	D. Breakwell (44*) & K.F. Jennings (51*), Somerset *v* Nottinghamshire, Trent Bridge, 1976.
9th	105	D.G. Moir (79) & R.W. Taylor (29*), Derbyshire *v* Kent, Derby, 1984.
10th	57	D.A. Graveney (27*) & J.B. Mortimore (26), Gloucestershire *v* Lancashire, Tewkesbury, 1977.

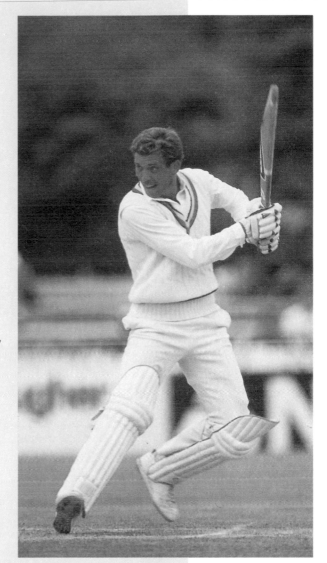

James Whitaker – a record stand with Peter Willey at Swansea in 1984.

Brian McMillan shared a record partnership on his first appearance in the John Player League.

BEST BOWLING PERFORMANCES

8 for 26   K.D. Boyce, Essex *v* Lancashire, Old Trafford, 1971.
7 for 15   R.A. Hutton, Yorkshire *v* Worcestershire, Headingley, 1969.
7 for 39   A. Hodgson, Northamptonshire *v* Somerset, Northampton, 1976.
7 for 41   A.N. Jones, Sussex *v* Nottinghamshire, Trent Bridge, 1986.

FIVE WICKETS IN AN INNINGS

6   D.L. Underwood (Kent).
5   D.P. Jones (Lancashire).
4   D.J. Brown (Warwickshire), R.E. East (Essex), J.K. Lever (Essex), H.R. Moseley (Somerset) and D.A. Marriott (Middlesex).

Marriott's five-wicket performances were all in the same season, 1973.

MOST WICKETS IN A SEASON

34 (av. 13.17)   R.J. Clapp (Somerset), 1974.
34 (av. 15.85)   C.E.B. Rice (Nottinghamshire), 1986.
33 (av. 12.69)   K.D. Boyce (Essex), 1971.
33 (av. 12.39)   D.L. Williams (Glamorgan), 1971.
33 (av. 16.78)   A.M. Ferreira (Warwickshire), 1981.

John Lever – the leading bowler in Sunday League cricket.

MOST WICKETS IN A CAREER

344 (av. 16.79)   D.L. Underwood (Kent).
344 (av. 18.69)   J.K. Lever (Essex).
303 (av. 23.86)   S. Turner (Essex).

The first bowler to 100 wickets was K.D. Boyce (Essex), 1972.
The first bowler to 200 wickets was S. Turner (Essex), 1978.
The first bowler to 300 wickets was J.K. Lever (Essex), who reached the target a quarter of an hour before D.L. Underwood reached it for Kent against Sussex at Hastings.

D.L. Underwood retired at the end of the 1987 season. He played in only two Refuge Assurance League matches in his final season, taking 2 for 67. J.K. Lever has given no indication of retirement; he will be forty in 1989. He played in 11 Refuge Assurance League matches in 1987, taking 13 wickets for 383 runs.

Richard Ellison (Kent).

Paul Jarvis (Yorkshire) — the youngest bowler to perform the hat-trick in the John Player League.

HAT-TRICKS

A. Ward (Derbyshire), R. Palmer (Somerset), K.D. Boyce (Essex), G.D. McKenzie (Leicestershire), R.G.D. Willis (Warwickshire), W. Blenkiron (Warwickshire), A. Buss (Sussex), J.M. Rice (Hampshire), M.A. Nash (Glamorgan), A. Hodgson (Northamptonshire), A.E. Cordle (Glamorgan), C.J. Tunnicliffe (Derbyshire), M.D. Marshall (Hampshire), I.V.A. Richards (Somerset), P.W. Jarvis (Yorkshire) and R.M. Ellison (Kent).

The most economical bowling figures are recorded earlier in the text.

Gary Sobers – 583 runs and 23 wickets for Notts in the John Player League, 1971.

John Murray (Middlesex, 28 dismissals in 1975.

MOST EXPENSIVE BOWLING

7.5–0–89–3	G. Miller, Derbyshire *v* Gloucestershire, Gloucester, 1984.
8–0–88–1	E.E. Hemmings, Nottinghamshire *v* Somerset, Trent Bridge, 1983.
8–0–85–0	A.M. Ferreira, Warwickshire *v* Essex, Colchester, 1982.
8–0–80–2	B.J. Griffiths, Northamptonshire *v* Sussex, Hastings, 1983.

E.E. Hemmings suffered during a partnership between I.V.A. Richards and I.T. Botham which realized 138 off 13 overs.

A.M. Ferreira suffered when K.S. McEwan took 24 off his last over to give him the worst analysis since the opening year of the competition.

MOST RUNS CONCEDED IN A SEASON

610 at 5.13 an over, E.E. Hemmings, Warwickshire, 1975.

ALL-ROUNDERS

Forty-three cricketers took 100 wickets or more and passed 1000 runs in the John Player League. Phil Bainbridge (Gloucestershire) scored 1433 runs and took 99 wickets in the League, but completed the double in the first Refuge Assurance League match of 1987.

500 RUNS AND 20 WICKETS IN A SEASON

583 runs & 23 wickets	G.StA. Sobers (Nottinghamshire), 1971.
532 runs & 20 wickets	Imran Khan (Worcestershire), 1976.
577 runs & 21 wickets	C.E.B. Rice (Nottinghamshire), 1976.
814 runs & 20 wickets	C.E.B. Rice (Nottinghamshire), 1977.
615 runs & 20 wickets	Imran Khan (Sussex), 1985.
571 runs & 34 wickets	C.E.B. Rice (Nottinghamshire), 1986.

Wicket-keeping

MOST DISMISSALS IN AN INNINGS

7, R.W. Taylor (c 6, st 1), Derbyshire *v* Lancashire, Old Trafford, 1975.

MOST CATCHES IN AN INNINGS

6	R.W. Taylor, as above.
	K. Goodwin, Lancashire *v* Worcestershire, Worcester, 1969.

MOST DISMISSALS IN A SEASON

28 (c 22, st 6)	J.T. Murray (Middlesex), 1975.
27 (c 23, st 4)	N. Smith (Essex), 1975.
25 (c 23, st 2)	R.W. Taylor (Derbyshire), 1974.

MOST STUMPINGS IN AN INNINGS

4, S.J. Rhodes, Worcestershire *v* Warwickshire, Edgbaston, 1986.

MOST STUMPINGS IN A SEASON

8, G.R. Stephenson (Hampshire), 1976.

MOST DISMISSALS IN A CAREER

236 (c 187, st 49)	R.W. Taylor (Derbyshire).
223 (c 184, st 39)	E.W. Jones (Glamorgan).
218 (c 183, st 35)	A.P.E. Knott (Kent).
215 (c 196, st 19)	D.L. Bairstow (Yorkshire).
201 (c 163, st 38)	G. Sharp (Northamptonshire).

Roger Harper. Economic bowling, hard-hitting batting and brilliance in the field.

Fielding

MOST CATCHES IN AN INNINGS

5, J.M. Rice, Hampshire *v* Warwickshire, Southampton, 1978.

MOST CATCHES IN A SEASON

16   J.M. Rice (Hampshire), 1978.
15   P.J. Watts (Northamptonshire), 1970.
14   G.M. Turner (Worcestershire), 1979.
13   G.M. Turner (Worcestershire), 1970; K. Higgs (Leicestershire), 1978;
     R.C.M. Gilliat (Hampshire), 1975; R.A. Harper (Northamptonshire),
     1986.

MOST CATCHES IN A CAREER

101   J.F. Steele (Leicestershire and Glamorgan).
 89   C.T. Radley (Middlesex).
 85   R.E. East (Essex).
 82   S. Turner (Essex) and K.W.R. Fletcher (Essex).
 81   G. Cook (Northamptonshire).
 80   G.R.J. Roope (Surrey) (Roope also took three catches as a wicket-
     keeper).

John Steele, 101 catches.

MOST APPEARANCES

261   J. Simmons (Lancashire).
256   C.T. Radley (Middlesex).
255   S. Turner (Essex).
252   J.K. Lever (Essex).

Six players – J.K. Lever and K.W.R. Fletcher (Essex); Dennis Amiss (Warwickshire); Peter Willey (Northamptonshire); Norman Gifford (Worcestershire) and Trevor Jesty (Hampshire) – all appeared in the opening John Player League matches in April 1969, and in the closing matches on 14 September 1986. Willey (Leicestershire), Gifford (Warwickshire) and Jesty (Surrey) had changed counties.

6 MATCHES OF MOMENT

From the first days of the Gillette Cup, limited-over cricket produced some memorable matches and thrilling finishes. We have already touched upon the deeds of Jack Bond, David Hughes, Mike Procter and Viv Richards and noted the number of times that a John Player League match was won when a batsman hit a six off the last ball of the innings; yet, with so much now at stake and with several counties having reached so high a standard that it is difficult to judge between them, the past decade has provided games where the sides were so evenly matched that the result has been in doubt until the last ball. The knock-out competitions, particularly in their later stages, have produced such excitement that, at times, mathematical calculation has been necessary to separate the teams.

No competition could have had a more exciting start than the NatWest Bank Trophy in 1981. Lancashire, in spite of looking rather ancient in the field on occasions, had shown signs of resurgence by beating Hampshire to qualify for the semi-final, while Essex, the favourites to win the Trophy, beat Sussex at Hove in the quarter-final in an enthralling contest which, on one of the hottest days of the summer, looked to be edging in favour of Sussex until Stuart Turner dismissed Ian Gould and Imran Khan in the same over.

The draw for the semi-finals took Lancashire to Northampton. Northamptonshire had won the Benson and Hedges Cup the previous season, beating Essex in the final, so that they were a capable one-day side with a particularly attractive batting line-up. Lancashire, in contrast, were an inconsistent side, heavily reliant on Fowler and the Lloyds in batting and expecting much from West Indian Michael Holding in their bowling.

It was a rather sombre day, which might

Brian Hardie is bowled by Watts for 0, and Essex are on their way to defeat by Northants, Benson and Hedges Cup Final, 1980. George Sharp is the wicketkeeper.

have influenced Geoff Cook's decision to ask Lancashire to bat first when he won the toss. Whatever his reasoning, he had immediate success when, having scored all the first six runs, Andrew Kennedy edged the Pakistan Test bowler Sarfraz to slip where Yardley took a fine, low catch. This was to be Northamptonshire's only success of the first session. Graeme Fowler, always eager to play his shots, and David Lloyd, resilient and determined, batted without any suggestion of trouble and carried their partnership past the hundred mark and into the fifth over of the afternoon before David Lloyd drove off-break bowler Richard Williams into the hands of extra-cover.

This precipitated a period of crisis for Lancashire, for two overs later Fowler was caught behind. In the next over came a decisive blow when Clive Lloyd, attempting to leg-glance, was splendidly caught behind by Sharp off the bowling of Tim Lamb. Reidy was lbw to the same bowler for 0 so that 3 wickets had gone down with the score on 123, and the Lancashire innings was in tatters.

There was to be no effective recovery. Abrahams went the way of Clive Lloyd with only another ten runs added, and David Hughes, aiming to drive to long-off, was caught on the third-man boundary. Having been 110 for 1 in the thirty-seventh over, Lancashire were 144 for 7 in the fifty-second.

Neither O'Shaughnessy nor Allott stayed long, but Holding joined Simmons in a last-wicket stand of 25, the product of violent assault and unorthodoxy. Northamptonshire, who owed much to Tim Lamb for a spell of bowling that was both economical and penetrative, were well content to have restricted Lancashire to 186 for 9, particularly as the wicket remained easy paced.

The home side began confidently, but just as it seemed that the opening batsmen had negotiated the initial fire of Holding and Allott, Wayne Larkins was lbw to the latter. Richard Williams seemed unable to settle, but he survived, and he and Geoff Cook took the score past fifty before, surprisingly, the Northamptonshire captain fell to the erratic O'Shaughnessy who had been preferred to the veteran medium-pace bowler Peter Lee, a selection which was hard to understand.

Williams grew in confidence, and Allan Lamb, on whom many hopes rested, started quietly. At tea all was well, but two overs into the last session Lamb was caught at backward short-leg off a ball from Simmons that turned, and in Simmons' next over, with only one run added, Williams was caught at mid-on. At 97 for 4 Northamptonshire, with a tail that looked long and vulnerable, were in a precarious position.

Jim Yardley, employing the sweep to great

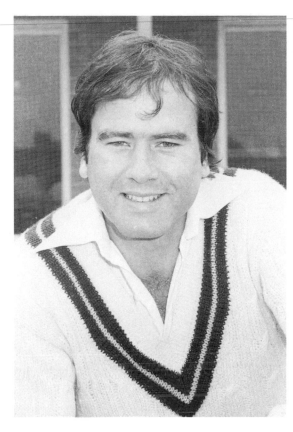

Tim Lamb – Man of the Match in Northants' tense victory over Lancashire, 1981.

effect, and Carter saw off the threatening Jack Simmons who had stunted the Northamptonshire run rate and taken two valuable wickets, and the runs began to come more freely. At 150, Northamptonshire appeared to have weathered the storm and to be moving smoothly towards victory. Then Yardley was caught at slip off Reidy, and two runs later Carter was lbw to David Lloyd, whose slow left-arm bowling had been pressed into service when O'Shaughnessy had failed to find either length or direction.

Now the game swung violently in favour of Lancashire. Sharp succumbed almost immediately. Sarfraz hit a few lusty blows before departing, and Mallender did not stay long. With Northamptonshire at 174 for 9, and only Jim Griffiths left to help Tim Lamb, Lancashire looked to be winners, for Griffiths was one of the renowned rabbits of county cricket. The highest score of his career was to be 16, and he was to end his career with a first-class average of 3.33. As 12 runs still separated the sides, the chances of a Northamptonshire victory seemed very remote indeed.

When Griffiths joined Lamb, eight overs of the match were left, and of those Holding and Allott could bowl two each. Whatever faint hopes Northamptonshire cherished were with Tim Lamb, not a batsman of talent but a thinking cricketer who nursed and cajoled his partner. Holding and Allott were pitched straight

The hero of the hour at Northampton, 1981, Jim Griffiths.

into the attack, but Holding in particular committed the worst of sins when he failed to make the batsmen play the ball. Fowler, a makeshift wicket-keeper, was not at his best behind the stumps, and the fielding was becoming excitable. There were flurries of leg-byes, and Griffiths hit a single, but most of the time Lamb shielded him from the bowling until, at the end of the fifty-ninth over, the scores were level and Griffiths was left to face the last over, which was to be bowled by David Lloyd.

Before that over began, Tim Lamb sent the umpires scurrying off to the score-box to query the rules of the competition with regard to the respective run rates. It was resolved that if Griffiths could survive the last over, Northamptonshire would have won as, with the scores level and both sides having lost 9 wickets, they had the superior run rate over the first thirty overs.

Four balls were bowled in what was now a Stygian gloom and with a crowd that suffered agonies at every delivery. The fifth ball turned from leg and beat Griffiths' forward prod. It also beat the groping gloves of Graeme Fowler, and the batsmen hurried through for a bye, continuing their run to the pavilion with bats held aloft in triumph as the crowd swarmed on to the field to celebrate.

Meanwhile, at Derby, gloom and drizzle

had brought the other semi-final to a premature closure with the game interestingly balanced. Barry Wood had won the toss and, on a green wicket under heavy cloud, had asked Essex to bat first to the surprise of no one. There was an early stoppage because of drizzle, but Derbyshire were soon celebrating when Tunnicliffe, left-arm medium pace, swung a ball late to have Hardie caught behind. Two runs later Gooch was brilliantly caught by Bob Taylor, diving in front of first slip, and Fletcher was yorked at 24.

Much depended on McEwan, who found an able ally in Keith Pont. They added 50 in twenty-one overs either side of lunch, which was ended when Pont fell to a steeply rising delivery from Hendrick. Two balls later came a great disaster from the Essex point of view. McEwan played a ball to leg and went for a quick single. It was not a wise run. Kim Barnett picked the ball up at mid-wicket and threw down the stumps at the bowler's end. It was a fine piece of fielding, a bad piece of judgement on McEwan's part, and Essex were 75 for 5.

They were soon 78 for 6, Turner edging to Taylor, and Pringle became the wicket-keeper's fifth victim after a most uneasy and unhappy brief period at the crease. Barry Wood now gambled on bowling out Essex within the sixty overs and brought back his main-line attack, but Norbert Phillip curbed his natural tendency to hit at everything and withstood the quick men. Ray East gave sound support before he was bowled by Newman at 98.

David East, in his first season in the Essex XI and with one Man of the Match award to his credit, showed qualities of defiance and aggression. He and Phillip were confident against Newman and Hendrick, and with the pace men having finished their quota, Essex were 117 for 8 with six overs remaining, which were to be bowled by the Derbyshire spinners who were unlikely to derive as much assistance from the pitch and conditions as the seam bowlers had done.

Phillip went on to the attack. The last six overs produced 36 runs, and the stand between Phillip and David East became worth 46 in ten overs. The partnership was not broken until the final over of the innings when Geoff Miller beat Phillip through the air and left him stranded. The last ball of the over accounted for David East, who attempted a massive hit and was well caught by Newman, running round the boundary at long-off. Essex could hardly be satisfied with 149, but it was a score far better than had looked likely when Phillip had come to the wicket in the thirty-fifth over.

Derbyshire began their innings in wretched weather, and the players soon left the field. They returned a few moments later and, in the fifth over of the innings, John Wright was lbw without offering a shot. In the eighth over Peter Kirsten was also lbw, so that when play was finally halted for the day Essex had clawed their way back into the game.

When Turner and Pringle came into the attack the following morning, Derbyshire began to gasp for runs. David Steele was bowled as he pushed forward, and Turner moved a ball across Miller to hit his leg stump. Alan Hill thought only of survival, providing a rock on which other could build, and his 21 runs took him beyond lunch and occupied forty overs. Ironically, he was run out; Barnett played the ball square on the off side, and Hill backed up so far that Fletcher's throw to the bowler beat him comfortably.

Kim Barnett and Barry Wood engaged in a resolute and vital stand of 51 in sixteen overs. They ran well between the wickets, and Barnett was particularly severe on anything down the leg side. It was not until Lever and Phillip returned for the final burst that the stand was broken. Wood swung at Phillip and was caught on the square-leg boundary. Seven runs later, Barnett also fell to the West Indian. He unwisely attempted to clout Phillip through the off side and the ball just clipped his off stump. With fifteen balls remaining, Derbyshire needed 18 to win, no easy task in a match in which runs had

Paul Newman – last ball winner at Derby, 1981.

been at a premium and where the bowlers had always held the advantage.

Colin Tunnicliffe, a powerful hitter, was bowled by the first ball of the fifty-ninth over, so that Newman joined Bob Taylor with eleven balls left. They conjured six runs from the last five balls of John Lever's last over. This meant that 11 were wanted from the final over, which was to be bowled by Norbert Phillip. If a wicket fell, the last man to come to the wicket would be Mike Hendrick, who had been in bed unwell earlier in the day but had been brought to the ground because a situation had arisen where his batting might be needed.

The field was spread widely; the boundaries were tenanted. Taylor drove the first ball straight, and the batsmen ran two. The second ball was run down to third man for a single, and the third produced another single when Newman pulled the ball to mid-on. Taylor pushed the fourth ball square for the third single in succession. The runs acquired from these first four balls had, in fact, brought Derbyshire a bonus, for they ensured that the home side now needed only to level the scores to win the match on the basis of having lost fewer wickets. Five runs were wanted from two balls.

Following his heroic innings, Norbert Phillip had bowled admirably, but at the most crucial stage of the match his nerve was to desert

Norbert Phillip — hero and villain for Essex at Derby in 1981.

NATWEST BANK TROPHY SEMI-FINAL, 1981

Northamptonshire *v* Lancashire at
Northampton, 19 August

Lancashire	
A. Kennedy c Yardley b Sarfraz Nawaz .	6
*G. Fowler c Sharp b Williams	57
D. Lloyd c Carter b Williams	52
C.H. Lloyd (capt) c Sharp b T.M. Lamb .	4
D.P. Hughes c T.M. Lamb b Sarfraz Nawaz	13
B.W. Reidy lbw b T.M. Lamb	0
J. Abrahams c Sharp b T.M. Lamb	2
J. Simmons not out	28
S.J. O'Shaughnessy b Griffiths	3
P.J.W. Allott lbw b Griffiths.	0
M.A. Holding not out	12
l-b 7, w 1, n-b 1	9
(9 wickets, 60 overs)	186

	O	M	R	W
Sarfraz Nawaz	12	2	35	2
Griffiths	12	1	46	2
Mallender	12	3	28	–
T.M. Lamb	12	1	28	3
Williams	12	–	40	2

Fall of wickets
1/6 2/116 3/123 4/123 5/123 6/133 7/144
8/160 9/161

Northamptonshire	
G. Cook (capt) b O'Shaughnessy	31
W. Larkins lbw b Allott	9
R.G. Williams c C.H. Lloyd b Simmons .	41
A.J. Lamb c D. Lloyd b Simmons	10
T.J. Yardley c C.H. Lloyd b Reidy	31
R.M. Carter lbw b D. Lloyd	14
*G. Sharp lbw b Reidy	1
Sarfraz Nawaz lbw b Reidy.	14
N.A. Mallender c Fowler b Allott	4
T.M. Lamb not out	10
B.J. Griffiths not out	1
B 2, l-b 16, w 1, n-b 2.	21
(9 wickets, 59.5 overs).	187

	O	M	R	W
Holding	12	2	36	–
Allott	12	2	32	2
O'Shaughnessy	4	–	25	1
Reidy	10	3	22	3
Simmons	12	4	17	2
D. Lloyd	9.5	–	34	1

Fall of wickets
1/24 2/58 3/96 4/97 5/150 6/152 7/162
8/170 9/174

Umpires: W.L. Budd and A.G.T. Whitehead
Man of the Match: T.M. Lamb

Northamptonshire won by 1 wicket

him. If he could prevent Derbyshire from scoring a boundary, Essex would most surely win. But the fifth ball of Phillip's over was a rank long-hop outside leg stump and Newman hooked it fiercely to the ropes. One run was needed from the one ball to be bowled.

Keith Fletcher spent much time adjusting his field, attempting to close every gap and to put pressure on the batsmen. Phillip bowled just short of a length on the line of the off stump. Newman pushed forward, and the ball just eluded Fletcher who had stationed himself at silly mid-off. Phillip, following through, picked up cleanly as Newman set off on an impossible single. Brian Hardie had taken up a position behind the stumps at the bowler's end, so that a gentle lob to him by Phillip would have left Newman well short of his ground and Essex as victors. But who can think rationally at such a moment? Phillip hurled wildly, some four to five feet high and wide of Hardie, and Newman made his ground comfortably. Derbyshire had reached the final.

So Derbyshire and Northamptonshire arrived at Lord's on a beautiful late summer day to contest the first NatWest Bank Trophy Final. Few believed that the final could rival either of the semi-finals in excitement or intensity. Northamptonshire welcomed back Willey after injury, and he replaced Carter. Derbyshire were unchanged.

Wood followed his customary policy of asking the opponents to bat first when he won the toss. Derbyshire started very nervously. The usually neat and accomplished Taylor conceded byes off the first delivery of the match. Tunnicliffe was unable to find a length and was taken off after a couple of overs, and the second over of the day produced 12 runs.

Larkins and Cook relished the situation, and

NATWEST BANK TROPHY SEMI-FINAL, 1981

Derbyshire *v* Essex at Derby, 19 and 20 August

Essex

B.R. Hardie c Taylor b Tunnicliffe.....	5
G.A. Gooch c Taylor b Newman......	14
K.W.R. Fletcher (capt) b Newman.....	4
K.S. McEwan run out.............	28
K.R. Pont c Taylor b Hendrick.......	20
N. Phillip st Taylor b Miller.........	42
S. Turner c Taylor b Hendrick.......	0
D.R. Pringle c Taylor b Tunnicliffe....	1
R.E. East b Newman..............	6
*D.E. East c Newman b Miller........	18
J.K. Lever not out................	4
l-b 4, n-b 3	7

(60 overs)...............	149

	O	M	R	W
Tunnicliffe	12	2	21	2
Hendrick	12	2	20	2
Newman	12	2	26	3
Wood	12	3	24	–
Steele	9	1	35	–
Miller	3	–	16	2

Fall of wickets
1/19 2/21 3/24 4/74 5/75 6/78 7/90
8/98 9/144

Derbyshire

J.G. Wright lbw b Lever...........	1
A. Hill run out..................	21
P.N. Kirsten lbw b Phillip..........	8
D.S. Steele b Pringle.............	7
G. Miller b Turner...............	0
K.J. Barnett b Phillip..............	59
B. Wood (capt) c R.E. East b Phillip...	18
*R.W. Taylor not out..............	9
C.J. Tunnicliffe b Lever............	1
P.G. Newman not out.............	7
M. Hendrick	
l-b 12, w 3, n-b 3............	18

(8 wickets, 60 overs)........	149

	O	M	R	W
Lever	12	4	22	2
Phillip	12	2	42	3
Pringle	12	5	19	1
Turner	12	4	18	1
Gooch	12	2	30	–

Fall of wickets
1/3 2/12 3/27 4/40 5/74 6/125 7/132
8/133

Umpires: D.O. Oslear and D.G.L. Evans
Man of the Match: K.J. Barnett

Derbyshire won by virtue of losing fewer
wickets with the scores level

Wood tried to stem the flow of runs by coming into the attack. He was partly successful, and was greatly aided by Taylor who had now found his best form and, standing up to the medium-pacers, represented a constant threat to the batsmen.

Containment did not last long, however, for Larkins pulled Wood over square-leg for six and flicked Newman in the same direction for four. Larkins was bustling with energy and aggression, and Cook was practical and effective, but in the twenty-ninth over Larkins pulled Wood high again to square-leg, and this time Miller took a well-judged catch on the ropes, to make Northamptonshire at 99 for 1.

Allan Lamb was the next man in, and the stage set for him to assault the Derbyshire bowling, but he fluttered and dithered. The Derbyshire bowling had steadied, and the fielding had found more resolution. Lamb faced forty deliveries and failed to produce a shot worthy of his reputation before being run out by Miller's direct throw from extra-cover. It was a very close decision, and the batsman may have considered himself a little unlucky.

Lamb had been promoted in the order to take advantage of the excellent start, but he had disappointed. It was left to Williams, chunky and belligerent, to provide the expected aggression, but just as he seemed set to tear the attack apart he was brilliantly caught by Alan Hill. Williams drove Miller straight and high to the Nursery End boundary where Hill, falling to his left, took the ball in front of the sight-screen.

Willey was wastefully run out, and the innings stuttered. Tunnicliffe returned to atone for the sins of the morning with an excellent spell. Cook, sensing loss of direction and purpose around him, hit Hendrick for three fours in an over to pass his century and reassert

Northamptonshire's authority, but with his score on 111, the dread of the superstitious, he was lbw to Tunnicliffe.

The Derbyshire fielders retreated to the boundary in anticipation of the final flourish, but it never came. Mallender was caught behind first ball, and Tim Lamb was out to the last ball of the innings when he swung wildly. 218 for 4 had become 235 for 9 – disappointing, but still a considerable target.

In their opening spell, Sarfraz and Griffiths swung the ball appreciably, and Hill, always professional and determined, and Wright concentrated on survival. The stand was broken when Hill uncharacteristically played across the line and was bowled. He had been in for fourteen overs, and the score was 41.

Without ever suggesting the fluency of the Cook–Larkins stand earlier in the day, Kirsten joined Wright in a partnership that was efficient in every detail and provided the platform from which a later assault could be mounted. Kirsten accumulated solidly rather than display his wide range of shots, but Wright, initially watchful with nose right over the ball, became more adventurous in his stroke-play. He is a beautiful player off the back foot, and he leant back to thump Sarfraz to the boundary square on either side of the wicket.

Northamptonshire needed 100 from the last seventeen overs. They scored 29 in the next five overs, but lost both Wright and Kirsten. In the forty-eighth over, Wright moved down the wicket and pulled Mallender high into the tavern area for six. Two balls later he was lbw. Wood got off the mark with a single, but Kirsten, like Wright, was lbw playing across the line. The game had taken a dramatic turn in favour of Northamptonshire.

Wood and Barnett batted with the surety that they had shown against Essex, and added 24 in five overs before Sarfraz moved a ball back off the seam to bowl Wood. From the last seven overs, Derbyshire needed 47 runs. This was not a situation to suit David Steele, and, like an animal in pain, he was thankfully soon put out of his misery. The enigmatic Miller did find the occasion to his liking, however, and he and Kim Barnett raced between the wickets. From the last four overs, 34 runs were needed.

The light was fading rapidly, and many of the fielders were having difficulty in sighting the ball, but with all bar two back on the boundary ropes, they excelled themselves with diving stops and lightning throws, one of which accounted for Barnett when he gambled on a second run.

Tunnicliffe, honest, strong and dependable in his cricket, had thrown off the nerves of early morning, and in the fifty-ninth over he produced the type of batting of which Derbyshire were in need. He took two off Sarfraz's first ball, and then hit a glorious square drive for four. Not content with that, he drove the ball back past the bowler to the pavilion rails, and a single left Derbyshire to conjure six from the last over to level the scores and win the match in the same manner as that by which they had won the semi-final.

The last over was bowled by Jim Griffiths, who had defied credibility with his batting in the semi-final to bring Northamptonshire to this point. Miller took two off the first ball and a single off the second, but a roar announced that the third ball had not produced a run. A single to Tunnicliffe was followed by a single to Miller, leaving Tunnicliffe to face the last ball of the match with one run separating the sides.

Cook deliberated in his field-placings, and the whole of Lord's fell still and quiet as Griffiths moved in to bowl. He pitched the ball just outside the line of the leg stump. Colin Tunnicliffe swung at it, but the ball hit him on the pad and squirted out on the leg side. Miller raced down the wicket as Allan Lamb, running in from mid-on, picked up and threw to hit the stumps, but Miller had dived in the dust and just made his ground. Before anyone could retrieve the ball, Tunnicliffe was safe at the bowler's end. Both batsmen raised their bats in jubilation as they met and embraced in mid-wicket a half-second before they were submerged in the sea of people which had engulfed the playing area.

It was Derbyshire's first triumph since they had won the Championship in 1936, and only the second in a history dating back to 1870.

Essex's experience at Derby was not their first disappointment in the sixty-over competition. In 1978 they had reached the semi-final and travelled to play Somerset at Taunton. They needed three to snatch victory on the last ball of a pulsating match. Lever swung the ball to the outfield where Rose did not gather cleanly, but his throw still beat Neil Smith as he dived for the crease and what would have been the third run. The scores were level, but Essex had lost more wickets.

Two years later, in the quarter-final at Chelmsford, they restricted Surrey to 195 for 7 and reached 185 for 6 with five overs left. The incredible happened, and Ray East was run out on the penultimate ball of the match with the scores level to leave Surrey as victors.

In that same season they lost the Benson and Hedges Cup Final to Northamptonshire by 6 runs, but they were back at Lord's for the final of the same competition in 1983 when their opponents were Middlesex. It was probably one of the rare occasions when the two best sides in the country have contested a Lord's final. They were first and second in the County

NATWEST BANK TROPHY FINAL, 1981

Derbyshire *v* Northamptonshire at Lord's, 5
September

Northamptonshire

G. Cook (capt) lbw b Tunnicliffe	111
W. Larkins c Miller b Wood	52
A.J. Lamb run out	9
R.G. Williams c Hill b Miller	14
P. Willey run out	19
T.J. Yardley run out	4
*G. Sharp c Kirsten b Tunnicliffe	5
Sarfraz Nawaz not out	3
N.A. Mallender c Taylor b Newman	0
T.M. Lamb b Hendrick	4
B.J. Griffiths	
B 2, l-b 9, w 1, n-b 2	14
(9 wickets, 60 overs)	235

	O	M	R	W
Hendrick	12	3	50	1
Tunnicliffe	12	1	42	2
Wood	12	2	35	1
Newman	12	–	37	1
Steele	5	–	31	–
Miller	7	–	26	1

Fall of wickets
1/99 2/137 3/168 4/204 5/218 6/225
7/227 8/235

Derbyshire

A. Hill b Mallender	14
J.G. Wright lbw b Mallender	76
P.N. Kirsten lbw b Mallender	63
B. Wood (capt) b Sarfraz Nawaz	10
K.J. Barnett run out	19
D.S. Steele b Griffiths	0
G. Miller not out	22
C.J. Tunnicliffe not out	15
*R.W. Taylor	
P.G. Newman	
M. Hendrick	
B 5, l-b 7, w 3, n-b 1	16
(6 wickets, 60 overs)	235

	O	M	R	W
Sarfraz Nawaz	12	2	58	1
Griffiths	12	2	40	1
Mallender	10	1	35	3
Willey	12	–	33	–
T.M. Lamb	12	–	43	–
Williams	2	–	10	–

Fall of wickets
1/41 2/164 3/165 4/189 5/191 6/213

Umpires: D.J. Constant and K.E. Palmer
Man of the Match: G. Cook

Derbyshire won by virtue of losing fewer
wickets with the scores level

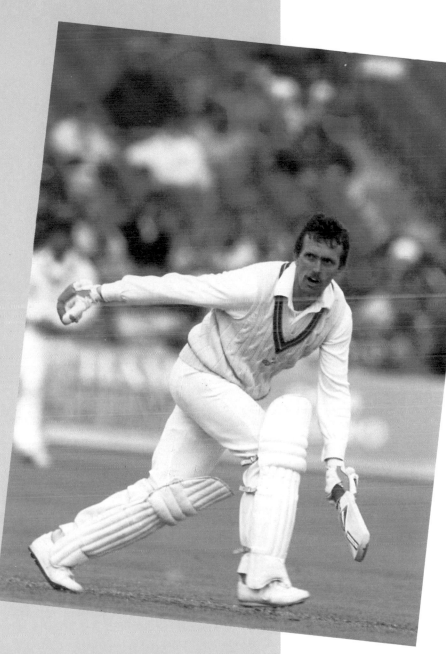

*A Man of the Match
award, but no victory for
Geoff Cook, Northants'
captain, in the NatWest
Bank Trophy Final,
1981.*

Lord's on Benson and Hedges Cup Final day, 1983.

Championship and fielded fourteen Test players between them. Indeed, it would have been sixteen but for the fact that Roland Butcher had been struck in the face by a ball from West Indian fast bowler Ferris when playing against Leicestershire, and that Essex had decided to leave out Norbert Phillip. This decision was a debatable one, for John Lever had undergone surgery for a stomach abscess only a week earlier and his fitness was in doubt, although he had announced himself well enough to play.

The week before the final the weather had been glorious, but the Saturday began with a disappointing drizzle, and play began fifty minutes late in an atmosphere of steaming damp. Fletcher won the toss and deliberated long on what to do. He consulted Gooch and Lever and asked Middlesex to bat first.

Barlow began confidently. He hit Lever through the off-side field to the boundary three times in the left-arm bowler's first two overs, so raising doubts as to the wisdom of playing Lever so soon after his operation. Foster on the other hand seemed in top form, menacing and smooth in his approach. In his second over he found the edge of Slack's bat, and Gooch took a

magnificent catch, right-handed and low down at slip.

As always, Radley determined to play off the front foot, and slowly and unobtrusively he began to build an innings. In the tenth over of the innings, however, he lost Barlow, who had his middle stump knocked back by another fine delivery from Foster which moved in to him.

Having bowled seven overs apiece, Lever and Foster were replaced by Pringle and Turner. Pringle had been uneasy in his run-up in the weeks before the match and had bowled a spate of no-balls. Perhaps nervous of repeating this sin on so important an occasion, he seemed hesitant in his approach, and after two ineffective overs which lacked both accuracy and threat he was replaced by Gooch.

Gooch and Turner now threatened to suffocate the Middlesex batting. Maintaining a relentlessly accurate length and moving the ball appreciably, they frustrated Gatting and Radley so that by the twenty-ninth over the score was only 72. Gatting was fretting to get the score moving. He turned Gooch square to the boundary in front of the Mound Stand. Foster set off in pursuit of the ball and picked up,

116

turned and threw in one movement as Gatting set off on an unwise third run. Foster's throw was straight over the top of the stumps into the gloves of David East, and Gatting was out by a foot. Tomlins was lbw first ball, and Middlesex were 74 for 4.

By the end of the thirty-sixth over, which saw the conclusion of Turner's economical spell, Middlesex were still short of the hundred. Emburey was struggling to put bat to ball, but Radley was pushing and nudging, crouching lower and lower over the bat as he did so. Emburey was dropped at mid-off when he swung desperately, but he perished in the forty-fourth over, by which time Radley had reached a defiant fifty.

Radley had been dropped the over before Emburey's dismissal, and this lapse cost Essex dearly for, from the last eleven overs, Radley cajoled Downton, Edmonds, Williams and Daniel into helping him to add 73 runs. Pringle and Lever were the main sufferers, and it was difficult to understand why Ray East had been chosen if his slow left-arm bowling were not to be used. Although the Middlesex total of 196 was not a good one, it was far better than had been expected for much of the innings, and for that they had Radley to thank. His 89 had spanned the last fifty-six overs of the innings, and he had shown, as ever, that professional determination which made him one of the most valuable cricketers in the limited-over game.

Essex began as if they were intent on winning the game inside twenty overs. Hardie crashed Daniel through the covers in the opening over, and the second, for Middlesex and for Norman Cowans in particular, was traumatic. Gatting set an attacking off-side field, but Cowans bowled short. Three times Gooch bludgeoned him to leg for four; twice he hit him for two. The England opener had begun with a display of awesome power.

Cowans was replaced by Williams after two overs, and Williams was immediately driven wide of mid-on for another boundary. A no-ball by Williams brought the fifty up in the eighth over, and after ten overs Essex were 71 for 0. It was heady stuff.

The battery continued. In the twelfth over of the innings, Gooch drove Williams straight and majestically to the Nursery End sight-screen. He aimed to repeat the shot next ball, but he edged to Downton who took a good, low catch. The thirteenth over was the first maiden, and McEwan, troubled by a wrist injury, found it hard to settle to his customary fluency. Hardie, too, was less confident and aggressive against Edmonds, but at tea, off twenty-five overs, Essex were 113 for 1, Hardie 34, McEwan 26, and victory seemed a formality.

Ultimate hero of the 1983 Benson and Hedges Cup Final – Norman Cowans.

Keith Pont is struck by a ball from Williams and is out, hit wicket, 1983.

In the thirtieth over, McEwan drove Edmonds low to mid-off, and there was suddenly a sense of anxiety in the Essex batting. Fletcher dithered and prodded before being taken, bat-pad, at silly mid-off. Hardie had managed only 13 runs in twenty overs, but Essex were within 61 runs of victory, had seven wickets in hand and twenty-three overs in which to get the runs.

In the thirty-eighth over the 150 came up, but Pont, who had been dropped by Cowans, was dismissed in a most unfortunate manner. Williams bowled a bouncer which Pont misjudged and took on the side of the helmet. The impact pressed a stud into Pont's temple and, stunned, he dropped his bat. In doing so he dislodged the off bail and was out, hit wicket. Essex needed 46 from seventeen overs with six wickets in hand.

Hardie, flat-footed against the spinners, had become becalmed. Since Gooch's departure he had scored 22 from twenty-nine overs. In the sixteen overs since tea he had made 15 runs. Cowans had been brought back from the pavilion end, and, perhaps in desperation, Hardie flashed at a widish ball and was caught behind in the forty-first over.

Middlesex had regained faith and hope. Gatting supported his bowlers with attacking fields, and Emburey induced strokelessness. Pringle and Turner nudged and ran sensibly. There was not the avalanche of runs that there had been at the start, but in nine overs they added 24 so that with five overs left, Essex were only 17 short of victory and had five wickets in hand.

Pringle struck two heartening boundaries and Turner one, before, with the first ball of the fifty-second over, Wayne Daniel had Pringle lbw. This meant that, with four wickets standing, Essex needed 12 runs from 23 balls.

David East managed a single and there was a leg-bye, but Turner, who had remained watchful against Emburey when he might have been more adventurous, clouted Cowans high to deep mid-on where, in the gathering gloom, John Carr, fielding as substitute for Williams, took a brilliant running catch.

This seemed to matter little to Essex when David East touched a ball to the fine-leg boundary, for at 191 for 7, Essex had more than two overs in which to score six runs. But, having hit the leg-side boundary, David East attempted to pull the next ball over mid-wicket

to the Tavern boundary. Gatting, who was fielding at mid-wicket, jumped and just got a hand to the ball, impeding its momentum. Spinning round, he caught the ball at the second attempt as it dropped behind him.

Ray East and Neil Foster, who was batting for the only time in the season in a limited-over match, were now at the wicket. Daniel bowled a wide to bring the score to 192, but with the fifth ball of the over he struck Ray East on the pad. The ball squirted out on the off side, and the batsman scampered up the wicket in search of an improbable leg-bye. Foster sent him back, but before he could regain his ground Radley had thrown down the stumps from point. Lever played out the last ball of the over so that the final over of the match arrived with Essex needing 5 runs to win, their last pair together.

Foster is bowled by Cowans and Middlesex have won the Benson and Hedges Cup, 1983.

119

The first ball of the final over ended the match. Cowans yorked Foster, who stood forlorn and bewildered among the wreckage. It was ten minutes to nine and almost dark. Cowans, recovering from the mauling he had received from Gooch, had taken three wickets in his last four balls to win the match. It was Essex who had suffered the final trauma.

BENSON AND HEDGES CUP FINAL, 1983

Middlesex *v* Essex at Lord's, 23 July

Middlesex

G.D. Barlow b Foster	14
W.N. Slack c Gooch b Foster	1
C.T. Radley not out	89
M.W. Gatting (capt) run out	22
K.P. Tomlins lbw b Gooch	0
J.E. Emburey c D.E. East b Lever	17
*P.R. Downton c Fletcher b Foster	10
P.H. Edmonds b Pringle	9
N.F. Williams c and b Pringle	13
W.W. Daniel not out	2
N.G. Cowans	
B 3, l-b 9, w 4, n-b 3	19
(8 wickets, 55 overs)	196

	O	M	R	W
Lever	11	1	52	1
Foster	11	2	26	3
Pringle	11	–	54	2
Turner	11	2	24	–
Gooch	11	2	21	1

Fall of wickets
1/10 2/25 3/74 4/74 5/123 6/141 7/171
8/191

Essex

G.A. Gooch c Downton b Williams	46
B.R. Hardie c Downton b Cowans	49
K.S. McEwan c Cowans b Edmonds	34
K.W.R. Fletcher (capt) c Radley b Edmonds	3
K.R. Pont hit wkt b Williams	7
D.R. Pringle lbw b Daniel	16
S. Turner c sub (Carr) b Cowans	9
*D.E. East c Gatting b Cowans	5
R.E. East run out	0
N.A. Foster b Cowans	0
J.K. Lever not out	0
l-b 12, w 3, n-b 8	23
(54.1 overs)	192

	O	M	R	W
Daniel	11	2	34	1
Cowans	10.1	–	39	4
Williams	11	–	45	2
Emburey	11	3	17	–
Edmonds	11	3	34	2

Fall of wickets
1/79 2/127 3/135 4/151 5/156 6/185
7/187 8/191 9/192

Umpires: H.D. Bird and B.J. Meyer
Gold Award: C.T. Radley

Middlesex won by 4 runs

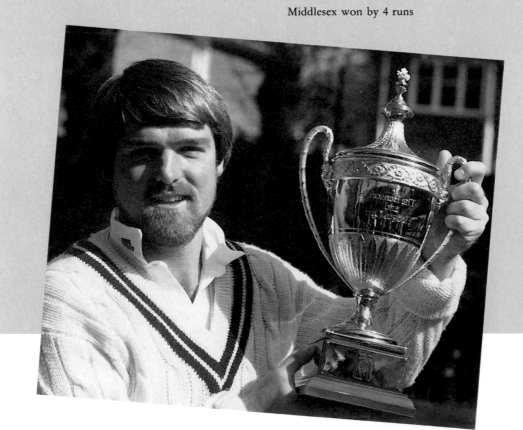

Gatting with the Cup. It is 9.00 p.m.

Robin Dyer is caught by Maynard off Watkinson for 11, and Warwickshire begin their slide to defeat in the Benson and Hedges Cup Final of 1984.

Another catch for Maynard. Humpage falls to Allott.

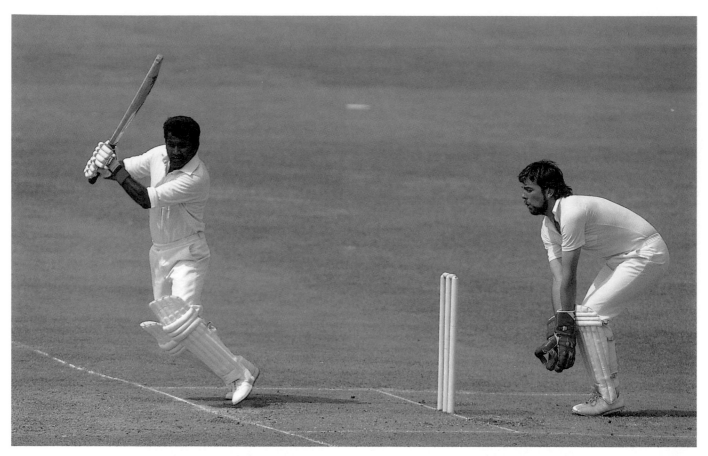

Warwickshire's lone hope, Alvin Kallicharran.

Willis bowls to Fairbrother, Lord's, 1984.

Fowler is caught behind off Willis, but Lancashire are close to taking the Benson and Hedges Cup, 1984.

David Hughes, 35 not out, as Lancashire win the one trophy that eluded them.

John Abrahams holds the Benson and Hedges Cup and the fans celebrate at Lord's, 1984.

Tim Robinson is clapped from the field at Worcester, 1985, after a brilliant century which put Notts in the final of the NatWest Bank Trophy. He batted well in the final, but still ended on the losing side.

Derek Pringle scored some pulsating runs in the 1985 NatWest Bank Trophy Final, and then bowled a dramatic last over.

The agonies that Essex endured at that Benson and Hedges final were compounded by the fact that they had also surrendered their interest in the NatWest Bank Trophy three days earlier when they had lost to Kent at Chelmsford by the same margin as that at Lord's, and in much the same manner.

Kent had found the going hard early on, but they had recovered, mainly due to the brilliance of Chris Cowdrey, and then slumped again to 182 for 7. The last fifteen overs, however, produced 72 runs, and with Pringle sprinkling no-balls about liberally, Kent reached 274 for 8. Chris Cowdrey finished with an exciting 122 not out, which included three sixes and fifteen fours.

This seemed to matter little, however, when Gooch and Hardie opened the Essex reply with a stand of 147, and Gooch and Fletcher took the score to 210 before Gooch was caught behind for 122. As at Lord's, it was from the moment of his departure that things began to go wrong for Essex, but they still moved to 262 for 5. Thirteen were needed from 15 balls, but Phillip was caught and Ellison bowled a maiden, so that the last over was reached with Essex needing six to win with three wickets standing.

Ellison bowled David East with the third ball and Pringle, swinging despairingly, with the last, to give him figures of 4 for 12 from his final four overs.

Essex, who had won three of the four major competitions within the space of three years, began to despair, believing that they were destined never to win the sixty-over competition. When they ultimately did gain the Trophy, it was not without a moment of high drama.

In 1984 Essex became the first county to win the Championship and the Sunday League in the same season. The Championship had been won in extraordinary circumstances, for Essex, having completed a victory at Old Trafford, had to listen to Nottinghamshire battling for a win at Taunton, a win which would have taken them ahead of Essex on the last afternoon of the season. They failed bravely, Mike Bore being caught on the boundary by substitute fielder Ollis off a hit that would have won the match. It was the fifth ball of the last over.

Essex were to retain their John Player League title in 1985, finish fourth in the Championship, reach the Benson and Hedges Cup Final where, Fletcher-less, they lost to Leicestershire, and, for the first time, find themselves in the final of the NatWest Bank Trophy where their opponents were Nottinghamshire, thirsting for revenge after their experiences of the previous season.

The summer of 1985 was, in the main, a wretched one, with players spending more time in the pavilion watching the rain than on the field playing the game. But the first Saturday in September was bright, crisp, warm and welcoming. For Essex, there was unexpected dismay on the morning of the match when it was revealed that Neil Foster, now the spearhead of their attack, was unable to play because of a viral infection. He was replaced by Ian Pont, younger brother of Keith who had played in the Benson and Hedges finals of 1979, 1980 and 1983. Ian Pont was a quick bowler of promise who had, ironically, assisted Nottinghamshire for a couple of seasons, but who was very inexperienced.

Clive Rice, the Nottinghamshire captain, won the toss and asked Essex to bat first. (The general reasoning for taking such a decision is that whatever assistance a Lord's wicket may give the bowler is to be found in the early morning rather than later.) The evidence of the first few overs suggested that Rice's decision was the right one, for the ball moved and lifted quite sharply, and Richard Hadlee, from the Pavilion End, was quick and menacing. Kevin Cooper began with a maiden, the first run did not come until the third over, and after six overs Essex had scored just 6 runs.

Gooch, with the confidence of a mammoth innings against Australia at The Oval a week earlier to support him, looked solid and assured. Hardie, in contrast, began to appear happily carefree and started to throw the bat at almost everything. After nineteen overs Essex were 55 for 0, and Hardie had scored 41. His fifty came

Ian Pont, late replacement for the sick Neil Foster, came through his ordeal well and ran out Chris Broad at Lord's, 1985.

in the twenty-fifth over when he drove Andy Pick for two, and Gooch's half-century, his fourth in five Lord's finals, came nine overs later. At lunch, Essex were 145 for 0 in thirty-eight overs.

There was no respite for Nottinghamshire in the early afternoon. Gooch and Hardie were quickly on to the attack again, and the first three overs after the break produced 18 runs. Hardie's century, off 136 deliveries with fourteen fours, came in the forty-fourth over at the end of which Essex were 175 without loss.

Brian Hardie has never batted better. There was an amusing eccentricity in his play; he would slash fiercely, the ball skimming fast and fine to the third-man boundary, and would then produce a shot of grandeur, driving regally through the covers to the Grand Stand boundary.

If Hardie provided the panache, Gooch, recognizing the responsibility that had been thrust upon him, concentrated on blunting the Nottinghamshire attack and offering an unyielding barrier. He was quick to seize any chance to increase the run rate, once moving casually down the wicket to hit Pick high into 'Q' Stand. He escaped a difficult leg-side stumping chance when on 70, Hemmings being the bowler, but he was finally bowled by Pick, the ball coming back a little, in the forty-ninth

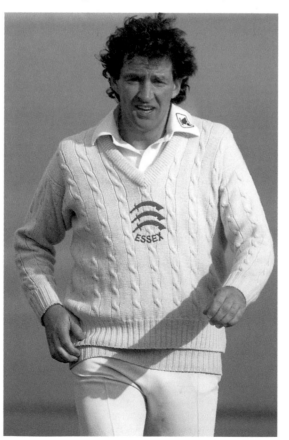

Man of the Match, Brian Hardie.

over. He had scored 91, and he and Hardie had put on 202, a record for any wicket in the NatWest Bank Trophy competition.

Ken McEwan came in to a standing ovation, for this was to be his last game at Lord's; his retirement from English cricket had been announced. He was to play a gem of an innings.

In the fifty-first over, Hardie was run out by Hemmings' throw to the non-striker's end from mid-off. Fletcher sent in Pringle to join McEwan, and they engaged in a stand which effectively put the match some ten runs beyond Nottinghamshire's reach. They added 77 in the last nine overs of the innings, batting with an audacity and eagerness that thrilled the capacity crowd.

McEwan was missed by Broad at mid-on in the fifty-sixth over, but in the fifty-eighth he drove Saxelby into the Mound Stand for six. Seventeen runs came from the over. Pringle, employing the reverse sweep to good effect, batted with confidence and aggression. They took the score to 280, and Nottinghamshire faced a daunting task, for no side had approached such a score when batting second in a sixty-over final.

Robinson and Broad began in workmanlike fashion. Their stand almost mirrored that of Hardie and Gooch, and at tea, after thirty-five overs, they had put on 124 and the Essex score began to look less frightening. Nevertheless, Nottinghamshire still needed another 157 runs at 6.28 an over.

The demands of such a scoring rate meant that after the break the batsmen had to play with a greater sense of urgency and take more risks. The Essex bowling offered few loose deliveries, and their fielding looked more dependable than the Nottinghamshire fielding had done. In fact, it was to be a fine piece of fielding and throwing which broke the opening stand.

Robinson played the ball towards the Grand Stand, the longer boundary, and the batsmen ran a brisk, comfortable single. Broad turned for a second run, but Robinson did not respond. Seemingly unaware of any danger, Broad attempted to regain his ground but was beaten by Ian Pont's long, fast and accurate throw to the wicket-keeper.

Rice joined Robinson, but the impetus of the innings had been lost, and in attempting to regain it, Robinson perished. Turner had begun to exert a stranglehold on the batsmen, and in an effort to break free Robinson hit him high to the square-leg boundary where Hardie took a comfortable catch. Randall took time to settle, and with the run rate required now more than seven an over, Rice clipped Turner to mid-wicket where Hardie held another simple catch.

Nottinghamshire's hopes now rested firmly with Richard Hadlee, and he hit a mighty six over long on to bring up the 200. Ian Pont, who had been nursed wisely by Fletcher and used in short spells, was brought back at the Nursery End to complete his quota. Hadlee hit him majestically to the long-off boundary, but next ball Pont knocked Hadlee's leg stump, and Nottinghamshire were 214 for 4.

Like Essex, Nottinghamshire had been deprived of a crucial player when appendicitis robbed them of the services of Paul Johnson. His deputy, Duncan Martindale, joined Randall to play with maturity. There were some good shots and intelligent running, but every over saw the required run rate climb so that when Pringle came to bowl the last over to Randall, 18 runs were needed and an Essex victory seemed assured.

One cannot think that there has ever been a more dramatic last over in a Lord's match. Pringle decided to attack leg stump, and the field was set accordingly, guarding the boundaries and leaving a gap only on the off-side Tavern boundary. Pringle's first ball, on a length and on the line of the leg stump, was driven into the off-side field for two. Randall repeated the shot next ball, but this time he pierced the field and reached the Tavern boundary. Two more runs came from the third ball, and the fourth, bowled outside leg stump, was crashed to the Tavern for another four.

Fletcher adjusted his field. The gap on the Tavern boundary was closed. Randall responded by stepping outside leg stump again and hitting a magnificent off-drive. The ball sped past Turner at long-off as he stood motionless, unable to sight the ball in the evening light.

So, after more than eight hours of cricket and 559 runs, we had arrived at the last ball of the match with Nottinghamshire needing two runs to snatch a victory which, for most of the day, had seemed totally out of their reach.

Pringle persisted with his leg-stump attack, and there are those who believe that had Randall stood his ground the last ball would have been declared a leg-side wide, but as Pringle bowled, Randall had committed himself to moving down the wicket. It is possible that Pringle anticipated his movement and pulled the ball down more sharply, for it pitched almost on Randall's toes. The fullness of the length cramped Randall's swing of the bat, and he could only clip the ball to mid-wicket where Paul Prichard jumped to take a comfortable catch. Essex had won by one wicket.

Randall walked down the wicket and shook hands with Pringle as the Essex players ran for the safety of the pavilion, away from the invading crowds.

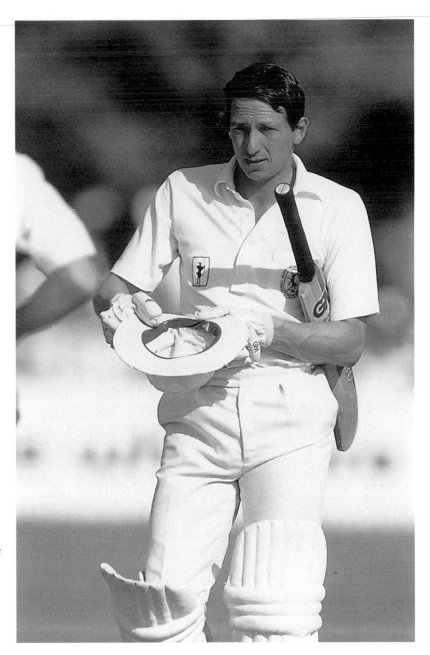

Heroic failure, Derek Randall.

NATWEST BANK TROPHY FINAL, 1985

Essex *v* Nottinghamsh. ·e at Lord's, 7 September

Essex

G.A. Gooch b Pick	91
B.R. Hardie run out.	110
K.S. McEwan not out	46
D.R. Pringle not out	29
P.J. Prichard	
K.W.R. Fletcher (capt)	
A.W. Lilley	
S. Turner	
*D.E. East	
I.L. Pont	
J.K. Lever	
B 1, l-b 3.	4
(2 wickets, 60 overs)	280

	O	M	R	W
Hadlee	12	4	48	–
Cooper	9	3	27	–
Saxelby	12	–	73	–
Rice	7	–	38	–
Pick	8	–	36	1
Hemmings	12	1	54	–

Fall of wickets
1/202 2/203

Nottinghamshire

R.T. Robinson c Hardie b Turner	80
B.C. Broad run out	64
C.E.B. Rice (capt) c Hardie b Turner . . .	12
D.W. Randall c Prichard b Pringle.	66
R.J. Hadlee b Pont	22
D.J.R. Martindale not out.	20
*B.N. French	
E.E. Hemmings	
R.A. Pick	
K. Saxelby	
K.E. Cooper	
l-b 14, n-b 1.	15
(5 wickets, 60 overs)	279

	O	M	R	W
Lever	12	2	53	–
Pont	12	–	54	1
Turner	12	1	43	2
Gooch	12	–	47	–
Pringle	12	1	68	1

Fall of wickets
1/143 2/153 3/173 4/214 5/279

Umpires: D.J. Constant and B.J. Meyer
Man of the Match: B.R. Hardie

Essex won by 1 run

Nottinghamshire had to wait only two years before returning to Lord's to claim the NatWest Bank Trophy. Their win over Northamptonshire in 1987 was as exciting as their defeat had been in 1985, and we have already touched upon it in analysing the tactics of the game. Rice's calm authority, and sensible support from Birch, set the platform from which Hadlee was able to take Nottinghamshire to victory with his innings of 70 off 61 balls.

Nottinghamshire needed 51 runs from the last five overs of that match, and they were indebted not only to Hadlee but also to Bruce French, who scored 35 runs from 27 deliveries before he was bizarrely run out. At one time, Hadlee and French plundered 35 from three overs.

Many people had sympathy for Northamptonshire in 1987 for, two months before they lost to Nottinghamshire in the NatWest Bank Trophy Final, they had lost to Yorkshire in the Benson and Hedges Cup Final by the narrowest of margins. But perhaps Kent's experience had been even worse. They had lost a sensational Benson and Hedges Cup semi-final to Northamptonshire because of a breathtaking hundred from Allan Lamb and a dropped catch, while in both 1984 and 1986 they had contrived to lose to Middlesex, in the final of the Nat West Bank Trophy in the first instance and in the Benson and Hedges Cup Final in the second, and on both occasions on the last ball of the match. In 1984, Edmonds and Emburey had brought Middlesex victory by their batting. In 1986, it was their bowling that was decisive.

The Benson and Hedges Cup Final of 1986 smouldered uneasily at first. Chris Cowdrey won the toss and decided that Kent should field in overcast conditions. Dilley began with a wide, and this was a portent. A wide or a no-ball is the worst crime that a bowler can commit in one-day cricket, for not only does it concede a run but it gives the opponents an extra delivery, and the game is about *limited* overs. In this match, Kent were to give Middlesex the equivalent of two and a half extra overs.

Slack was very uncertain and was close to being run out in the opening over following a dreadful mix-up with Miller. He was not to survive long, and was bowled by Dilley in the

The Cowdrey brothers, Chris and Graham, gallant losers in the Benson and Hedges Final, 1986.

Dermot Reeve, 4 for 20 and Man of the Match, NatWest Bank Trophy Final, 1986, Sussex v Lancashire.

third over. Gatting did not seem happy with the conditions, and Miller, in his anxiety to get forward, took the rising deliveries on his body so that runs did not come smoothly. The first boundary arrived in the sixth over when Miller edged Baptiste, quick but lacking in control, through the slips.

The first ten overs brought 28 runs, and Chris Cowdrey then made a double change. He took over himself from Dilley at the Pavilion End, while Ellison replaced Baptiste at the Nursery End. Gatting found luck with him in Chris Cowdrey's opening over when he twice hit the ball over the head of Graham Cowdrey at cover and was close to being caught both times. The Middlesex captain also slashed Ellison past Tavaré at slip, but Ellison, the most impressive of the Kent bowlers, had his revenge when, in the twentieth over, he had Gatting and Butcher caught behind off successive deliveries.

This had the effect of tranquillizing Middlesex, who added only another 23 runs in the remaining fourteen overs until lunch. They also lost another wicket when, in the thirty-first over, Miller became the third victim of Steve Marsh, who had an outstanding game behind the stumps for Kent. Middlesex lunched uneasily at 89 for 4 from thirty-four overs, but Radley was 8 not out and he was already determining the length at which the bowler should be allowed to bowl, moving down the wicket to smother any venom that Underwood might offer.

In the first over of the afternoon Middlesex added 10 runs, and the necessary acceleration had begun. Cowdrey changed his bowling frequently, and in the forty-second over Downton was lbw to Ellison. Radley's fifty came six overs later, and Kent's problems were centred mainly on Baptiste, who could find no sort of rhythm. Emburey collected runs briskly, but Radley's fine innings came to an end when he was run out by the remarkable Marsh, the wicket-keeper reacting quickly and throwing the ball to the bowler's end.

Once again Radley had shown an intelligent mastery of the demands of batting in the one-day game. Without any hint of a rush of blood or a loss of composure, he had hit Underwood over the top and run him down to third man for fours, and when the same bowler threatened to dampen the Middlesex innings he had driven him through the covers and pulled him over mid-wicket to the boundary.

Baptiste bowled Emburey, but Hughes and Edmonds plundered well to take the score close to 200. It was a score which left the game open, for if the Kent batting could match the energy of much of their fielding, the hop county must surely win.

The Middlesex opening bowling was altogether tighter than Kent's had been. Only five runs came from the first four overs, and Benson in particular was struggling to put bat on to ball. It was something of a mercy killing when he was caught behind in the ninth over. Wayne Daniel was generating a lively pace, and it was he who captured the important wicket of Tavaré. The batsman sliced the ball to Downton off the face of the bat, and when in the next over Hinks fell to Cowans, Middlesex had captured 3 wickets for 20 runs in thirteen overs, and Kent were in despair.

The first bowling change came after fifteen overs, and surprisingly, Gatting brought himself into the attack. He conceded 18 runs in four overs and gave Kent some respite. Chris Cowdrey showed signs of rallying his side, batting with his usual positive and pugnacious air, but Taylor seemed intimidated and failed to profit from what loose deliveries there were. He was always intent on pushing forward to smother the ball, whatever its length or direction. In sixteen overs 42 runs were added, and then Cowdrey attempted to run the ball down through the slip area and was magnificently caught by Emburey. The fielder dived to his right to hold the ball one-handed and kicked the air with his feet in jubilation as he lay on the ground. At tea Kent were 71 for 4 in thirty-five overs, and the match looked dead and buried.

Taylor added only one run to his score after tea before hitting rashly at Edmonds. He had batted for twenty-five overs. When Baptiste joined Graham Cowdrey, 128 runs were needed and the asking rate was nearly seven an over.

Suddenly, the Kent innings burst into life. Graham Cowdrey had square-cut Edmonds for four in the first over after the break, and now Baptiste hit a boundary. Graham Cowdrey displayed a varied and delightful array of shots; in the forty-third over he pulled Edmonds over mid-wicket for six.

The light was worsening and it began to drizzle, but the runs were flowing more freely. The forty-fifth over realized 11 runs, and when Daniel was brought back he was hit for 7 and 10 in successive overs. Baptiste was hitting cleanly and running furiously, but he escaped two stumping chances, the first when he was beaten by a ball from Edmonds and stranded well down the wicket. The second chance was more difficult, and that it was missed did not matter, for Baptiste tried to cut the next ball, which was too close to him, and was bowled. He and Graham Cowdrey had added 69 in twelve overs.

Ellison kept the momentum going. He drove with splendour, and 37 runs came in four overs. But Graham Cowdrey's exciting innings came to an end when he hit a full toss into the

BENSON AND HEDGES CUP FINAL, 1986

Middlesex *v* Kent at Lord's, 12 July

Middlesex

W.N. Slack b Dilley	0
A.J.T. Miller c Marsh b C.S. Cowdrey	37
M.W. Gatting (capt) c Marsh b Ellison	25
R.O. Butcher c Marsh b Ellison	0
C.T. Radley run out	54
*P.R. Downton lbw b Ellison	13
J.E. Emburey b Baptiste	28
P.H. Edmonds not out	15
S.P. Hughes not out	4
N.G. Cowans	
W.W. Daniel	
l-b 8, w 11, n-b 4	23
(7 wickets, 55 overs)	199

	O	M	R	W
Dilley	11	2	19	1
Baptiste	11	–	61	1
C.S. Cowdrey	11	–	48	1
Ellison	11	2	27	3
Underwood	11	4	36	–

Fall of wickets
1/6 2/66 3/66 4/85 5/131 6/163 7/185

Kent

M.R. Benson c Downton b Cowans	1
S.G. Hinks lbw b Cowans	13
C.J. Tavaré c Downton b Daniel	3
N.R. Taylor c Miller b Edmonds	19
C.S. Cowdrey (capt) c Emburey b Hughes	19
G.R. Cowdrey c Radley b Hughes	58
E.A.E. Baptiste b Edmonds	20
R.M. Ellison b Edmonds	29
*S.A. Marsh not out	14
G.R. Dilley not out	4
D.L. Underwood	
l-b 9, w 8	17
(8 wickets, 55 overs)	197

	O	M	R	W
Cowans	9	2	18	2
Daniel	11	1	43	1
Gatting	4	–	10	
Hughes	9	2	35	2
Emburey	11	5	16	–
Edmonds	11	1	58	3

Fall of wickets
1/17 2/20 3/20 4/62 5/72 6/141 7/178
8/182

Umpires: D.J. Constant and D.R. Shepherd
Gold Award: J.E. Emburey

Middlesex won by 2 runs

hands of mid-wicket. His 58 had come off 70 balls, and he had revived the Kent cause when all had seemed lost.

The drizzle had now become forceful rain. Kent needed 19 runs from the last two overs. Phil Edmonds had bowled with admirable control and intelligence, asserting the cause of the spinner in circumstances when others would have denied him a hearing. He struck the vital blow when he bowled Ellison in the penultimate over of the match. The Kent left-hander had hit 29 off 18 deliveries.

From the last over, bowled by Simon Hughes, Kent needed 14 runs. The batsman was Steve Marsh, who had kept wicket so splendidly; he missed the first ball and took two off the second, so that the game seemed lost. But then he pulled the third ball of the over high into the Grand Stand for six. Kent needed six runs from three balls, and victory was once again a possibility.

Hughes responded with a near-yorker which Marsh did well to survive, and the batsmen could only scramble a single from the fifth ball of the over, so that Dilley was left to hit the last ball of the match for six if Kent were to win. He swung the ball towards the Tavern boundary. Momentarily it looked as if it might carry, but it dropped well short. The batsmen ran two, and Dilley slumped disappointedly, but in the pouring rain he was one who had contributed much to a splendid game of cricket.

*Top left, David Capel
hit an exciting 97 for
Northants in the Benson
and Hedges Cup, 1987,
but finished on the losing
side.*

*Bottom left, Ashley
Metcalfe took a record
four Gold Awards in the
Benson and Hedges Cup,
1987, and put Yorkshire
on the road to success in
the final.*

*Top right, Bairstow is
run out, but Yorkshire
go on to win the Benson
and Hedges Cup, 1987.*

*Bottom right, moment of
joy for Yorkshire
skipper, Phil Carrick,
Lord's, 1987.*

7 INTERNATIONAL ONE-DAY CRICKET

When one considers the success and popularity of the domestic limited-over competitions in England, and the immediate interest, sponsorship and financial reward that they brought to the game, it is surprising how long it took the authorities to stage a one-day international. The first was to be played eight years after the inaugural Gillette Cup match, two years after the instigation of the John Player League and some months after the first Benson and Hedges Cup competition had been announced and scheduled, and even then it was hastily arranged as a brief entertainment only because a Test match had had to be abandoned.

Test matches hold a most important place in the history and traditions of cricket. They have produced great deeds and great players. They are epic in conception, and victory or defeat in them is often taken as a national triumph or calamity. They impose a sense of grandeur on all who are associated with them, and what happens in them becomes part of cricket legend. Or so it was until they became too frequent.

By its very nature cricket is conservative, as are those who run it, and the idea of tampering with the established order of international cricket was abhorrent to the administrators of the game. But fate was to play a hand.

There had been a custom of staging an exhibition match in an afternoon if a Test match ended surprisingly early and there was a large crowd to be entertained. One of these exhibition matches had a sad result, for when England met South Africa on what should have been the fourth afternoon of a Test match at Lord's in 1960, Griffin, the South African fast bowler, was no-balled for throwing, and his career was virtually at an end. He had been no-balled by umpire F.S. Lee eleven times during the course of the Test, and in the one over that he bowled in the exhibition game he was no-balled four times out of five by Syd Buller and eventually finished the over bowling underarm.

Except in an instance such as this, however, the details of exhibition matches were never recorded, and they had little meaning to crowd

Ahmedabad – the venue for a one-day international between England and India, 1981.

INAUGURAL ONE-DAY INTERNATIONAL MATCH, 1971

Australia *v* England at Melbourne Cricket Ground, 5 January

England

G. Boycott c Lawry b Thomson	8
J.H. Edrich c Walters b Mallett	82
K.W.R. Fletcher c G.S. Chappell b Mallett	24
B.L. D'Oliveira run out	17
J.H. Hampshire c McKenzie b Mallett	10
M.C. Cowdrey c Marsh b Stackpole	1
R. Illingworth (capt) b Stackpole	1
*A.P.E. Knott b McKenzie	24
J.A. Snow b Stackpole	2
K. Shuttleworth c Redpath b McKenzie	7
P. Lever not out	4
B 1, l-b 9	10
(39.4 overs)	190

	O	M	R	W
McKenzie	7.4	–	22	2
Thomson	8	2	22	1
Connolly	8	–	62	–
Mallett	8	1	34	3
Stackpole	8	–	40	3

Fall of wickets
1/21 2/87 3/124 4/144 5/148 6/152 7/156
8/171 9/183

Australia

W.M. Lawry (capt) c Knott b Illingworth	27
K.R. Stackpole c and b Shuttleworth	13
I.M. Chappell st Knott b Illingworth	60
K.D. Walters c Knott b D'Oliveira	41
I.R. Redpath b Illingworth	12
G.S. Chappell not out	22
*R.W. Marsh not out	10
A.A. Mallett	
G.D. McKenzie	
A.N. Connolly	
A.L. Thomson	
l-b 4, w 1, n-b 1	6
(5 wickets, 34.6 overs)	191

	O	M	R	W
Snow	8	–	38	–
Shuttleworth	7	–	29	1
Lever	5.6	–	30	–
Illingworth	8	1	50	3
D'Oliveira	6	1	38	1

Fall of wickets
1/19 2/51 3/117 4/158 5/165

Umpires: T.F. Brooks and L.P. Rowan
Man of the Match: J.H. Edrich

Australia won by 5 wickets

or players. But in Australia in January 1971, events were rather different.

England and Australia were scheduled to play a six-match Test series. The Third Test was due to begin at Melbourne on 31 December 1970, but three days of continuous rain caused the game to be abandoned without a ball being bowled. A special meeting was convened between members of the Australian Board, led by Sir Donald Bradman, and visiting dignitaries of the MCC, Sir Cyril Hawker and G.O. (later Sir George) Allen, together with the England tour manager D.G. Clark, and a decision was taken that a seventh Test should be played to offset the complete loss of the Melbourne game. It was also agreed that, in an attempt to compensate the Melbourne public for the loss of cricket over the New Year period, a forty-over match would be played on what would have been the last day of the Test match, 5 January. Thus, the first one-day international match came into being.

Australia won by 5 wickets with 5.2 of their eight-ball overs unused. John Edrich became the first batsman to score fifty in a one-day international, and nine of the fourteen wickets that fell to bowlers were taken by spinners Mallett, Stackpole and Illingworth. Shuttleworth, Colin Cowdrey, Bill Lawry, 'Garth' McKenzie and Alan Connolly all played in what was to be their one and only limited-over international.

John Edrich was named Man of the Match by C.S. Elliott, the former Derbyshire batsman and Test-match umpire who was in Australia on a Churchill Fellowship, but the most significant fact of a rather ordinary game was that 46,000 people paid 33,000 Australian dollars to watch it. Such a response and revenue could not be ignored, and limited-over international cricket was born. Like Topsy, it has grown and grown.

By the end of 1974, 15 one-day internationals had been played. By 1979 the number had grown to 82. This doubled in three years. By the end of 1985, 329 had been staged.

The appeal of one-day cricket at international level was never better exemplified than when Pakistan met India in a charity match at Harrogate in 1986 before a capacity crowd. Saleem Malik pulls a ball to the boundary.

Crowds spill onto the pitch in the match at Harrogate.

The proliferation in the number of limited-over internationals in recent years has given cause for concern in many quarters, yet initially, those who administer the game were slow to realize the full potential of the exciting product they were marketing. Nevertheless, the success of the match at Melbourne encouraged the governing bodies to seek sponsorship for a series of three limited-over games to be played at the conclusion of the Test series.

The Prudential Assurance Company offered a new trophy for which the teams could compete, and a sponsorship of £30,000 was provided, of which £4000 was to be prize money. The matches were played over the Bank Holiday weekend in August 1972, and England won the first and third matches.

Ray Illingworth withdrew from the party because of injury, and he was succeeded as captain by Brian Close, who had just taken over at Somerset. England selected fifteen men for the three-match series, but Old, Underwood and Roope did not appear in any of the games.

In the first match at Old Trafford, which England won by six wickets, Dennis Amiss hit 103 and became the first batsman to score a century in a one-day international. He and Keith Fletcher shared a second-wicket stand of 125 in 86 minutes, the first century partnership in such a match. Fletcher was bowled by Massie for 60.

The third match of the series, at Edgbaston, saw Geoff Arnold of Surrey, the England pace bowler, become the first man to take four wickets in an innings of a limited-over international.

Prudential continued to sponsor one-day series until 1984 when Texaco took over, but the timing of the matches was an initial problem. The decision to play the games after the Test series was, as it transpired, a bad one, for they had an anti-climatic feeling, with both public and players somewhat jaded.

The question of timing arose, too, in Australia, when, on England's tour of 1974/5, the only one-day international was played immediately after a pulsating Third Test match and suffered in consequence. The game was played in scorching heat, the mood was somnolent, and the attendance was disappointing. Nevertheless, the crowd still numbered 18,977.

This match did have a significant place in the overall pattern of a tour which was dominated by the fast bowling of Lillee and Thomson. The England captain, Mike Denness, had had an unhappy time against them and pushed himself down the order to number eight for the one-day international in which, although Lillee did not play, Denness made only 12. Later, he dropped himself from the Test side.

It was not until 1977 that Prudential Trophy matches were staged before the Test series, and this tradition has since been maintained with great success. In recent seasons matches have been played before capacity crowds, and the Texaco Trophy has been the first highlight of the season, producing keen and exciting cricket with players fresh and eager.

The early one-day internationals provided some oddities and some points of interest. On 11 February 1973, New Zealand met Pakistan at Lancaster Park, Christchurch, and this was the only one-day international played before the Prudential World Cup of 1975 which did not involve either England or Australia. It was also the first one-day international to be played on a Sunday. The match began at noon and ended at 6.30 p.m. in near darkness. It was played in between the second and third matches of a three-match Test series, and New Zealand won by 22 runs.

It was a forty-over match, with eight-ball overs being played. The New Zealand innings was opened by Glenn Turner and Peter Coman. Coman was a right-handed batsman from Christchurch who was to play two more one-day internationals, against Australia, a year later, but he was never to play Test cricket, and so he ranks as the first international cricketer to be considered solely as a one-day specialist.

There were six awards given in this match, which seems rather excessive. Top scorers Burgess (47) and Sadiq Mohammad (37) were given batting awards, while Sarfraz Nawaz (4 for 46) and Dayle Hadlee (4 for 34) took the bowling honours. Fielding awards were given to Glenn Turner and Asif Iqbal.

When New Zealand came to England a few months later for a tour which occupied only the first half of the season, they played two Prudential Trophy matches, but the second had to be abandoned before the completion of the England innings. The first match was played at Swansea, and this was one of only two occasions when a limited-over international has been played in Wales, the second being when Pakistan met Sri Lanka in the World Cup in 1983.

What was remarkable about the England victory at St Helen's in July 1973 was that Boycott and Amiss began England's bid to score 159 to win with an opening stand of 96, of which Boycott made only 20. Dennis Amiss, having hit the first century in one-day international cricket, hit the second, exactly 100, in this match.

Later the same season, England met West Indies at Headingley and The Oval. West Indies had won the Test series convincingly, and England chose the Prudential Trophy matches to try to reshape their side. Mike Denness took

Roger Binny, India, an ideal one-day international cricketer with his medium-pace bowling and hard-hitting batting. Here, he takes a magnificent return catch to dismiss Richard Ellison in the Texaco Trophy match at The Oval, 1986.

David Gower has prospered in one-day international cricket. He played magnificently in the Texaco Trophy at Lord's against Australia, 1985, to restore his confidence after a lean spell.

Allan Lamb – one of the most successful batsmen that the one-day game has known.

over as captain for the first time, hit 66 in the first game at Leeds and took the individual award as England won by one wicket with three balls to spare.

At lunch, West Indies were 127 for 3 from thirty-two overs, but in the afternoon they collapsed, losing 5 wickets for 27 runs at one period, including Sobers and Julien in the space of three balls from Old, neither batsmen scoring. Sobers' 'duck' was to be the only innings he was to play in one-day international cricket, and his one wicket, that of Chris Old, was to cost him 31 runs, a meagre record for one of the greatest cricketers the world has known.

If the match saw the last of Sobers, it also saw the first of Bob Taylor and Bob Willis among others, of whom one was Mike Smith, the Middlesex opener. Smith scored 31 in this game, sharing a second-wicket stand of 71 with Mike Denness after Boycott had gone at 3. He was to play five one-day internationals in all and to be called up to the England party on the eve of a Test match, but he was never to play for England in a Test, nor to be selected as a member of a touring party.

This victory by England over West Indies, which came on the third ball of the fifty-fifth over after Willis and Underwood had bravely added 6 for the last wicket, was to be their last over the men from the Caribbean until the Benson and Hedges World Series in Australia in 1979–80. When they met again at The Oval in 1973 the match was won resoundingly by West Indies, who scored 190 for 2 in reply to England's 189 for 9. Roy Fredericks hit 105 as he and Kallicharran put on 143 for the second wicket, which stood as a record partnership until the first World Cup.

It was not until August 1974 that a match was played in which a century was scored on both sides. This was when England met Pakistan at Trent Bridge. Rain delayed the start and caused the match to be reduced to one of fifty overs per innings. David Lloyd batted throughout the England innings to score 116 not out of a total of 244 for 4. Sadiq Mohammad and Majid Khan began Pakistan's reply with a stand of 113 in 18.2 overs. Majid went on to hit 109 in thirty-one overs. His knock included a six and sixteen fours, and Pakistan romped to victory with 7.1 overs to spare.

In contrast, the second match at Edgbaston was reduced to thirty-five overs because of rain, and England made 81 for 9, their lowest score in a one-day international. Pakistan won by 8 wickets.

The first World Cup a year later excited such interest that one-day internationals proliferated in its wake, although the game seemed to have little fascination at first for the

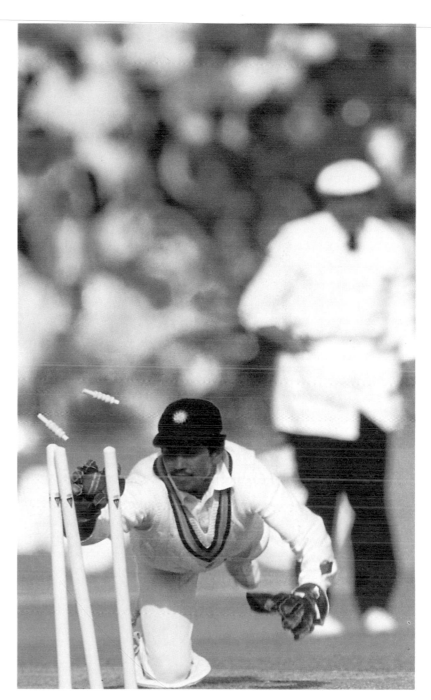

The excitement mounts. Pandit attempts a run out, India v England at The Oval, 1986.

Kapil Dev, an exciting all-rounder and captain, holds the Texaco Trophy after India had beaten England, 1986.

Indian sub-continent. In England, its following was growing rapidly.

On Saturday 28 August 1976, England met West Indies at Lord's. Viv Richards hit 97, and West Indies made 221 in 47.5 overs. England began disastrously and were 47 for 4 from fourteen overs when play had to be abandoned. For the first time, international cricket was staged at Lord's on a Sunday, and in spite of England's dreadful position and the apparent hopelessness of their cause, 6000 people arrived to see the completion of the match.

England were quickly reduced to 48 for 5 and 62 for 6, but Derek Randall entertained the crowd with a brave knock of 88, sharing stands of 63 with Knott and 55 with Jackman. England lost by 36 runs.

When Australia toured England a year later, the Prudential Trophy matches were played before the Test series for the first time, but the whole summer was clouded by the news that most of the tourists, along with Greig, Knott, Amiss and Underwood, would be defecting the following winter to the 'World Series Cricket' organized by Australian entrepreneur Kerry Packer. These events were to launch Mike Brearley on his successful career as captain of England and to change the face of cricket, particularly through Packer's emphasis on one-day internationals.

The 1977 series itself was something of a watershed. England won the first game by 2 wickets, and the second game at Edgbaston was a remarkable affair.

At lunch England were 90 for 7, but Chris Old and John Lever rallied the side splendidly in the afternoon and added 55. England were finally all out for 171. Greg Chappell took 5 for 20, and Gary Cosier took 5 for 18, and this has so far been the only occasion in limited-over internationals when two bowlers have each taken five wickets in an innings.

When Australia batted, Bob Willis sent back the openers for 0 and 2, and John Lever followed his 27 not out with 4 wickets in 15 balls for 2 runs. He finished with 4 for 29, and Australia were bowled out for 70, their lowest total in one-day internationals.

With England having taken the series two matches to nil, the third game was of only academic interest, but 15,000 people arrived at The Oval to see it. Dennis Amiss and Mike Brearley put on 161 for England's first wicket. Brearley hit 78, and Amiss, with 108, achieved his fourth century in what was to be his last one-day international.

Australia responded with a second-wicket stand of 148 between Robinson and Greg Chappell, who hit 125 not out, his first hundred in limited-over internationals. There was a stoppage for rain, but as the following day was Jubilee Day, the captains agreed to finish the game that evening. The match was continued in torrential rain. Large pools of water were lying all over The Oval as Australia won by 2 wickets with ten balls to spare. The time was 8.15 p.m.

The events in Australia were watched with interest by the rest of the world. Large crowds saw a reshaped England side in the one-day internationals in Pakistan, while in West Indies, an uneasy series was contested with Australia at the beginning of 1978.

Australia asked Bobby Simpson to return to international cricket to lead a side which had been crippled by defections to the Packer organization, so that Simpson played his two one-day internationals at the age of forty-one. The two matches were for the Guinness Trophy, and the West Indies won the first on a faster scoring rate. Nine of the Australian side had not played in a one-day international before. Desmond Haynes, one of five West Indians making their debut in this form of cricket, scored 148.

The West Indian Board of Control had formed an uneasy truce with its senior players, but when it was learned that Haynes, Austin and Murray had also signed to play for Kerry Packer, the truce broke down. These three players were omitted from the West Indian side, and Clive Lloyd led a walk-out of experienced internationals, so that the second of the Guinness Trophy games saw six more players make their debuts for West Indies, and Australia won by 2 wickets.

A few months later, a Pakistan side which had also been devastated by the Packer affair was crushed by England. Pakistan reinstated their WSC players in October 1978, when India were their opponents. The one-day international at Quetta on 1 October was the first meeting between the two countries for seventeen years. Two decades of political and religious disagreement had kept India and Pakistan apart on the cricket field. The match at Quetta witnessed Kapil Dev's debut in international cricket, and India gained a surprise victory by 4 runs, although they were to lose at Sialkot and Sahiwal.

By the time of the second World Cup in 1979, only Australia, severely handicapped, and England had not reinstated their Packer players, but by the end of the year the Australian Cricket Board and the Packer organization had come to an agreement. The initial argument had been caused by Packer's desire to claim the television rights for international cricket in Australia for his Channel Nine company. When his offer had been rejected by the Board he had set up his own 'World Series Cricket', hiring the best

Saadat Ali of Pakistan. An exciting opening batsman who was a success in his country's limited-over side, but could never establish himself at Test level. He was the leading run-scorer in the series against England, 1983–4.

Bobby Simpson played his one-day internationals for Australia when in his forties, but he managed the Australian side that won the World Cup in 1988.

A fast bowler who could rout an attack with his batting, New Zealand's Lance Cairns.

Far right, Zaheer Abbas of Pakistan.

Floodlights have been installed on Australian grounds as day/night cricket has drawn large crowds. Australia v England, Melbourne, 1985.

players, emphasizing limited-over competition and introducing floodlit cricket and coloured clothing. His television coverage of these matches was exceptional, and his marketing of the game, and of the advertisers who supported him, was exemplary.

When he reached agreement with the Australian Board (who in effect gave him exactly what he wanted), Packer, and Australian cricket, needed an injection of funds, and that was best provided by a series between the top teams. A triangular tournament was hastily arranged for 1979–80 which would involve Australia, England and the West Indies in twelve one-day internationals and a best-of-three-match final between the two top teams. The tournament, Benson and Hedges World Series, was not brought into being without some bloodshed, notably that of countries such as Pakistan and New Zealand who should have been touring Australia but were brushed aside to make way for the more commercially exploitable England and West Indies, but in the decade since its inception it has established itself as the most financially successful feature of Australian cricket.

Initially, in that season of 1979–80, Australian cricket enthusiasts were in a state of bewilderment, not quite knowing what to expect next, especially as it was the two visiting sides that reached the final; but the series was significant in several respects.

The matches were restricted to fifty six-ball overs, the first time that six-ball overs had been

144

used in limited-over competition in Australia. The opening match of the tournament, Australia *v* West Indies at Sydney, was the first official one-day international to be played under floodlights, the game beginning in the afternoon and finishing in a 5-wicket victory for Australia at night.

The following day, 28 November 1979, England also played West Indies under floodlights, and it was this match which hastened the introduction of fielding circles. England made 211 for 8 from their fifty overs, with Peter Willey hitting 58 not out. Rain reduced West Indies' target to 199 off forty-seven overs, and the last ball was reached with Colin Croft needing to hit Botham for three to win the match. Brearley positioned all his fielders, including wicket-keeper David Bairstow, around the boundary, to the amazement and derision of the crowd. In the event, Botham bowled Croft to give England one of her rare victories over the West Indies, but the tactics of Brearley and Clive Lloyd during the series had brought about the introduction of the fielding circles.

In the fourth match, when the West Indies met Australia at Melbourne, Viv Richards (who had received a pain killing injection for a back injury and hobbled through his innings) played a mighty knock. Dennis Lillee had Greenidge caught behind at 28, and Richards then proceeded to hit 153 not out off 131 deliveries, with a six and sixteen fours. He and Desmond Haynes put on 205 in thirty-four overs, the first double-century stand in limited-over internationals, and 40,000 people witnessed one of the greatest and most sustained attacks ever launched on quality bowling.

England were beaten only twice in the preliminary matches, finishing with eleven points to seven by the West Indies and six by Australia, but West Indies won the final, two matches to nil.

What the first Benson and Hedges World Series had demonstrated was a higher quality of cricket than had previously been seen in the limited-over game, outside the World Cup, and the floodgates opened as more and more one-day internationals were scheduled.

The infamous third final in the Benson and Hedges World Series, 1980-1, which ended with Trevor Chappell's underarm ball to McKechnie, was watched by 52,990 people, and when the West Indies beat Australia in Melbourne in January 1982, a record crowd of 78,142 was in attendance. A year later, on the same ground, 84,153 saw Australia beat England, and this record was to stand for only a year for, on 22 January 1984, 86,133 filled the Melbourne Cricket Ground for a World Series game between Australia and the West Indies.

That match saw another amazing innings

One-day international cricket has proliferated in Australia with every season bringing an excuse for another tournament. Coloured clothing is the norm. Chris Broad was an England hero in the Perth Challenge, January, 1987.

Ewen Chatfield of New Zealand, a relentlessly accurate bowler.

Desmond Haynes, the West Indian opening batsman, enjoyed a phenomenal one-day series against New Zealand, March to April, 1985, when he hit 54, 4, 146 not out, 85 not out and 116. This last innings brought him his eighth century in one-day internationals, a record he shared with Viv Richards.

The one-day international between West Indies and England at Queen's Park Oval, Port of Spain, 1986. Gooch hit 129 not out and England gained her only victory of the tour.

from Viv Richards. Australia had begun well, in spite of the fact that Haynes had gone off with a flourish, but Wessels, who had a good match, missed Richards off a skier which went behind the wicket-keeper. Richards then hit 106 off 96 balls in 116 minutes. His innings included a six and thirteen fours. He played havoc with the Australian bowling and field-placing with his perfect timing and magnificent placements of the ball. Haynes was overshadowed by Richards in a stand of 90, and Dujon and Lloyd plundered well.

Needing 253 at more than five an over, Australia were given a sound start by Ritchie and Wessels who put on 62 in 80 minutes, but they rarely looked like forcing victory. Richards added to his earlier glory by capturing the wickets of Wessels and Hookes. There was bravery from Kim Hughes whose 71 came off 73 balls in 85 minutes, but the fact that his innings included only three boundaries was an indication both of the vastness of the Melbourne Cricket Ground and of the greatness of Richards' innings.

Viv Richards had now come to bestride the one-day international scene like a Colossus. Clive Lloyd brought the West Indian side to England in 1984 to play a five-match Test series which was preceded by the first Texaco Trophy matches. The first of the three one-day games, at Old Trafford, produced one of the most amazing innings seen on any cricket ground.

Clive Lloyd won the toss and decided to bat first. All began well for England. Botham ran out Haynes in the first over, and then had Greenidge caught behind. Richardson was caught and bowled off a ball that held up a little, and Miller, the wicket giving him a little help, completely bemused Gomes, had Lloyd taken on the square-leg boundary and captured Dujon first ball when the batsman swept. Bairstow ran out Marshall with a magnificent throw, and at lunch West Indies were 107 for 7, and England were winning by a mile. But Richards was still at the crease; he had hit Botham for 16 in one over and was suggesting awesome power.

Baptiste was the first batsman other than Richards to reach double figures, and he stayed until the score was 161 when he was caught behind off Botham, who had been brought back into the attack. When Garner fell in the forty-first over, Richards was 96 not out and the score was 166. He had batted quite brilliantly up until this point; now he moved his innings on to a plain which transcended description. In fourteen overs, he and Holding added a record 106 for the last wicket, Richards making 93 of them. His century came from 112 balls. His next fifty came off 35 balls, and his 189 was made off 170 balls in 220 minutes. Holding was allowed to face only 27 of the 81 deliveries of the last-wicket partnership.

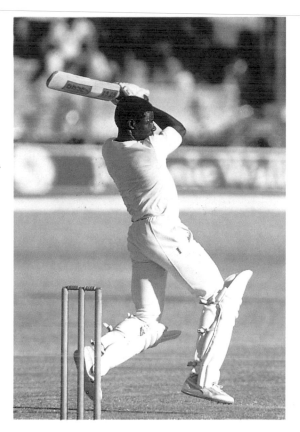

Richie Richardson, who is seen by many as the heir to Viv Richards in West Indian cricket.

Wasim Raja, the Pakistan left-hander, an aggressive batsman and fine fielder.

With swaggering confidence, he hit five sixes and twenty-one fours. All of his shots were majestic, and some of them – Botham into the pavilion, Pringle out of the ground, Foster over mid-off for six from outside leg stump – were breathtaking. His 189 not out is the highest innings ever played in a one-day international. Baptiste, with 26, was the next highest scorer, and Holding was the only other batsman to reach double figures.

Inevitably, what followed was an anti-climax. Fowler was taken at slip off Dujon's gloves. Gatting was completely out of his depth. Botham and Gower fell to fine catches, and Andy Lloyd, on his first international appearance, played encouragingly for eleven overs before falling to an outstanding catch by Dujon. Lamb, uncertain at first, stayed until the end, but the issue had long since been decided.

The grip that one-day international cricket now had on the public should not be underestimated. Having been granted full membership of the ICC in 1981, Sri Lanka staged its first home international four days before the

Kandy – one of the several beautiful grounds on which Sri Lanka play one-day internationals.

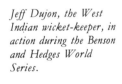

Jeff Dujon, the West Indian wicket-keeper, in action during the Benson and Hedges World Series.

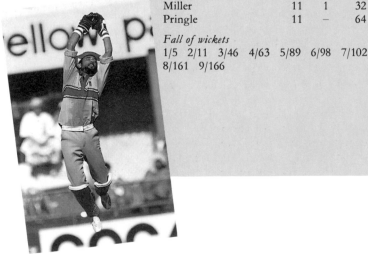

TEXACO TROPHY, 1984

England *v* West Indies at Old Trafford, Manchester, 31 May

West Indies		**England**	
C.G. Greenidge c Bairstow b Botham	9	G. Fowler c Lloyd b Garner	1
D.L. Haynes run out	1	T.A. Lloyd c Dujon b Holding	15
R.B. Richardson c and b Willis	6	M.W. Gatting lbw b Garner	0
I.V.A. Richards not out	189	D.I. Gower (capt) c Greenidge b Marshall	15
H.A. Gomes b Miller	4	A.J. Lamb c Richardson b Gomes	75
C.H. Lloyd (capt) c Pringle b Miller	8	I.T. Botham c Richardson b Baptiste	2
*P.J.L. Dujon c Gatting b Miller	0	*D.L. Bairstow c Garner b Richards	13
M.D. Marshall run out	4	G. Miller b Richards	7
E.A.E. Baptiste c Bairstow b Botham	26	D.R. Pringle c Garner b Holding	6
J. Garner c and b Foster	3	N.A. Foster b Garner	24
M.A. Holding not out	12	R.G.D. Willis not out	1
B 4, l-b 2, w 1, n-b 3	10	l-b 6, n-b 3	9
(9 wickets, 55 overs)	272	(50 overs)	168

	O	M	R	W		O	M	R	W
Willis	11	2	38	1	Garner	8	1	18	3
Botham	11	–	67	2	Holding	11	2	23	2
Foster	11	–	61	1	Baptiste	11	–	38	1
Miller	11	1	32	3	Marshall	6	1	20	1
Pringle	11	–	64	–	Richards	11	1	45	2
					Gomes	3	–	15	1

Fall of wickets
1/5 2/11 3/46 4/63 5/89 6/98 7/102
8/161 9/166

Fall of wickets
1/7 2/8 3/33 4/48 5/51 6/80 7/100
8/115 9/162

Umpires: D.J. Constant and D.R. Shepherd
Man of the Match: I.V.A. Richards

West Indies won by 104 runs

inaugural Test match against England in Colombo. England won a keenly contested game by 5 runs, but the second match, played the following day, 14 February 1982, saw Sri Lanka triumph by 3 runs in a remarkable finish.

The match was played at the Sinhalese Sports Club in Colombo. Put in to bat, Sri Lanka started badly, losing Warnapura and Mendis in Botham's fourth over. In the seventeenth over, Roy Dias lost his helmet, which fell onto his stumps as he tried to avoid a ball from John Lever, and Sri Lanka were a miserable 43 for 3.

Arjuna Ranatunga and Sidath Wettimuny added 87 in sixteen overs, and Wettimuny and his last three partners, Madugalle, de Mel and Somachandra de Silva, increased the score by 70 over the last ten overs. Wettimuny, who hit eight fours, faced 109 balls and carried his bat for 86.

Gooch and Geoff Cook began smoothly and efficiently with a stand of 109 which, against Sri Lanka's 215 for 7, seemed to have put England on the way to a comfortable victory. Both openers were beaten through the air by the slow left arm of Ajit de Silva, and both were stumped. The leg-breaks of Somachandra de Silva were also causing problems, so that England's scoring rate slumped and they reached the last ten overs needing 74 to win, with the light fading.

The Sri Lankans rejoiced when Botham gave a simple return catch to Warnapura, but Keith Fletcher, the England captain, hit 16 runs off the thirty-eighth over of the quota of forty-five, which was bowled by Somachandra de

Silva. The leg-spinner retaliated by bowling Tavaré with the first ball of his next over, so that England needed 46 from 35 balls.

The forty-first over, bowled by Ajit de Silva, realized 16 runs, including an on-driven six by Gatting. From the last four overs England needed 27. This was reduced to 19 from three and 14 from two. England had five wickets standing, but at this point they were gripped by a corporate insanity.

Gatting was run out on the first ball of the penultimate over, and Fletcher on the third ball. The first ball of the last over, bowled by de Mel, went through to the wicket-keeper. The second ball accounted for Bob Taylor, run out as he attempted the second run for a leg-glance. Derek Underwood was run out next ball, the first he had faced, and John Lever took a single off the fourth ball. This left Bob Willis facing with four runs wanted from two balls. He swung ferociously at de Mel for what would have been the winning hit, but Madugalle, at mid-wicket, plucked the ball out of the air, and Sri Lanka had won by 3 runs.

The crowd of 20,000 swept on to the pitch in adulation, and celebrations, including fireworks, went on late into the night. A national holiday was decreed to mark a famous victory. England could reflect that they had lost their last five wickets in eleven balls.

Sri Lanka can boast another famous victory, for, on 6 April 1984, they beat Pakistan by 5 wickets at the Sharjah Cricket Association Stadium in the opening match of the Rothmans Asia Cup. The significance of this match was

Batting hero of Sri Lanka's first one-day international victory over England, Sidath Wettimuny.

Above left, Somachandra de Silva, the veteran leg-spinner, who was one of Sri Lanka's heroes in their victory over England in 1981–2.

England captain Mike Gatting holds the trophy after his side has won the Perth Challenge, 1987.

Maninder Singh, the Indian slow left-arm bowler, who has demonstrated the value of the spinner in one-day international cricket.

A violent appeal by New Zealand wicket-keeper Ian Smith and captain Jeremy Coney for a stumping against Bill Athey is rejected, Texaco Trophy, Old Trafford, 1986. Athey went on to score 142 not out.

that it was the first international to be played in the United Arab Emirates.

Cricket had been played in Kuwait and Bahrain in the 1930s, but it did not take root in the UAE until after the Second World War. Now, mainly due to the enthusiasm of the many Indian, Pakistani and Sri Lankan expatriates, there are more than eighty clubs in the UAE. Thanks to the efforts of an Arab cricketer and enthusiast, Abdul Rehman Bukhatir, Sharjah has moved ahead of all other clubs in the Gulf. It boasts two grass cricket fields, one of which is the magnificent Sharjah Stadium where international tournaments have been staged in front of capacity crowds for very large prizes.

It is the custom to hold two international competitions a year in Sharjah, in April and November, and the first Asia Cup, played in April 1984, was won by India. Pakistan and Sri Lanka were the other competitors.

A year later, India were again the winners in a Four Nations Tournament which saw Australia as runners-up, Pakistan third, and England, with an unwisely weak side, a poor fourth.

By November 1985 the West Indians had been lured to Sharjah, and they beat Pakistan and India in a Three Nations Tournament. April 1986 saw Sharjah host the Australasia Cup and produce a match which excited the imagination of a continent. Like England in 1985, New Zealand sent a strangely weak side and were easily beaten by India and Pakistan. Australia and Sri Lanka were also losers, so that the final was contested, much to local delight, by India and Pakistan.

The energy, enthusiasm and vision which

had brought cricket to Sharjah were rewarded with a final which ranks among the most thrilling and dramatic one-day internationals ever seen. As the prize offered – 40,000 dollars – was the richest that had ever been provided for a cricket match, it was appropriate that the final should have been so hugely entertaining.

Put in to bat, India, in the shape of Gavaskar and Srikkanth, began gloriously with a flurry of exquisite strokes. Srikkanth, a thrilling batsman in any form of cricket, hit 75 out of 117 before falling to Abdul Qadir. Vengsarkar then joined Gavaskar in a stand of 99, but the later batsmen perished in the dash for quick runs.

Pakistan needed close to five an over to win, but they began quietly. The loss of Mudassar, Mohsin and Rameez with only 61 scored tipped the scales very much in favour of India. Maninder Singh, slow left-arm, bowled a particularly tight spell and threatened all batsmen, and it was only the durable Javed who steadied Pakistan.

Javed was given excellent support by Saleem Malik, but when he was run out Pakistan were faced with the formidable task of scoring 90 runs from the last ten overs. More support came from Abdul Qadir, who helped to lift the run rate, but Javed was superb. Characteristically, he ran two where others would have seen only one, and hit violently when the opportunity arose. Once he put the ball out of the ground, but that was one of only two sixes and two fours in the 110 that he had scored before he faced the last ball of the match.

The last over began with Pakistan on 235 for 8. Wasim Akram was run out and Zulqarnian bowled, but Tauseef Ahmed saw to it that Javed had the strike for the last ball of the match, from which Pakistan needed four to win the Cup. Kapil Dev and Chetan Sharma set the field to close all avenues to the boundary, but Javed pulled the ball into the crowd for six and a mighty victory.

The Australasia Cup was played as part of the Cricketers' Benefit Fund series, and Vijay Hazare, Dilip Vengsarkar, Wazir Mohammad and Javed himself were beneficiaries of the tournament, yet Javed was to benefit in other ways from that last, dramatic gesture. He returned to Pakistan a hero, and was feted by many who also gave sizeable donations to his bank balance, for his achievement was seen as being of great national importance.

Tony Lewis described the significance of the innings and the final six in *Benson and Hedges Cricket Year, Five*:

It was probably the most famous blow struck between the two countries, because it was the most watched. My role in Sharjah is to lead the television commentary team. Having described this exciting contest, I was rather shocked by the information which came later, that we had been broadcasting to India and Pakistan 'live'. The estimated viewing was 70 million television sets. Multiply that by twenty-four to a room . . . !

Lewis wrote that he had seen nothing to surpass Javed's century in that final, and that Javed was the batsman above all others whom he would choose to play for his life.

He has the warring instincts of the alley cat. He is not distracted by schoolboy strains of loyalty, or noblesse or dignity in the battle. He is hell-bent on self-preservation and the demolition of those who threaten to demolish him. His hundred was the best I have ever seen in a one-day match which could not have meant more to either side. India and Pakistan do not play friendlies.

AUSTRALASIAN CUP FINAL, 1986

India *v* Pakistan at Sharjah CA Stadium, 18 April

India

K. Srikkanth c Wasim Akram b Abdul Qadir	75
S.M. Gavaskar b Imran Khan	92
D.B. Vengsarkar b Wasim Akram	50
K.B.S. Azad b Wasim Akram	0
R.N. Kapil Dev (capt) b Imran Khan	8
C.J. Sharma run out	10
R.J. Shastri b Wasim Akram	1
*C.S. Pandit not out	0
M. Azharuddin	
U.S. Madan Lal	
Maninder Singh	
l-b 6, w 2, n-b 1	9
(7 wickets, 50 overs)	245

	O	M	R	W
Imran Khan	10	2	40	2
Wasim Akram	10	1	42	3
Abdul Qadir	10	2	49	1
Manzoor Elahi	5	–	33	–
Mudassar Nazar	5	–	32	–
Tauseef Ahmed	10	1	43	–

Fall of wickets
1/117 2/216 3/216 4/229 5/242 6/245
7/245

Pakistan

Mudassar Nazar lbw b Sharma	5
Mohsin Khan b Madan Lal	36
Rameez Raja b Maninder Singh	10
Javed Miandad not out	116
Saleem Malik run out	21
Abdul Qadir c sub (Lamba) b Kapil Dev	34
Imran Khan (capt) b Madan Lal	7
Manzoor Elahi c Shastri b Sharma	4
Wasim Akram run out	3
*Zulqarnain b Sharma	0
Tauseef Ahmed not out	1
l-b 11	11
(9 wickets, 50 overs)	248

	O	M	R	W
Kapil Dev	10	1	45	1
Sharma	9	–	51	3
Madan Lal	10	–	53	2
Maninder Singh	10	–	36	1
Shastri	9	–	38	–
Azharuddin	2	–	14	–

Fall of wickets
1/9 2/39 3/61 4/110 5/181 6/209 7/215
8/236 9/241

Umpires: D.M. Archer and A. Gaynor (West Indies)
Man of the Match: Javed Miandad

Pakistan won by 1 wicket

If one needed further evidence of the important part that one-day cricket had come to play in the world game, one had only to look at the Champions Tournament in Sharjah in November 1986, which was won by West Indies, and at the Four Nations Tournament in April 1987, when England, at last realizing the stature of the Sharjah competitions, sent a more representative side and beat Pakistan and India on run rate.

On the financial side, when Pakistan beat Australia and Javed hit 74 not out, Haji Abdulla, a local businessman, presented the Pakistani with a gift of £17,500. In the next game, when Azharuddin hit 84, also against Australia, he received £8000 from Haji Abdulla.

With a cricket stadium at Dubai now being built and the large amount of money generously donated as competition prizes, one can foresee a time when the World Cup will be played in the United Arab Emirates. The World Cup has become a four-yearly celebration of cricket, the most exciting tournament that the game has known, and it is now time we turned our attention to it. It is naïve to believe that England or India could be the only venue.

The richest of international cricket centres. Mohammad Azharuddin, the fine Indian batsman, in action in Sharjah.

RESULTS SUMMARY OF ONE-DAY INTERNATIONAL MATCHES UP TO THE END OF THE ENGLAND SEASON, 1987

England	P	W	L	Abandoned
v Australia	41	22	18	1
v India	18	11	7	–
v New Zealand	23	11	9	3
v Pakistan	22	15	7	–
v Sri Lanka	4	3	1	–
v West Indies	27	9	18	–
v Canada	1	1	—	–
v East Africa	1	1	—	–

Australia	P	W	L	Abandoned
v England	41	18	22	1
v India	27	15	10	2
v New Zealand	30	18	10	2
v Pakistan	19	7	10	2
v Sri Lanka	10	5	3	2
v West Indies	45	13	31	one match tied
v Canada	1	1	—	–
v Zimbabwe	2	1	1	–

India	P	W	L	Abandoned
v England	18	7	11	–
v Australia	27	10	15	2
v New Zealand	18	7	11	–
v Pakistan	25	9	15	1
v Sri Lanka	15	11	3	1
v West Indies	14	3	11	–
v East Africa	1	1	—	–
v Zimbabwe	2	2	—	–

New Zealand	P	W	L	Abandoned
v England	23	9	11	3
v Australia	30	10	18	2
v India	18	11	7	–
v Pakistan	14	7	6	1
v Sri Lanka	13	10	3	–
v West Indies	13	1	11	1
v East Africa	1	1	—	–

Pakistan	P	W	L	Abandoned
v England	22	7	15	–
v Australia	19	10	7	2
v India	25	15	9	1
v New Zealand	14	6	7	1
v Sri Lanka	17	13	3	1
v West Indies	10	1	8	1
v East Africa	1	1	—	–

Sri Lanka	P	W	L	Abandoned
v England	4	1	3	–
v Australia	10	3	5	2
v India	15	3	11	1
v New Zealand	13	3	10	–
v Pakistan	17	3	13	1
v West Indies	8	—	8	–

West Indies	P	W	L	Abandoned
v England	27	18	9	–
v Australia	45	31	13	one match tied
v India	14	11	3	–
v New Zealand	13	11	1	1
v Pakistan	10	8	1	1
v Sri Lanka	8	8	—	–
v Zimbabwe	2	2	—	–

Imran Khan, the Pakistan captain, relaxes between matches.

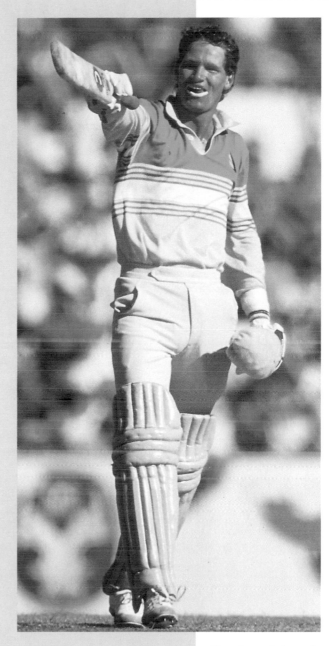

Dean Jones of Australia who hit centuries in successive matches in the Perth Challenge, 1987.

RECORDS

HIGHEST INDIVIDUAL SCORE

189 not out, I.V.A. Richards, West Indies *v* England, Old Trafford, 1984.

BEST BOWLING

7 for 15, W.W. Davis, West Indies *v* Australia, Leeds, 1983 (World Cup).
6 for 14, G.J. Gilmour, Australia *v* England, Leeds, 1975 (World Cup).
6 for 14, Imran Khan, Pakistan *v* India, Sharjah, 1984–5.

RECORD PARTNERSHIPS FOR EACH WICKET

1st	212	G.R. Marsh & D.C. Boon, Australia *v* India, Jaipur, 1986–7.
2nd	221	C.G. Greenidge & I.V.A. Richards, West Indies *v* India, Jamshedpur, 1983–4.
3rd	224*	D.M. Jones & A.R. Border, Australia *v* Sri Lanka, Adelaide, 1984–5.
4th	173	D.M. Jones & S.R. Waugh, Australia *v* Pakistan, Perth, 1986–7.
5th	152	I.V.A. Richards & C.H. Lloyd, West Indies *v* Sri Lanka, Brisbane, 1984–5.
6th	144	Imran Khan & Shahid Mahboob, Pakistan *v* Sri Lanka, Leeds, 1983 (World Cup).
7th	115	P.J.L. Dujon & M.D. Marshall, West Indies *v* Pakistan, Gujranwala, 1986–7.
8th	68	B.E. Congdon & B.L. Cairns, New Zealand *v* England, Scarborough, 1978.
9th	126*	R.N. Kapil Dev & S.M.H. Kirmani, India *v* Zimbabwe, Tunbridge Wells, 1983 (World Cup).
10th	106*	I.V.A. Richards & M.A. Holding, West Indies *v* England, Old Trafford, 1984.

8 THE WORLD CUP

The World Cup was a logical extension of one-day international competition, and in many ways it is surprising that it took so long to come into being. As long ago as 1912, when there were only England, Australia and South Africa as Test-playing nations, a triangular Test tournament had been staged in England in an attempt to determine 'world champions', but wretched weather and the strength of the two visiting sides had limited its appeal and its value.

If one man can be said to have had the idea of staging a World Cup, that man was Ben Brocklehurst, a former captain of Somerset and managing director of *The Cricketer* magazine. The idea was taken up, and the Prudential Assurance Company agreed to sponsor the first competition, which was held in England in 1975. At the time, one-day international cricket was still in its infancy, popularized only by England and Australia, but the impact of the World Cup was to be enormous, and it can be said to have engendered the excess of one-day internationals that dominate the cricket calendar today.

For the inaugural World Cup, six Test-playing countries were automatic participants – England, India, Australia, West Indies, Pakistan and New Zealand (South Africa having been excluded from international cricket). At short notice, Sri Lanka, still only an associate member of the ICC but pressing hard for full membership, eagerly accepted an invitation to participate. No other associate member country was able to even up the number of contestants with so little warning, mostly because of financial considerations, but East Africa finally agreed to field a side.

The eight countries were divided into two groups, and West Indies found themselves in the stronger group alongside Pakistan, Australia and Sri Lanka. England were grouped with India, New Zealand and East Africa, whose party included the late D.J. Pringle whose son was later to play for England in the World Cup of 1987. The competition was condensed into the fortnight between 7 and 21 June. Within the two groups each side played the others once, and the top two sides from each met in the semi-finals.

The World Cup did not start well, in that England overwhelmed India in the opening match at Lord's. Dennis Amiss and Keith Fletcher put on 176 for the second wicket. At lunch, England were 150 for 1, and Amiss was on 98. His 137 was made out of 245 in fifty-one overs, and the last nine overs of the innings produced 89 runs, with Chris Old hitting 51 off 28 balls. In reply, India gave a miserable exhibition. They had as yet found no appetite for limited-over cricket and made no attempt to get the runs. Gavaskar batted throughout the sixty overs to finish with 36 not out.

Meanwhile, at Edgbaston, Glenn Turner managed 171 not out in sixty overs as New Zealand overwhelmed East Africa. At the time, this was the highest individual score ever made in a limited-over international.

At Headingley, where the gates were closed for the first time in nineteen years, an enthralling match took place. Chasing 279, Pakistan looked as if they might beat Australia when they reached 172 for 4 in forty overs. Then, with Dennis Lillee in devastating form, Pakistan slipped from 181 for 4 to 205 all out at the end of the fifty-third over.

West Indies beat Sri Lanka with the ease with which New Zealand beat East Africa. Put in to bat on a wicket that assisted the bowlers, Sri Lanka crumbled before the West Indian pace men.

With Fletcher again in excellent form, England assured themselves of a place in the semi-finals when they brushed aside the New Zealand challenge, while East Africa gave further evidence that they were out of their depth, being trounced by India.

In the other group, contests were more keen, and Pakistan and the West Indies engaged in a memorable game at Edgbaston. From the start, Pakistan followed the example of their skipper Majid Khan and went for their shots in an exciting manner, savaging anything that was not on a length. Mushtaq Mohammad and Wasim Raja were both unfortunate not to play when going well, but Pakistan must have been pleased with their 266 for 7.

West Indies began poorly and at 99 for 5 and 166 for 8, they looked doomed. The ninth wicket fell in the forty-sixth over with the West Indies still 64 runs short of victory but, incredibly, the last pair, Deryck Murray and Andy Roberts, scored the runs necessary, the winning run coming off the fourth ball of the last over.

At The Oval, Australia won the match and lost a few friends. They made an impressive 328 for 5 against Sri Lanka, who responded gallantly and never stopped trying to win. Frustrated, the Australian bowlers – Jeff Thomson in particular – unleashed a stream of bouncers against the diminutive, and at the time inexperienced, Sri Lankan batsmen. Wettimuny, hit on the foot and the body, and Mendis, hit on the head, were both forced to retire hurt, and Thomson aroused the wrath of the crowd when he tried to run out Wettimuny as the batsman staggered after being hit. Eventually, Sri Lanka fell 52 short of the Australian score, and Australia, like West Indies, were assured of a place in the semi-final.

These two, who had emerged as the strongest sides in the tournament, met at The Oval in the third round. Put in to bat on a cloudy morning, Australia struggled to 192, and West Indies, enjoying better conditions, won with fourteen overs unused.

Pakistan and England won their remaining matches predictably, and with another glorious array of strokes, Glenn Turner led his New Zealand side to victory over India and into the semi-finals.

It was the Australians who had learned most from this latest round of matches, for whatever their bowlers had achieved against Sri Lanka, whenever they bowled short against the West Indians Fredericks and Kallicharran they were viciously hooked to the boundary. It was a lesson they took to heart.

The semi-finals paired England and Australia at Headingley, and New Zealand and

Glenn Turner, captain of New Zealand in 1975 and later manager of the national side, hit 171 not out against East Africa in the opening match of the first World Cup tournament at Edgbaston, 7 June 1975.

Jeff Thomson, the Australian fast bowler, a hero and a villain of the first World Cup.

West Indies at The Oval.

From the time that Clive Lloyd won the toss and asked New Zealand to bat first, West Indies were always on top. Turner and Geoff Howarth battled valiantly in a second-wicket stand of 90, but the sustained West Indian pace attack first restricted and then destroyed the New Zealanders. West Indies, with Greenidge and Kallicharran adding 125 for the second wicket, won with five wickets and nearly twenty overs to spare.

At Headingley, things were very different. A wicket which was unsuitable for such an occasion produced a semi-final of excitement and fine bowling figures. Put in to bat, England were bowled out for 93 in 36.2 overs. Denness was top scorer with 27, and he and Arnold saved the side from complete ignominy with a ninth-wicket stand of 21. Gary Gilmour's left-arm medium pace was a potent weapon in such conditions, and his 6 for 14 was a bowling record for a one-day international at the time.

Australia had no easy task to get the runs. They were 39 for 6 when Gilmour joined Walters and threw caution aside as he attacked the bowling so that 55 were added, Gilmour hit 28 not out, and the match was won by 4 wickets in 28.4 overs.

WORLD CUP FINAL, 1975

The longest day of the year beckoned the final, and, indeed, a long day was needed to decide a splendid match.

Throughout the competition West Indies had fielded first, so that it could have been part of Ian Chappell's policy to frustrate them when he put them in on winning the toss. Whatever his reasons, he had early success. Gilmour had given West Indies encouragement with three no-balls in his first over, but with the score on 12, Roy Fredericks hooked a Lillee bouncer over the boundary ropes only to lose his balance as he did so and tread on his wicket.

Kallicharran began confidently, but he tried to cut a ball from Gilmour that was too close to him and was caught behind. Greenidge had been groping ineffectively for eighty minutes before he edged a ball low to Marsh and West Indies, at 50 for 3, were in some trouble.

Clive Lloyd now joined Rohan Kanhai. Lloyd was always a most unlikely looking cricketer as he approached the wicket. His slouch, his stoop, his spectacles, all suggested laziness and inertia, but once the bat was in his hands he was like a cat ready to pounce on its prey. Almost immediately he hooked Lillee for six and then drove Walker through the covers off the back foot for four.

Rohan Kanhai curbed his natural aggression to play the role of anchor man, and for eleven overs he was scoreless. Lloyd, meanwhile, was lashing the ball to every part of the field, and once Kanhai felt free to open his shoulders, runs came at a brisk rate. In thirty-six overs they added 149. With two sixes and twelve fours, Lloyd reached a thrilling century off 82 balls in 108 minutes. He was out in somewhat controversial fashion, caught behind on the leg side when he seemed to gesture that he had not touched the ball.

It was Gilmour who captured his wicket, and in an economical second spell he also captured Kanhai and Richards to leave West Indies on 209 for 6 in the forty-sixth over, with Australia recovering poise.

Keith Boyce, uncurling like a spring, and Bernard Julien added 52 whirlwind runs to regain the initiative for West Indies, and useful runs from Deryck Murray, emphasizing the West Indian batting strength by being placed as low as number nine, took West Indies to a formidable 291.

The pressure to score too quickly too soon led the Australians into trouble. McCosker fretted across the line and was taken at slip. Turner and Ian Chappell settled and runs began to come briskly, but an illogicality seeped into the Australian batting as Turner and the Chappell brothers were all run out in going for unwise and unnecessary short runs. It was three throws from Viv Richards, two of them direct hits which could have been made only by one of the world's great fielders, that accounted for the trio. At 162 for 4, Australia needed 130 from twenty-two overs.

Walters and Marsh flurried briefly, but 76 were needed from the last ten overs, with four wickets standing. Ross Edwards played well before skying the ball. Gilmour did the same, and Walker ran himself out so that Jeff Thomson joined Dennis Lillee on the last ball of the fifty-third over. Australia needed 59 runs off 43 balls from this last pair.

The two great fast bowlers summoned their natural hostility for their batting. They hit at everything, and if they did not always connect with the middle of the bat, they hit so hard that they still cleared the field. The West Indies were literally forced back on the ropes.

There was panic, misfielding and overthrows. From two overs, Australia needed 21 runs. In the constant roar of excitement, the crowd failed to hear a cry of no-ball, and, believing that Fredericks had caught Thomson, invaded the pitch. Fielders were knocked over, and the ball was lost from sight as Thomson and Lillee ran up and down the wicket. Finally the umpires called 'dead ball', the crowds were ushered off and three runs were added to the score.

PRUDENTIAL WORLD CUP, 1975

Group A

at Lord's, 7 June
England 334 for 4 (D.L. Amiss 137, K.W.R. Fletcher 68)
India 132 for 3
England won by 202 runs

at Edgbaston, 7 June
New Zealand 309 for 5 (G.M. Turner 171 not out, J.M. Parker 66)
East Africa 128 for 8
New Zealand won by 181 runs

at Trent Bridge, Nottingham, 11 June
England 266 for 6 (K.W.R. Fletcher 131)
New Zealand 186 (J.F.M. Morrison 55, A.W. Greig 4 for 45)
England won by 80 runs

at Headingley, 11 June
East Africa 120
India 123 for 0 (S.M. Gavaskar 65 not out, F.M. Engineer 54 not out)
India won by 10 wickets

at Old Trafford, Manchester, 14 June
India 230 (S. Abid Ali 70)
New Zealand 233 for 6 (G.M. Turner 114 not out)
New Zealand won by 4 wickets

at Edgbaston, 14 June
England 290 for 5 (D.L. Amiss 88, B. Wood 77, F.C. Hayes 52)
East Africa 94 (J.A. Snow 4 for 11)
England won by 196 runs

Group A Final Table

	P	W	L	Pts
England	3	3	–	12
New Zealand	3	2	1	8
India	3	1	2	4
East Africa	3	–	3	0

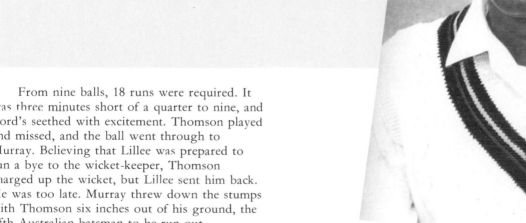

Rohan Kanhai who played a vital part in West Indies triumph in 1975.

From nine balls, 18 runs were required. It was three minutes short of a quarter to nine, and Lord's seethed with excitement. Thomson played and missed, and the ball went through to Murray. Believing that Lillee was prepared to run a bye to the wicket-keeper, Thomson charged up the wicket, but Lillee sent him back. He was too late. Murray threw down the stumps with Thomson six inches out of his ground, the fifth Australian batsman to be run out.

West Indies were the first champions of the world, and the World Cup had captured the public's imagination at the first attempt.

Group B

at Headingley, 7 June
Australia 278 for 7 (R. Edwards 80 not out)
Pakistan 205 (Majid J. Khan 65, Asif Iqbal 53, D.K. Lillee 5 for 34)
Australia won by 73 runs

at Old Trafford, Manchester, 7 June
Sri Lanka 86 (B.D. Julien 4 for 20)
West Indies 87 for 1
West Indies won by 9 wickets

at Edgbaston, 11 June
Pakistan 266 for 7 (Majid J. Khan 60, Wasim Raja 58, Mushtaq
Mohammad 55)
West Indies 267 for 9 (D.L. Murray 61 not out, C.H. Lloyd 53, Sarfraz
Nawaz 4 for 44)
West Indies won by 1 wicket

at The Oval, 11 June
Australia 328 for 6 (A. Turner 101, R.B. McCosker 73, K.D. Walters 59,
G.S. Chappell 50)
Sri Lanka 276 for 4 (S. Wettimuny 53 retired hurt, M. Tissera 52)
Australia won by 52 runs

at The Oval, 14 June
Australia 192 (R. Edwards 58, R.W. Marsh 52 not out)
West Indies 195 for 3 (A.I. Kallicharran 78, R.C. Fredericks 58)
West Indies won by 7 wickets

at Trent Bridge, Nottingham, 14 June
Pakistan 330 for 6 (Zaheer Abbas 97, Majid J. Khan 84, Sadiq
Mohammad 74)
Sri Lanka 138
Pakistan won by 192 runs

Group B Final Table

	P	W	L	Pts
West Indies	3	3	–	12
Australia	3	2	1	8
Pakistan	3	1	2	4
Sri Lanka	3	–	3	0

Semi-finals

at Headingley, 18 June
England 93 (G.J. Gilmour 6 for 14)
Australia 94 for 6
Australia won by 4 wickets

at The Oval, 18 June
New Zealand 158 (G.P. Howarth 51, B.D. Julien 4 for 27)
West Indies 159 for 5 (A.I. Kallicharran 72, C.G. Greenidge 55)
West Indies won by 5 wickets

Man of the Match awards

2   G.M. Turner and A.I. Kallicharran.
1   D.L. Amiss, D.K. Lillee, B.D. Julien, K.W.R. Fletcher, F.M.
     Engineer, A. Turner, Sarfraz Nawaz, J.A. Snow, Zaheer Abbas,
     G.J. Gilmour and C.H. Lloyd.

PRUDENTIAL WORLD CUP FINAL, 1975

Australia *v* West Indies at Lord's, 21 June

West Indies

R.C. Fredericks hit wkt b Lillee	7
C.G. Greenidge c Marsh b Thomson . . .	13
A.I. Kallicharran c March b Gilmour . . .	12
R.B. Kanhai b Gilmour	55
C.H. Lloyd (capt) c Marsh b Gilmour . .	102
I.V.A. Richards b Gilmour	5
K.D. Boyce c G.S. Chappell b Thomson.	34
B.D. Julien not out	26
*D.L. Murray c and b Gilmour.	14
V.A. Holder not out	6
A.M.E. Roberts	
l-b 6, n-b 11.	17
(8 wickets, 60 overs).	291

	O	M	R	W
Lillee	12	1	55	1
Gilmour	12	2	48	5
Thomson	12	1	44	2
Walker	12	1	71	–
G.S. Chappell	7	–	33	–
Walters	5	–	23	–

Fall of wickets
1/12 2/27 3/50 4/199 5/206 6/209 7/261
8/285

Australia

A. Turner run out	40
R.B. McCosker c Kallicharran b Boyce . .	7
I.M. Chappell (capt) run out	62
G.S. Chappell run out	15
K.D. Walters b Lloyd	35
*R.W. Marsh b Boyce	11
R. Edwards c Fredericks b Boyce.	28
G.J. Gilmour c Kanhai b Boyce	14
M.H.N. Walker run out	7
J.R. Thomson run out	21
D.K. Lillee not out	16
B 2, l-b 9, n-b 7	18
(58.4 overs)	274

	O	M	R	W
Julien	12	–	58	–
Roberts	11	1	45	–
Boyce	12	–	50	4
Holder	11.4	1	65	–
Lloyd	12	1	38	1

Fall of wickets
1/25 2/81 3/115 4/162 5/170 6/195 7/221
8/231 9/233

Umpires: H.D. Bird and T.W. Spencer
Man of the Match: C.H. Lloyd

West Indies won by 17 runs

*The ICC Trophy, 1979.
Holland v Wales at
Enville.*

*The ICC Trophy, 1979.
Bermuda v Papua New
Guinea at Stourbridge.*

Ole Mortensen, the Danish fast bowler, whose performances in the ICC Trophy, 1979, led him into county cricket with Derbyshire.

Such was the success of the first World Cup tournament that the future of the competition was assured, and although India were anxious to stage the second world championship, it was decided that England should again be hosts in 1979. The associate members of the ICC were now aware of the benefits in terms of finance, prestige and experience that participation in the World Cup would give them, and they planned to play a qualifying competition for the ICC Trophy, the winners and runners-up taking the two places that were available in the World Cup itself. The tournament was staged in the Midlands the month before the World Cup.

Unfortunately the weather was wretched, but the competition between the fourteen nations was keen. This was a splendid entry, leaving only three associations as non-contestants, one of them, Gibraltar, a late withdrawal for financial reasons. A Welsh eleven was brought in to give five in each group, but Wales were not allowed to gain points.

The three groups were won by Bermuda, Denmark and Sri Lanka, and Canada qualified for the fourth semi-final place as the group runner-up with the fastest scoring rate. Canada were surprise victors over Bermuda, while Sri Lanka beat Denmark who were probably the second-best side in the competition. (Denmark revealed one of the outstanding players of the tournament in fast bowler Ole Mortensen, who was later to play for Derbyshire with great success.)

Sri Lanka and Canada took their places alongside the six Test-playing countries for the World Cup a month later, and once again there were two qualifying groups from which four

sides were to come forward to the semi-finals.

West Indies began by showing that they were determined to hold on to their title, overwhelming India in the opening match. The other match in the same group followed an almost identical pattern, as New Zealand routed Sri Lanka.

The Australian side had been badly depleted by defections to Packer's 'World Series Cricket', and they quietly succumbed to England at Lord's, while Canada proved no match for Pakistan.

New Zealand assured themselves of a place in the semi-finals by beating India with considerable ease in the second round of matches, but for the first and only time in the history of the competition, a match – that between West Indies and Sri Lanka – was abandoned without a ball being bowled.

Canada trod a miserable path in the gloom at Old Trafford, being bowled out for 45, but occupying 40.3 overs in scoring the runs. England won the match in near darkness, taking only 13.5 overs to reach their target. This win put England in the semi-finals, where they were joined by Pakistan, far too strong for the weakened Australian side.

It was the third and last round of matches which provided the most competitive contests of the qualifying rounds. At Old Trafford, Sri Lanka gained a memorable victory over India; it was this win which strengthened their claim for full membership of the ICC and with it, Test status. By the next World Cup, in 1983, this ambition had been realized.

West Indies clinched their semi-final place, but New Zealand, for whom Ewen Chatfield made his one-day international debut, ran them very closely. Even Canada gave Australia a fright when Rodney Hogg was hit for 26 in his first two overs. In fact, he was taken off and did not bowl again, but Canada collapsed from 50 for 1 to 105 all out, and Australia won by 7 wickets.

England and Pakistan engaged in a thrilling game at Headingley in which Mike Hendrick produced a devastating spell of bowling which settled the match. This game was mentioned earlier, when discussing tactics and the options open to a captain. In this instance, Brearley chose to bowl Hendrick out and had to rely on Boycott at the last. The win was important to England for it meant that they avoided West Indies in the semi-finals, entertaining New Zealand at Old Trafford instead.

Another huge crowd witnessed a tense battle. Richard Hadlee gave England considerable problems after they had been put in to bat, and both Boycott and Larkins went cheaply. Brearley, playing authoritatively, and Gooch, batting with confidence, took England to

Ian Botham hits out for England in the semi-final of the 1979 World Cup against New Zealand.

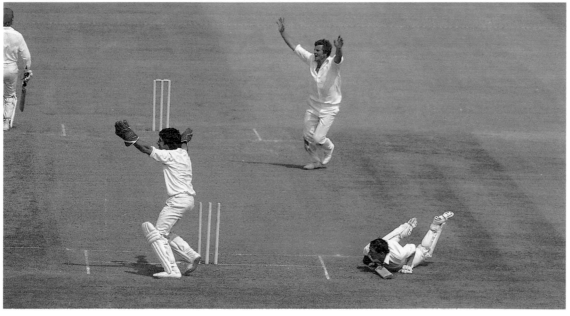

Derek Randall narrowly escapes being run out in the semi-final, England v New Zealand.

Viv Richards played a prominent part in West Indies' semi-final victory and dominated the final against England.

a healthier position, but Brearley cut Coney to the wicket-keeper, and Gower was run out for 1. But Botham and Randall made valuable runs, and England's 221 left the game in the balance.

A solid start from Wright and Edgar was undermined when Edgar was lbw, and Howarth went the same way to a Boycott full toss. With the England attack reduced to the walking wounded, New Zealand threatened to take the match, but they found a target of 14 off Botham's last over just a little too much.

An opening stand of 132 between Greenidge and Haynes gave West Indies a chance to thrive against Pakistan, and when Holding sent back Sadiq at 10, West Indies looked set for an easy win. Majid and Zaheer joined in a wonderful partnership of 166 in thirty-six overs, which put the match within Pakistan's reach, but Croft dismissed both batsmen and Javed within the space of twelve balls for 4 runs, and Pakistan lost their way.

WORLD CUP FINAL, 1979

With Willis unfit to play, England faced the 'fifth' bowler problem in the final, and this proved to be their undoing. Yet all began well for the hosts. Greenidge and Haynes were in circumspect mood and moved uneventfully to 22 before Greenidge, who had been one of the great successes of the competition, was run out by the effervescent Randall. Richards began uncertainly, but survived. Haynes did not, edging Old to second slip. Hendrick, who took the catch, was brought back to clip Kallicharran's off bail, and West Indies were 55 for 3.

Clive Lloyd began to strike the ball firmly, suggesting a West Indian revival, but Old took a fine return catch, one-handed low to his left, and England seemed well on top. Collis King joined Richards, and they survived until lunch when England's hopes were high. But in the hour after the break, they were somewhat dashed.

In one of the most powerful displays of batting ever seen at Lord's, Richards and King added 139 in 77 minutes. From 76 balls, King scored 86. Hitting with tremendous power, he smote three sixes and ten fours. He hit cleanly to all parts of the ground and displayed all the text-book shots. He was out in the fifty-first over, well caught on the square-leg boundary.

Irrelevant wickets fell in the last nine overs as West Indies plundered more runs, and Richards finished the innings with his third six, the one described earlier when he pulled an intended yorker from Hendrick into the Mound Stand. He also hit eleven fours, and once more he had dominated the stage.

Faced by a target of 287, England needed a solid start, and they got it. Boycott and Brearley

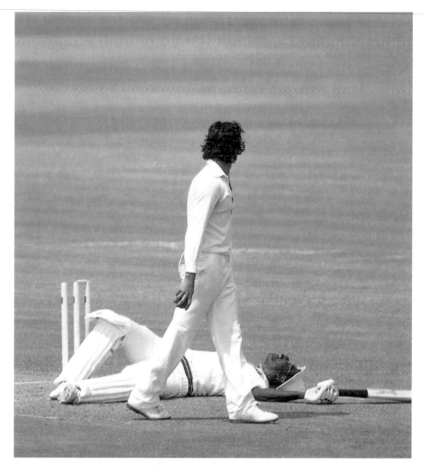

Clive Lloyd falls flat in an attempt to avoid being run out in the semi-final against Pakistan.

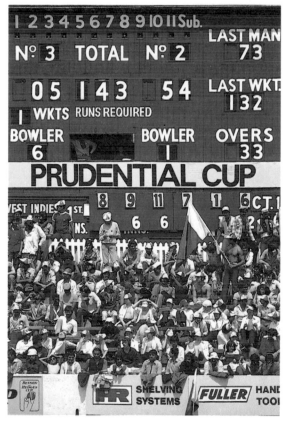

The score-board shows the West Indies romping away in the semi-final of the 1979 World Cup against Pakistan. Number two is Haynes, number three is Richards. Haynes was out for 65, Richards for 42. The last man, Greenidge, made 73 out of an opening stand of 132.

THE PRUDENTIAL WORLD CUP, 1979

Group A

at Edgbaston, 9 June
India 190 (G.R. Viswanath 75, M.A. Holding 4 for 33)
West Indies 194 for 1 (C.G. Greenidge 106 not out)
West Indies won by 9 wickets

at Trent Bridge, Nottingham, 9 June
Sri Lanka 189 (A.P.B. Tennekoon 59)
New Zealand 190 for 1 (G.M. Turner 83 not out, G.P. Howarth 63 not out)
New Zealand won by 9 wickets

at Headingley, 13 June
India 182 (S.M. Gavaskar 55)
New Zealand 183 for 2 (B.A. Edgar 84 not out)
New Zealand won by 8 wickets

at The Oval
West Indies *v* Sri Lanka
Match abandoned

at Trent Bridge, Nottingham, 16 June
West Indies 244 for 7 (C.H. Lloyd 73 not out, C.G. Greenidge 65)
New Zealand 212 for 9
West Indies won by 32 runs

at Old Trafford, Manchester, 16 and 18 June
Sri Lanka 238 for 5 (S.R. de S. Wettimuny 67, L.R.D. Mendis 64, R.L. Dias 50)
India 191
Sri Lanka won by 47 runs

Group A Final Table

	P	W	L	Ab	Pts
West Indies	3	2	–	1	10
New Zealand	3	2	1	–	8
Sri Lanka	3	1	1	1	6
India	3	–	3	–	0

Group B

at Lord's, 9 June
Australia 159 for 9
England 160 for 4 (G.A. Gooch 53)
England won by 6 wickets

at Headingley, 9 June
Canada 139 for 9
Pakistan 140 for 2 (Sadiq Mohammad 57 not out)
Pakistan won by 8 wickets

at Old Trafford, Manchester, 13 and 14 June
Canada 45 (R.G.D. Willis 4 for 11, C.M. Old 4 for 8)
England 46 for 2
England won by 8 wickets

at Trent Bridge, Nottingham, 13 and 14 June
Pakistan 286 for 7 (Majid J. Khan 61, Asif Iqbal 61)
Australia 197 (A.M.J. Hilditch 72)
Pakistan won by 89 runs

at Headingley, 16 June
England 165 for 9
Pakistan 151 (Asif Iqbal 51, M. Hendrick 4 for 15)
England won by 14 runs

at Edgbaston, 16 June
Canada 105 (A.G. Hurst 5 for 21)
Australia 108 for 3
Australia won by 7 wickets

Group B Final Table

	P	W	L	Pts
England	3	3	–	12
Pakistan	3	2	1	8
Australia	3	1	2	4
Canada	3	–	3	0

Semi-finals

at Old Trafford, Manchester, 20 June
England 221 for 8 (G.A. Gooch 71, J.M. Brearley 53)
New Zealand 212 for 9 (J.G. Wright 69)
England won by 9 runs

at The Oval, 20 June
West Indies 293 for 6 (C.G. Greenidge 73, D.L. Haynes 65, Asif Iqbal 4 for 56)
Pakistan 250 (Zaheer Abbas 93, Majid J. Khan 81)
West Indies won by 43 runs

Man of the Match awards

2 G.A. Gooch and C.G. Greenidge.
1 G.P. Howarth, Sadiq Mohammad, B.A. Edgar, Asif Iqbal, C.M. Old, L.R.D. Mendis, C.H. Lloyd, A.G. Hurst, M. Hendrick and I.V.A. Richards.

PRUDENTIAL WORLD CUP FINAL, 1979

England *v* West Indies at Lord's, 23 June

West Indies

C.G. Greenidge run out	9
D.L. Haynes c Hendrick b Old	20
I.V.A. Richards not out	138
A.I. Kallicharran b Hendrick	4
C.H. Lloyd (capt) c and b Old	13
C.L. King c Randall b Edmonds	86
*D.L. Murray c Gower b Edmonds	5
A.M.E. Roberts c Brearley b Hendrick	0
J. Garner c Taylor b Botham	0
M.A. Holding b Botham	0
C.E.H. Croft not out	0
B 11	11
(9 wickets, 60 overs)	286

	O	M	R	W
Botham	12	2	44	2
Hendrick	12	2	50	2
Old	12	–	55	2
Boycott	6		38	–
Edmonds	12	2	40	2
Gooch	4	–	27	–
Larkins	2	–	21	–

Fall of wickets
1/22 2/36 3/55 4/99 5/238 6/252 7/258
8/260 9/272

England

J.M. Brearley (capt) c King b Holding	64
G. Boycott c Kallicharran b Holding	57
D.W. Randall b Croft	15
G.A. Gooch b Garner	32
D.I. Gower b Garner	0
I.T. Botham c Richards b Croft	4
W. Larkins b Garner	0
P.H. Edmonds not out	5
C.M. Old b Garner	0
*R.W. Taylor c Murray b Garner	0
M. Hendrick b Croft	0
l-b 12, w 2, n-b 3	17
(51 overs)	194

	O	M	R	W
Roberts	9	2	33	–
Holding	8	1	16	2
Croft	10	1	42	3
Garner	11	–	38	5
Richards	10	–	35	–
King	3	–	13	–

Fall of wickets
1/129 2/135 3/183 4/183 5/186 6/186
7/188 8/192 9/192

Umpires: H.D. Bird and B.J. Meyer
Man of the Match: I.V.A. Richards

West Indies won by 92 runs

---

batted with great resolution, but the overs ebbed away. It took Boycott seventeen overs to reach double figures, and in the thirty-fourth he was dropped by Lloyd at mid-on, a simple chance. The stand ended in the thirty-eighth over when Brearley swung Holder high to square-leg. The opening partnership had been a fine platform, but the batsmen had never been able to change gear, and the rest of the batting was left the unenviable task of trying to hit 159 off Holding, Garner, Roberts and Croft at seven runs an over.

Gooch played gloriously, but briefly, and Joel Garner took 5 wickets in 11 balls to bring a mercifully quick death. At lunch, West Indies had been 125 for 4 from thirty-four overs. The twenty-six overs of the afternoon had produced 161 runs, but England had no Richards or King to provide such a burst, nor were they opposed to such bowling as that of Boycott, Larkins and Gooch who, between them, had conceded 86 runs in twelve overs.

It will be remembered, however, as a magnificent final when England twice appeared to have victory within their reach, only to be most emphatically denied.

With Sri Lanka now a fully fledged Test nation, the ICC Trophy of 1982 was able to supply only one country, the winner, for the World Cup a year later, and with Zimbabwe now having gained independence and associate membership of the ICC, there was never much doubt as to who the winners would be. In absolutely dreadful weather, the competition was again fought out in the Midlands, and the strength of the Zimbabwe side was too much for all opposition. Denmark, for financial reasons, and Argentina, for political ones, did not compete, and Zimbabwe won their group with ease before overcoming Bangladesh in the semi-final and Bermuda in the final.

In the World Cup itself, Zimbabwe were to be grouped with Australia, India and West Indies, and a change in the format of the competition decreed that each side in the group should play the others twice. This proved to be a most successful amendment, keeping interest alive until the end of the tournament for all eight sides.

England began in fine style, beating New Zealand with ease on a batting paradise at The

The teams parade for the third World Cup.

Oval. Martin Snedden conceded 105 runs from his twelve overs, an unwanted record, and Allan Lamb opened his shoulders to produce some powerful drives.

Another batting paradise at Swansea saw Pakistan sweep Sri Lanka aside, while the other group opened with two sensations. A supremely fit Zimbabwe side, intelligently led by Duncan Fletcher, edged out Australia. One of the decisive factors in the Zimbabwe win was the bowling of John Traicos, who had played Test cricket for South Africa. The off-spinner kept an immaculate length and conceded only 27 runs in twelve overs.

Equally sensationally, India, whose World Cup record had been less than moderate, beat West Indies at Old Trafford. It was the West Indies' first defeat in three World Cups, and they were victims of a balanced and spirited Indian side, strong in medium-pace seam bowling ideally suited to English conditions.

This time inspired by the elegant David Gower, England again reached a big score and trounced Sri Lanka at Taunton as India took a

grip on Group B with victory over Zimbabwe. New Zealand and West Indies showed better form in gaining their first wins, but the West Indies victory was gained in poor conditions at Headingley where Australia suffered on a crumbling wicket on the second day. Wood was hit and forced to retire hurt, and Winston Davis returned figures of 7 for 51, a record for a one-day international.

England's success continued in a rather poor game against Pakistan, and New Zealand secured second place with a comfortable win. West Indies brushed aside Zimbabwe, and by beating India, Australia opened up the second group, for each side had lost at least one match.

New Zealand, fancied by many to win the title, beat England with one ball to spare at Edgbaston and joined them on twelve points. Pakistan won a narrow victory over a valiant Sri Lankan side whose attack was limited, and West Indies gained revenge over India, who seemed to be on their way out of the competition as the men from the Caribbean looked ominously as if they were moving into top gear and were about

*Australia in a muddle as
they lose to Zimbabwe at
Trent Bridge, 1983.*

*Zimbabwe celebrate a
famous victory.*

*Botham is caught by
Warren Lees off Richard
Hadlee for 22, England
v New Zealand, The
Oval, 1983.*

*Botham is run out for 0,
but England pile on the
runs against Sri Lanka
at Taunton.*

170

*Javed falls lbw to
Chatfield for 35,
Edgbaston, 1983.*

*Richard Hadlee bowls
Zaheer Abbas and
Pakistan are 0 for 3
against New Zealand at
Edgbaston, 1983.*

A sad sight at Headingley. Graeme Wood is felled by a ball from Holding and taken to hospital.

to claim their third World Cup.

At Southampton, Australia had another fright against Zimbabwe, but the running out of Heron and Pycroft and a fine late spell from Rodney Hogg brought them success.

England and West Indies both moved towards the semi-finals with comparative ease with victories in the fifth-round matches, but New Zealand slipped surprisingly at Derby and left Pakistan with a chance to reach the last four.

The most significant match of the competition, however, took place at Tunbridge Wells. The Nevill Ground, with its banks of rhododendrons, seems an unlikely setting for a game between India and Zimbabwe, but the beautiful Kent ground staged one of the greatest matches in the history of any competition, and

A mix up at Lord's. Ian Gould, the England wicket-keeper, runs out Javed Miandad who was acting as runner for Imran Khan.

saw one of the finest innings ever played.

On a bright morning with a light breeze, Kapil Dev chose to bat first when he won the toss. To the last ball of the opening over, bowled by Rawson, Gavaskar was lbw. There was no run until a leg-bye was recorded in the third over, and in the fifth, having hit a boundary, Amarnath was caught behind. The exciting Srikkanth, ignoring the responsibility that had been thrust upon him, drove Curran high to the outfield where Butchart took a fine running catch. Patil scooped Curran to the wicket-keeper, and Yashpal Sharma also touched the ball to Houghton so that, after thirteen overs, India were 17 for 5.

At last there was some relief for India with a sensible stand of 60 between Kapil Dev and Roger Binny, but Traicos, as naggingly accurate as ever, broke the stand when he had Binny lbw. The next over Shastri played a wretched shot, and India were back in trouble at 78 for 7.

Kapil Dev's fifty and India's hundred came in the thirty-sixth over, and in the period immediately after lunch Kapil Dev took command of the game. He hit 12 in one over from Rawson, and he and Madan Lal put on 62 in sixteen overs before Madan Lal provided Houghton with his fourth catch of the day. Kirmani, his head shaved, joined Kapil Dev, resolute, mature and confident.

The Indian captain had played himself in with care; now he let loose a stream of glorious shots. He was majestic in all that he did. His century came in the forty-ninth over, and he scored at seven an over for the last eleven overs of the innings. Kirmani gave intelligent support, and they added 100 in thirteen overs.

India had been 9 for 4 in the tenth over when Kapil Dev came to the wicket. They closed at 266 for 8. Kapil Dev's 175 included six sixes and sixteen fours and was, at the time, the highest score ever made in a one-day international. It remains the most stirring and romantic.

To their credit, Zimbabwe battled bravely, and Curran played an innings that gave a glimpse of victory, but in the end they fell 31 runs short.

On the Monday, India destroyed Australia at Chelmsford with a fine team performance, and reached the semi-final. England and West Indies joined them as did, surprisingly, Pakistan who, in spite of Imran Khan's inability to bowl at any time in the competition, ousted New Zealand at the last.

Their luck ran out in the semi-final when they batted laboriously and fell easy prey to the West Indians. The impetus that India had gained from the victory at Tunbridge Wells was sustained at Old Trafford where a thoroughly efficient performance saw them brush England aside and win with 5.2 overs to spare.

PRUDENTIAL WORLD CUP FINAL, 1983

In the final, Clive Lloyd won the toss and followed his custom of asking the opponents to bat first. There was an air of menace in the West Indian pace attack, and in the fifth over Gavaskar pushed indecisively at Roberts and was caught behind.

Amarnath played with calm, and suddenly Srikkanth unleashed dazzling shots, once hooking Roberts for six. He hit 38 off 57 balls and was threatening to take the West Indians apart when he fell to Marshall. Yashpal and Amarnath batted watchfully, but both fell before lunch, Amarnath bowled between bat and pad and Yashpal wastefully caught as he tried to hit over the top.

Kapil Dev played a couple of blistering shots and then perished at long-on, and the fall of Kirti Azad and Binny meant that 5 wickets had fallen in seven overs for 40 runs. At 130 for 7 India were in gloom, and the predictions of a one-sided final were coming true. There was spirit from the tail, but India failed to bat out their sixty overs, and a West Indian win looked a formality.

There was early encouragement for India when Greenidge was bowled offering no shot, but Richards began with an air of contempt and arrogance, determined to end this nonsense as soon as possible. He savaged Sandhu and Kapil Dev and hit Madan Lal for three fours in his first over. That Madan Lal had Haynes caught at extra cover in his next over seemed to matter little. Haynes was soon to reappear as runner for a limping Clive Lloyd.

Madan Lal now turned the course of the game. In the fourteenth over, Richards swung the ball contemptuously over mid-wicket for what looked to be six, but running back, Kapil Dev held a fine catch. Madan Lal then had Gomes caught at slip, and Lloyd thumped Binny into the hands of mid-off. West Indies were suddenly 76 for 5 from twenty-five overs, and they took tea uneasily.

Immediately after the break, Bacchus chased a widish ball from Sandhu and was spectacularly caught by Kirmani. Dujon and Marshall batted with great sense, and 47 runs were added unfussily.

Madan Lal's fine spell was at an end, and Kapil Dev's options were becoming fewer. He turned to the slow medium pace of Amarnath, and Dujon played his first gentle loosener into his stumps. Five runs later, an innocent-looking seamer was edged to slip by Marshall. There was no stopping India now, and Kapil Dev returned to dismiss Roberts, but the last blow went to Amarnath who beat Holding's shuffle and hit him on the pad. Umpire Bird's finger went up, and India were world champions.

THE PRUDENTIAL WORLD CUP, 1983

Gavaskar is caught behind by Gould off Allott in the semi-final at Old Trafford, but India went on to reach the final.

Group A

at The Oval, 9 June
England 322 for 6 (A.J. Lamb 102)
New Zealand 216 (M.D. Crowe 97)
England won by 106 runs

at Swansea, 9 June
Pakistan 338 for 5 (Mohsin Khan 82, Zaheer Abbas 82, Javed Miandad 72, Imran Khan 56 not out)
Sri Lanka 288 for 9 (D.S.B.P. Kuruppu 72, R.G. de Alwis 59 not out)
Pakistan won by 50 runs

at Taunton, 11 June
England 333 for 9 (D.I. Gower 130, A.J. Lamb 53)
Sri Lanka 286 (R.G. de Alwis 58 not out, L.R.D. Mendis 56, V.J. Marks 5 for 39, G.R. Dilley 4 for 45)
England won by 47 runs

at Edgbaston, 11 and 12 June
New Zealand 238 for 9 (Abdul Qadir 4 for 21)
Pakistan 186
New Zealand won by 52 runs

at Lord's, 13 June
Pakistan 193 for 8 (Zaheer Abbas 83 not out)
England 199 for 2 (G. Fowler 78 not out)
England won by 8 wickets

at Bristol, 13 June
Sri Lanka 206 (R.S. Madugalle 60, R.J. Hadlee 5 for 25)
New Zealand 209 for 5 (G.P. Howarth, 76, G.M. Turner 50)
New Zealand won by 5 wickets

at Edgbaston, 15 June
England 234 (D.I. Gower 92 not out, G. Fowler 69)
New Zealand 238 for 8 (J.V. Coney 66 not out, G.P. Howarth 60, R.G.D. Willis 4 for 42)
New Zealand won by 2 wickets

at Headingley, 16 June
Pakistan 235 for 7 (Imran Khan 102 not not, Shahid Mahboob 77, A.L.F. de Mel 5 for 39)
Sri Lanka 224 (S. Wettimuny 50, Abdul Qadir 5 for 44)
Pakistan won by 11 runs

at Old Trafford, Manchester, 18 June
Pakistan 232 for 8 (Javed Miandad 67)
England 233 for 3 (G. Fowler 69, C.J. Tavaré 58)
England won by 7 wickets

at Derby, 18 June
New Zealand 181 (A.L.F. de Mel 5 for 32)
Sri Lanka 186 for 7 (R.L. Dias 64 not out, D.S.B.P. Kuruppu 62)
Sri Lanka won by 3 wickets

at Headingley, 20 June
Sri Lanka 136
England 137 for 1 (G. Fowler 81 not out)
England won by 9 wickets

at Trent Bridge, Nottingham, 20 June
Pakistan 261 for 3 (Zaheer Abbas 103 not out, Imran Khan 79 not out)
New Zealand 250 (J.V. Coney 51)
Pakistan won by 11 runs

Group A Final Table

	P	W	L	*pts*	*Run rate*
England	6	5	1	20	4.67
Pakistan	6	3	3	12	4.01
New Zealand	6	3	3	12	3.93
Sri Lanka	6	1	5	4	3.75

Group B

at Trent Bridge, Nottingham, 9 June
Zimbabwe 239 for 6 (D.A.G. Fletcher 69 not out)
Australia 226 for 7 (K.C. Wessels 76, R.W. Marsh 50 not out, D.A.G. Fletcher 4 for 42)
Zimbabwe won by 13 runs

at Old Trafford, Manchester, 9 and 10 June
India 262 for 8 (Yashpal Sharma 89)
West Indies 228
India won by 34 runs

at Headingley, 11 and 12 June
West Indies 252 for 9 (H.A. Gomes 78)
Australia 151 (W.W. Davis 7 for 51)
West Indies won by 101 runs

at Leicester, 11 June
Zimbabwe 155
India 157 for 5 (S.M. Patil 50)
India won by 5 wickets

at Trent Bridge, Nottingham, 13 June
Australia 320 for 9 (T.M. Chappell 110, G.N. Yallop 66 not out, K.J. Hughes 52, R.N. Kapil Dev 5 for 43)
India 158 (K.H. MacLeay 6 for 39)
Australia won by 162 runs

at Worcester, 13 June
Zimbabwe 217 for 7 (D.A.G. Fletcher 71 not out, D.L. Houghton 54)
West Indies 218 for 2 (C.G. Greenidge 105 not out, H.A. Gomes 75 not out)
West Indies won by 8 wickets

at Southampton, 16 June
Australia 272 for 7 (G.M. Wood 73)
Zimbabwe 240 (D.L. Houghton 84)
Australia won by 32 runs

at The Oval, 15 June
West Indies 282 for 9 (I.V.A. Richards 119)
India 216 (M.B. Amarnath 80)
West Indies won by 66 runs

at Lord's, 18 June
Australia 273 for 6 (K.J. Hughes 69, D.W. Hookes 56, G.N. Yallop 52 not out)
West Indies 276 for 3 (I.V.A. Richards 95 not out, C.G. Greenidge 90)
West Indies won by 7 wickets

at Tunbridge Wells, 18 June
India 266 for 8 (R.N. Kapil Dev 175 not out)
Zimbabwe 235 (K.M. Curran 73)
India won by 31 runs

at Chelmsford, 20 June
India 247
Australia 129 (U.S. Madan Lal 4 for 20, R.M.H. Binny 4 for 29)
India won by 118 runs

at Edgbaston, 20 June
Zimbabwe 171 (K.M. Curran 62)
West Indies 172 for 0 (D.L. Haynes 88 not out, S.F.A. Bacchus 80 not out)
West Indies won by 10 wickets

Group B Final Table

	P	W	L	Pts	Run rate
West Indies	6	5	1	20	4.31
India	6	4	2	16	3.87
Australia	6	2	4	8	3.81
Zimbabwe	6	1	5	4	3.49

India celebrate as Bacchus falls to Sandhu, caught by Kirmani, in the final.

Semi-finals

at The Oval, 22 June
Pakistan 184 for 8 (Mohsin Khan 70)
West Indies 188 for 2 (I.V.A. Richards 80 not out, H.A. Gomes 50 not out)
West Indies won by 8 wickets

at Old Trafford, Manchester, 22 June
England 213
India 217 for 4 (Yashpal Sharma 61, S.M. Patil 51 not out)
India won by 6 wickets

Man of the Match awards

3 I.V.A. Richards.
2 M.B. Amarnath and Abdul Qadir.
1 A.J. Lamb, Yashpal Sharma, D.A.G. Fletcher, Mohsin Khan, D.I. Gower, U.S. Madan Lal, W.W. Davis, R.J. Hadlee, T.M. Chappell, C.G. Greenidge, Zaheer Abbas, J.V. Coney, D.L. Houghton, A.L.F. de Mel, R.N. Kapil Dev, G. Fowler, Imran Khan, R.M.H. Binny, S.F.A. Bacchus and R.G.D. Willis.

PRUDENTIAL WORLD CUP FINAL, 1983

India *v* West Indies at Lord's, 25 June

India

S.M. Gavaskar c Dujon b Roberts	2
K. Srikkanth lbw b Marshall	38
M.B. Amarnath b Holding	26
Yashpal Sharma c sub (Logie) b Gomes .	11
S.M. Patil c Gomes b Garner	27
R.N. Kapil Dev (capt) c Holding b Gomes	15
K.B.S. Azad c Garner b Roberts	0
R.M.H. Binny c Garner b Roberts	2
U.S. Madan Lal b Marshall	17
*S.M.H. Kirmani b Holding	14
B.S. Sandhu not out	11
B 5, l-b 5, w 9, n-b 1	20
(54.4 overs)	183

	O	M	R	W
Roberts	10	3	32	3
Garner	12	4	24	1
Marshall	11	1	24	2
Holding	9.4	2	26	2
Gomes	11	1	49	2
Richards	1	–	8	–

Fall of wickets
1/2 2/59 3/90 4/92 5/110 6/111 7/130
8/153 9/161

West Indies

C.G. Greenidge b Sandhu	1
D.L. Haynes c Binny b Madan Lal	13
I.V.A. Richards c Kapil Dev b Madan Lal	33
C.H. Lloyd (capt) c Kapil Dev b Binny .	8
H.A. Gomes c Gavaskar b Madan Lal . .	5
S.F.A. Bacchus c Kirmani b Sandhu	8
*P.J.L. Dujon b Amarnath	25
M.D. Marshall c Gavaskar b Amarnath . .	18
A.M.E. Roberts lbw b Kapil Dev	4
J. Garner not out	5
M.A. Holding lbw b Amarnath	6
l-b 4, w 10	14
(52 overs)	140

	O	M	R	W
Kapil Dev	11	4	21	1
Sandhu	9	1	32	2
Madan Lal	12	2	31	3
Binny	10	1	23	1
Amarnath	7	–	12	3
Azad	3	–	7	–

Fall of wickets
1/5 2/50 3/57 4/66 5/66 6/76 7/119
8/124 9/126

Umpires: H.D. Bird and B.J. Meyer
Man of the Match: M.B. Amarnath

India won by 43 runs

India are world champions, 1983. Kapil Dev whose innings at Tunbridge Wells saved India from eclipse smiles as Man of the Match, Mohinder Amarnath, holds the cup.

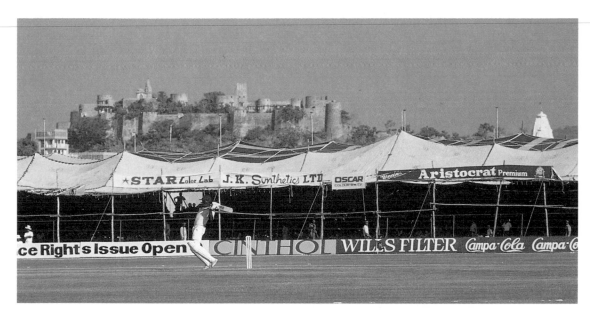

The fourth World Cup was the first to be played outside England. India and Pakistan had offered to stage the event, and the sponsorship and prize money that they obtained was so great that the offer could not be refused.

In 1986, the ICC Trophy took place in the Midlands, and Zimbabwe again emerged as clear winners although Denmark, with an entirely Danish-born side, and Holland, with a number of overseas players, showed that they had advanced much.

The fourth World Cup proved to be the best so far. Entertaining cricket of high quality drew huge crowds even when the host countries were not involved, so that the fourth-round match between New Zealand and Zimbabwe when neither side had much hope of qualifying for the semi-finals drew a capacity crowd of 50,000 – testimony to the success of the competition.

Pakistan began with a victory over Sri Lanka, while England won magnificently against West Indies. Needing 244 to win, England seemed to have slipped against Hooper's gentle off-breaks and were 162 for 7. Emburey and De Freitas both hit lustily, but the major contribution came from Allan Lamb, a consistently fine player in one-day cricket. He took 15 off the forty-eighth over, bowled by Walsh, and saw that the 13 needed from the last over by the same bowler were obtained. A two to mid-wicket, a four to third man, four wides and a single left Foster to play the ball to third man for the winning boundary.

Meanwhile, India were surprisingly beaten by Australia. Boon and Marsh, as they were to do throughout the tournament, provided a sound opening, but the Australian middle order fell away. India reached the forty-seventh over with 15 runs needed and four wickets in hand, but in the last three overs there was wild haste, and the last man, Maninder Singh, faced Waugh's last over with six needed. Twice Maninder tucked the ball away for two, but he swung massively at the fifth delivery and was bowled.

A century of heroic proportions by Dave Houghton could not save Zimbabwe against New Zealand, but the Kiwis slumped in their second match when Navjot Singh Sidhu emerged as an exciting stroke-maker. England's form against West Indies was not sustained against the impressive Pakistanis, while Viv Richards hit a record 181 off 125 balls to show that the West Indies were far from dead. Australia quietly and effectively notched up their second win.

The prospect of West Indies failing to reach the final for the first time loomed large when Pakistan won a thrilling encounter in the last over. Abdul Qadir was the hero of the moment, lashing a six off Walsh to win the match. Fourteen runs had been needed off the over. Qadir took a single first ball, Saleem Jaffer a single off the second. A misfield allowed Qadir two off the third, and he hit the fourth over long off for six. A drive into the covers brought two, and Qadir sliced the last ball past slip for the winning runs.

England and India both won comfortably, but Australia had to rely again on Waugh's last-over heroics to give them victory over New Zealand in a match reduced to thirty overs by rain.

Pakistan became the first side assured of a semi-final place when they trounced England, and West Indies kept their hopes alive with an easy win over Sri Lanka. Australia were beaten for the first time by an Indian side showing ever-increasing form and confidence.

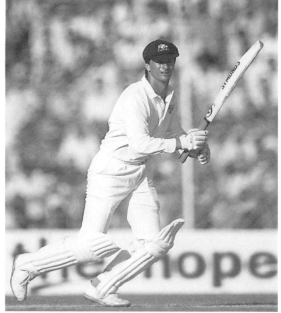

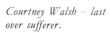

Dave Houghton, the Zimbabwe wicket-keeper, hit a valiant century against New Zealand, but his side was beaten.

Last over hero – Steve Waugh of Australia.

Courtney Walsh – last over sufferer.

Abdul Qadir, the Pakistan leg-spinner and outstanding bowler in the 1987 World Cup.

Australia are due to meet New Zealand at Indore, and the ground staff work furiously to clear the flooded pitch.

179

The Merchant stand at Bombay during the semi-final between England and India.

Graham Gooch on his way to 115 in the semi-final against India.

In spite of a delightful knock from Roy Dias, Sri Lanka were beaten, and West Indies ended Pakistan's winning streak. The excitement came at Nagpur where India needed to score at a very fast rate to top Group A. They did. Chasing 222 to beat New Zealand, they averaged seven runs an over. Gavaskar and Srikkanth opened with 136 in seventeen overs, and Gavaskar's first century in one-day internationals came off 85 balls. Earlier, Chetan Sharma had recorded the first World Cup hat-trick.

The favourites to meet in the final, India and Pakistan, had safely reached the semi-finals, but there they were thwarted. Border chose to bat first against Pakistan, and Boon and Marsh again began well. Jones batted fluently, and Veletta made valuable runs at a difficult time after Imran had returned to take 3 for 17 in five overs. Waugh took 18 runs from Saleem Jaffer's last over, however, and this proved decisive.

Pakistan made a wretched start. Rameez was run out on the third ball of the innings, and they slipped to 38 for 3 in the eleventh over. Javed and Imran put on 112 in twenty-six overs, but the last three wickets could not realize the 56 runs that were left to them.

The fifth round of matches proved decisive. Pakistan clinched first place, and England second with another exciting win over West Indies, who conceded 22 wides. A mighty innings from Gooch took England to 269, 83 of which had been conjured from the last ten overs. Richards and Richardson put on 82 in eighteen overs, but when Hemmings bowled Richards the nature of the game changed. Hemmings caught Logie and ran out Harper, and the last 6 West Indian wickets went down for 30 runs in eight overs.

Gooch swept his way to an amazing hundred at Bombay, and Lamb and Gatting gave good support. India received a dreadful shock

Hemmings has Azharuddin lbw, and England are close to victory over India and a place in the final.

The semi-final at Lahore. Javed Miandad swings wildly and is bowled by Reid for 70, and Pakistan's hopes of a final place fade.

David Boon, Man of the Match in the World Cup Final, 1987, and consistent throughout the competition. He hits Hemmings to leg.

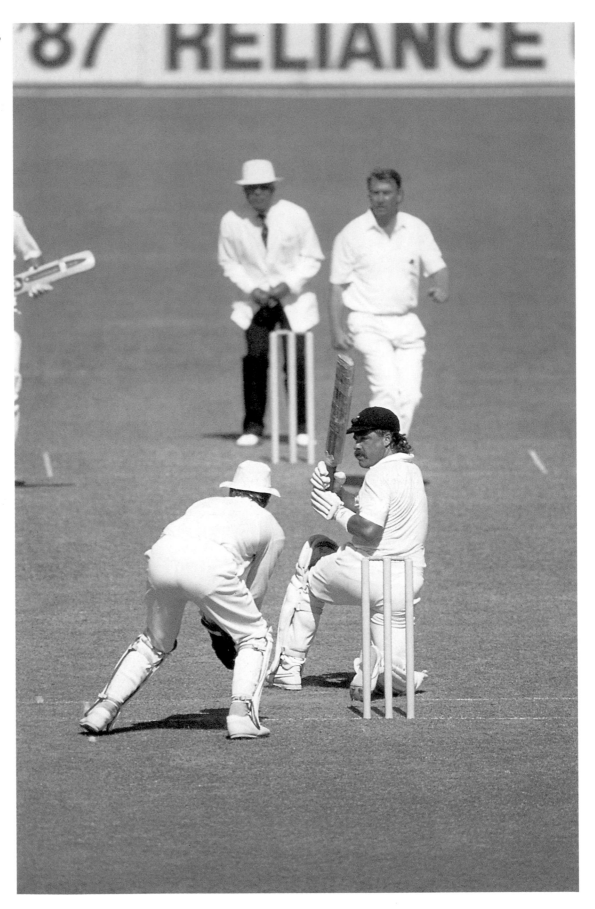

David Boon, Man of the Match in the World Cup Final, 1987, and consistent throughout the competition. He hits Hemmings to leg.

when De Freitas bowled Gavaskar in the third over, but there was some revival from Srikkanth and Sidhu. Kapil Dev came in at 121 for 4, and he and Azharuddin added 47 off 32 balls. Kapil Dev fell, caught on the square-leg boundary off Hemmings, Azharuddin was lbw to the same bowler, and India lost nerve and rushed to defeat.

THE RELIANCE WORLD CUP FINAL, 1987

Border won the toss in the final, and again chose to bat first. Marsh and Boon once more gave their side a good start, but then it was left to Border and Veletta as Australia threatened to fall, and 65 runs came from the last six overs.

Robinson was lbw to the first ball he received, but Gooch and Athey put on 65 in seventeen overs. Gatting and Athey then appeared to have England firmly in control, and there were signs of despair in the Australian camp when, at the beginning of the thirty-second over, England were 135 for 2. Border now introduced his own slow left arm into the attack. The result was immediate. Gatting played the reverse sweep described earlier in the book, and England began to falter.

Athey and Lamb added 35 in eight overs, and England needed 75 from the last ten, 46 from the last five. The dismissal of Lamb in the forty seventh over was crucial, but De Freitas took 14 in an over from McDermott before Waugh had him caught going for a big hit. England needed 17 from the last over, but McDermott kept calm, and Australia, the most organized, disciplined and balanced side, won the World Cup for the first time.

Bill Athey dives but is run out for 58, and England's collapse begins.

The moment of truth. Gatting reverse sweeps at Border and loops the ball to wicket-keeper Greg Dyer.

THE RELIANCE WORLD CUP, 1987

Group A

at Madras, 9 October
Australia 270 for 6 (G.R. Marsh 110)
India 269 (N.S. Sidhu 73, K. Srikkanth 70, C.J. McDermott 4 for 56)
Australia won by 1 run

at Hyderabad, 10 October
New Zealand 242 for 7 (M.D. Crowe 72, M.C. Snedden 64)
Zimbabwe 239 (D.L. Houghton 141)
New Zealand won by 3 runs

at Madras, 13 October
Australia 235 for 9 (A.R. Border 67, G.R. Marsh 62)
Zimbabwe 139 (S.P. O'Donnell 4 for 39)
Australia won by 96 runs

at Bangalore, 14 October
India 252 for 7 (N.S. Sidhu 75, R.N. Kapil Dev 72 not out)
New Zealand 236 for 8 (K.R. Rutherford 75, A.H. Jones 64)
India won by 16 runs

at Bombay, 17 October
Zimbabwe 135 (A.J. Pycroft 61, M. Prabhakar 4 for 19)
India 136 for 2
India won by 8 wickets

at Indore, 19 October
Australia 199 for 4 (D.C. Boon 87, D.M. Jones 52)
New Zealand 196 for 9 (M.D. Crowe 58)
Australia won by 3 runs

at New Delhi, 22 October
India 289 for 6 (D.B. Vengsarkar 63, S.M. Gavaskar 61, M. Azharuddin
54 not out, N.S. Sidhu 51)
Australia 233 (D.C. Boon 62)
India won by 56 runs

at Calcutta, 23 October
Zimbabwe 227 for 5 (A.J. Pycroft 52 not out, K.J. Arnott 51, D.L.
Houghton 50)
New Zealand 228 for 6 (J.J. Crowe 88 not out, M.D. Crowe 58)
New Zealand won by 4 wickets

at Ahmedabad, 26 October
Zimbabwe 191 for 7 (K.J. Arnott 60)
India 194 for 3 (N.S. Sidhu 55, S.M. Gavaskar 50)
India won by 7 wickets

at Chandigarh, 27 October
Australia 251 for 8 (G.R. Marsh 126, D.M. Jones 56)
New Zealand 234 (J.G. Wright 61)
Australia won by 17 runs

at Cuttack, 30 October
Australia 266 for 5 (D.C. Boon 93, D.M. Jones 58 not out)
Zimbabwe 196 for 6
Australia won by 70 runs

at Nagpur, 31 October
New Zealand 221 for 9
India 224 for 1 (S.M. Gavaskar 103 not out, K. Srikkanth 75)
India won by 9 wickets

Group A Final Table

	P	W	L	Pts	Run rate
India	6	5	1	20	5.39
Australia	6	5	1	20	5.19
New Zealand	6	2	4	8	4.88
Zimbabwe	6	—	6	0	3.76

184

Group B

at Hyderabad, 8 October
Pakistan 267 for 6 (Javed Miandad 103, Rameez Raja 76)
Sri Lanka 252 (R.S. Mahanama 89)
Pakistan won by 15 runs

at Gujranwala, 9 October
West Indies 243 for 7 (R.B. Richardson 53)
England 246 for 8 (A.J. Lamb 67 not out)
England won by 2 wickets

at Rawalpindi, 13 October
Pakistan 239 for 7 (Saleem Malik 65, Ijaz Ahmed 59)
England 221 (Abdul Qadir 4 for 31)
Pakistan won by 18 runs

at Karachi, 13 October
West Indies 360 for 4 (I.V.A. Richards 181, D.L. Haynes 105)
Sri Lanka 169 for 4 (A. Ranatunga 52 not out)
West Indies won by 191 runs

at Lahore, 16 October
West Indies 216 (I.V.A. Richards 51, P.V. Simmons 50, Imran Khan 4 for 37)
Pakistan 217 for 9 (Saleem Yousuf 56, C.A. Walsh 4 for 40)
Pakistan won by 1 wicket

at Peshawar, 17 October
England 296 for 4 (G.A. Gooch 84, A.J. Lamb 76, M.W. Gatting 58)
Sri Lanka 158 for 8
England won by 109 runs – faster run rate

at Karachi, 20 October
England 244 for 9 (C.W.J. Athey 86, M.W. Gatting 60, Imran Khan 4 for 37)
Pakistan 247 for 3 (Rameez Raja 113, Saleem Malik 88)
Pakistan won by 7 wickets

at Kanpur, 21 October
West Indies 236 for 8 (P.V. Simmons 89, A.L. Logie 65 not out)
Sri Lanka 211 for 8 (A. Ranatunga 86 not out)
West Indies won by 25 runs

at Faisalabad, 25 October
Pakistan 297 for 7 (Saleem Malik 100)
Sri Lanka 184 for 8 (L.R.D. Mendis 58, A. Ranatunga 50)
Pakistan won by 113 runs

at Jaipur, 26 October
England 269 for 5 (G.A. Gooch 92)
West Indies 235 (R.B. Richardson 93, I.V.A. Richards 51)
England won by 34 runs

at Pune, 30 October
Sri Lanka 218 for 7 (R.L. Dias 80)
England 219 for 2 (G.A. Gooch 61, R.T. Robinson 55)
England won by 8 wickets

at Karachi, 30 October
West Indies 258 for 7 (R.B. Richardson 110, I.V.A. Richards 67)
Pakistan 230 for 9 (Rameez Raja 70)
West Indies won by 28 runs

Group B Final Table

	P	W	L	Pts	Run rate
Pakistan	6	5	1	20	5.01
England	6	4	2	16	5.12
West Indies	6	3	3	12	5.16
Sri Lanka	6	–	6	0	4.04

Semi-finals

at Lahore, 4 November
Australia 267 for 8 (D.C. Boon 65)
Pakistan 249 (Javed Miandad 70, Imran Khan 58, C.J. McDermott 5 for 44)
Australia won by 18 runs

at Bombay, 5 November
England 254 for 6 (G.A. Gooch 115, M.W. Gatting 56)
India 219 (M. Azharuddin 64, E.E. Hemmings 4 for 52)
England won by 35 runs

Man of the Match awards

3   D.C. Boon and G.A. Gooch.
2   A.J. Lamb, R.N. Kapil Dev and G.R. Marsh.
1   Javed Miandad, D.L. Houghton, Abdul Qadir, I.V.A. Richards, S.R. Waugh, Saleem Yousuf, M. Prabhakar, Imran Khan, P.V. Simmons, M. Azharuddin, J.J. Crowe, Saleem Malik, R.B. Richardson and C.J. McDermott.
    S.M. Gavaskar and C.J. Sharma shared the award in the match India *v* New Zealand at Nagpur.

RELIANCE WORLD CUP FINAL, 1987

England *v* Australia at Eden Gardens, Calcutta, 8 November

Australia	
D.C. Boon c Downton b Hemmings . . .	75
G.R. Marsh b Foster	24
D.M. Jones c Athey b Hemmings	33
C.J. McDermott b Gooch.	14
A.R. Border (capt) run out	31
M.R.J. Veletta not out	45
S.R. Waugh not out.	5
S.P. O'Donnell	
*G.C. Dyer	
T.B.A. May	
B.A. Reid	
B 1, l-b 13, w 5, n-b 7.	26
(5 wickets, 50 overs).	253

	O	M	R	W
De Freitas	6	1	34	–
Small	6	–	33	–
Foster	10	–	38	1
Hemmings	10	1	48	2
Emburey	10	–	44	–
Gooch	8	1	42	1

Fall of wickets
1/75 2/151 3/166 4/168 5/241

England	
G.A. Gooch lbw b O'Donnell.	35
R.T. Robinson lbw b McDermott	0
C.W.J. Athey run out.	58
M.W. Gatting (capt) c Dyer b Border. . .	41
A.J. Lamb b Waugh	45
*P.R. Downton c O'Donnell b Border . .	9
J.E. Emburey run out	10
P.A.J. De Freitas c Reid b Waugh.	17
N.A. Foster not out.	7
G.C. Small not out	3
E.E. Hemmings	
B 1, l-b 14, w 2, n-b 4.	21
(8 wickets, 50 overs).	246

	O	M	R	W
McDermott	10	1	51	1
Reid	10	–	43	–
Waugh	9	–	37	2
O'Donnell	10	1	35	1
May	4	–	27	–
Border	7	–	38	2

Fall of wickets
1/1 2/66 3/135 4/170 5/188 6/218 7/220
8/235

Umpires: R.B. Gupta and Mahboob Shah
Man of the Match: D.C. Boon

Australia won by 7 runs

Allan Border, the Australian captain, holds the Reliance World Cup, 1987.

The tournament is at an end. Celebratory fireworks.

CAREER RECORDS OF LEADING ENGLISH PLAYERS IN ONE-DAY INTERNATIONALS TO END OF 1987 SEASON

Batting	M	Inns	NOs	Runs	HS	Average	100s
C.W.J. Athey	20	20	1	607	142*	31.94	2
I.T. Botham	95	86	11	1703	72	22.70	
B.C. Broad	20	20		891	99	44.55	
P.A.J. De Freitas	19	13	6	128	33	18.28	
G.R. Dilley	34	18	1	114	31*	11.40	
P.R. Downton	17	14	4	193	44*	19.30	
J.E. Emburey	36	27	7	295	34	14.75	
N.A. Foster	34	17	6	96	24	8.72	
B.N. French	7	5	2	25	9*	8.33	
M.W. Gatting	63	60	14	1241	115*	26.97	1
G.A. Gooch	52	51	3	1792	129*	37.33	4
D.I. Gower	102	99	8	2905	158	31.92	7
A.J. Lamb	68	67	11	2315	118	41.33	3
D.R. Pringle	13	11	4	183	49*	26.14	
C.J. Richards	21	15	2	66	50	10.76	
R.T. Robinson	13	13		297	83	22.84	
E.E. Hemmings	5	2		4	3	2.00	
G.C. Small	13	6	3	23	8*	7.66	

Bowling	Overs	Runs	Wkts	Average	Best	4/inn
I.T. Botham	846	3398	116	29.29	4/56	1
P.A.J. De Freitas	184.1	621	25	24.84	4/35	1
G.R. Dilley	318.3	1182	45	26.26	4/23	3
J.E. Emburey	344.1	1356	42	32.28	4/37	1
N.A. Foster	301	1242	36	35.88	3/29	
M.W. Gatting	61.2	320	10	32.00	3/32	
G.A. Gooch	176.1	837	19	44.05	2/12	
D.R. Pringle	120.2	575	13	44.23	3/21	
E.E. Hemmings	41.3	175	5	35.00	3/11	
G.C. Small	128	490	12	40.83	3/28	

FIELDING

30 I.T. Botham and D.I. Gower
20 G.A. Gooch
18 M.W. Gatting
17 A.J. Lamb and C.J. Richards (c 16/st 1)

INDEX

PHOTOGRAPHIC ACKNOWLEDGEMENTS
The author and publishers would like to thank
Adrian Murrell of Allsport Photographic Ltd for
all his help in providing the pictures for this
book.

All photographs have been supplied by Allsport
Photographic, except as indicated below.

Page 45 – George Herringshaw.
Page 69 – Ken Kelly
Page 70 – Mark Leech.
Pages 82/83 – George Herringshaw.
Page 97 – George Herringshaw.
Page 107 – Tony Edenden.